Jesus
in Egypt

✠

Jesus in Egypt

Discovering the Secrets
of Christ's Childhood Years

Paul Perry

BALLANTINE BOOKS · NEW YORK

A Ballantine Book
Published by The Random House Publishing Group

Copyright © 2003 by Paul Perry

All rights reserved under International and Pan-American Copyright
Conventions. Published in the United States by The Random House Publishing
Group, a division of Random House, Inc., New York, and simultaneously in Canada
by Random House of Canada Limited, Toronto.

All photographs are from the author's collection.

Ballantine and colophon are registered trademarks of Random House, Inc.

www.ballantinebooks.com

Library of Congress Cataloging-in-Publication Data
Perry, Paul, 1950–
   Jesus in Egypt : discovering the secrets of Christ's childhood years / Paul Perry.— 1st ed.
     p. cm.
   ISBN 0-345-45145-7 (alk. paper)
   1. Jesus Christ—Flight into Egypt.   I. Title.
BT315.3.P47 2003
232.92'7—dc21   2003051851

Design by Joseph Rutt
Map by Mapping Specialists

Manufactured in the United States of America

First Edition: November 2003

10 9 8 7 6 5 4 3 2 1

For
Darleen

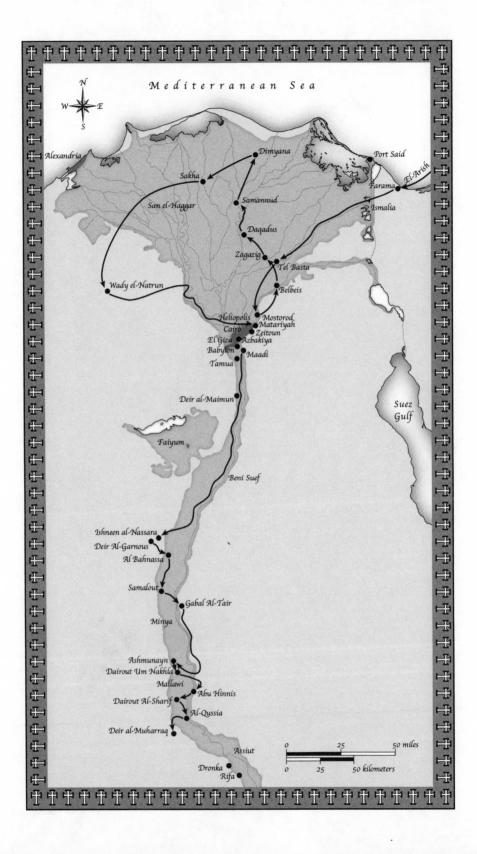

Contents

CONTENTS

Part II

Behold, the angel of the Lord appeareth to Joseph in a dream, saying, Arise, and take the young child and his mother, and flee into Egypt, and be thou there until I bring thee word: for Herod will seek the young child to destroy him.
—Matthew 2:13

Introduction to a Fulfillment Saga

Otto F. A. Meinardus

An unusual gathering of Egyptian religious and political leaders assembled on Thursday morning, June 1, 2000, on the banks of the Nile at the Coptic Orthodox Church of the Holy Virgin in Maadi, nine miles south of Cairo. The reason for this rare assembly of dignitaries was an interreligious festival commemorating the two thousandth anniversary of the Holy Family's arrival in Egypt. Egypt's prime minister, Atef Ebeid, the foreign minister, Amr Musa, Coptic Pope Shenouda III of Alexandria, Shaikh Mohammed Sayed al-Tantawi of al-Azhar University, the Rev. Dr. Safwat al-Bayadi, head of the Coptic Evangelical Community, the Catholic Patriarch Stephanus II, several cabinet ministers, and other celebrities watched an audiovisual opera on the Nile showing in eleven parts various stopovers of the journey of the holy fugitives. For the Egyptians, both Christians and Muslims, this spectacle was an important event, one that had united "cross and crescent" under the aegis of the visit of the Holy Family.

Ever since the fourth century Christians were puzzled by the brief references about the Holy Family's travels in Egypt as mentioned by

St. Matthew in his gospel. They wanted to know more about their redeemer. Which route did the Holy Family follow? Where did they eventually settle? How long did they remain in Egypt? How did they support themselves? They realized that the decision to flee from the wrath of Herod was based upon a dream. Dreams, visions, oracles, and apparitions used to have decisive, final functions in the history of God's people; this was true in the past and, at least in the Orient, it is true to this very day.

Many centuries ago—so goes the Old Testament story—Egypt had experienced an unexpected blessing. Joseph, the son of Jacob, was sold into slavery and gained the favor of the pharaoh by his interpretations of dreams. As prime minister of Upper and Lower Egypt, he obtained a high position, contributing to the economic prosperity of the land. The Egyptians believe that he built cities and canals and constructed the first Nilometer. The Bible called him a "dreamer." Would he have known that more than a thousand years later this gift would be interpreted as a prefiguration of the dreams of the carpenter of Nazareth? Joseph's dreams not only determined the time and direction of the journey of the Holy Family, they inspired also their departure and final destination.

In their search for locations associated with the travels of the Holy Family, the early Christian pilgrims seem to have been satisfied by visiting two or three sites in the Nile Valley. Thus, the seven late-fourth-century visitors coming from Palestine stopped in the Nile Valley in the city of Hermopolis Magna (Ashmunayn), where they heard that the visit of the Holy Family had fulfilled the prophecy of Isaiah: "Behold, the Lord is riding on a swift cloud and comes to Egypt, and the heart of the Egyptians will melt within them" (19:1). The early pilgrims understood the escape of the divine fugitives to Egypt as a fulfillment of the prophecy of Hosea: "When Israel was a child, I loved him, and out of Egypt I called my son" (11:1). In the Old Testament Israel is referred to as "God's son." In Moses' initial challenge to Pharaoh, Israel is called God's "first born son" (Exodus 4:22). St. Matthew and later the church fathers and doctors "individualized" the people of Israel and related the "son of God" to Jesus Christ.

One of the early visitors was the pilgrim Antonius of Piacenza, who visited Egypt in 570. In Memphis, where Upper and Lower Egypt meet, he noticed a church built on the site of a former temple, which had been visited by the Holy Family. There he saw the imprint of the face of the Redeemer on a linen pallium (tunic), a kind of predecessor of the holy shroud of Turin. Jesus had wiped his face with this linen, whereupon the mark of his face was indelibly fixed upon the cloth—so it was explained to Antonius.

It is not until the Middle Ages that curiosity and thirst for knowledge led to the unhampered growth of legends, fables, and myths pertaining to the experiences and miracles of the divine Child and His mother. Some of these stories clearly reflect biblical accounts. The raising of the dead son of a widow in the Nile Delta town of Bilbeis is an Egyptian double to the story of the raising of the son of a widow in Nain (Luke 7:11). In many cities visited by pilgrims they noticed that the ancient temples, columns, and statues had collapsed and fallen down. Already the early church fathers and historians had explained the destruction of the pharaonic monuments in terms of prophetic fulfillment— had not Isaiah prophesied that at His presence the idols of Egypt should be moved (19:1)? Other stories center around shade-providing trees, sheltering caves, and life-giving springs and wells.

One of the primary sources accepted by the Egyptian Christians is the Vision of Theophilus, a twelfth-century homily attributed to the fifth-century Pope Theophilus of Alexandria. Inspired by the Holy Virgin, Theophilus relates in detail the numerous miracles performed by the Child Jesus in the towns of Lower and Upper Egypt. In the twelfth century John ibn Said al-Kulzumi provided a geographical itinerary of the Holy Family in the *History of the Patriarchs of the Egyptian Church* and lists nine sites visited by the fugitives. A century later, Abu'l-Makarim (thirteenth century) mentioned in his *Churches and Monasteries of Egypt* fourteen stopovers of the Holy Family, while the medieval Coptic and Ethiopic *synaxaria* (calendars of saints) agree on nine towns and villages that were blessed by the Child Jesus and His mother. By the thirteenth century, a skeleton of an itinerary of the route of the divine travelers was clearly established.

Although the legends of the various Infancy Gospels were circulated in Europe in the works of Aurelius Prudentius and in the poetry of the Benedictine nun Hrosvitha, it is somewhat peculiar that the medieval Holy Land and Sinai pilgrims did not venture south of Cairo. True enough, between the fourteenth and sixteenth centuries, Western pilgrims on their return from St. Catherine's Monastery in Sinai visited the crypt with the well in the Church of Sts. Sergius and Bacchus in Old Cairo, "where Joseph drew water for washing the Child, for cooking and drinking." They also stayed in the Garden of Balm with the well of the Virgin in Matariyah. These bushes of balm, they were told, were brought by the Queen of Sheba on her visit to Solomon until they were transplanted to Egypt either by Augustus or Cleopatra. However, the pilgrims were confident that the plants never did well until the visit of the Holy Family. Neither the Franciscans, the Jesuits, or later the Protestant missionaries to Egypt seemed to care about the miracles and traditions of the Holy Family. To them these stories had their origin in the various apocryphal Infancy Gospels, which were duly condemned as being heretical forgeries by the so-called Gelasian decrees (sixth century). Moreover, for the Protestants they were rejected and repudiated by the sixteenth-century Reformation fathers, especially by Martin Luther.

It is praiseworthy and commendable that Paul Perry, an American Protestant with a conservative Bible-oriented upbringing, has shown the kind of genuine curiosity to inquire about the young Jesus in Egypt. From the days of his Sunday school in the local Baptist church, he had wondered about Jesus and His mother in the Nile Valley. It was this interest in the "historical Jesus" that convinced him that only a visit to Egypt could provide the answer.

Paul Perry was fortunate that for his investigations throughout Lower Egypt, the Nile Delta, and the traditional sites in Cairo he succeeded in obtaining the assistance of Ra'ed El-Sharqawi, an interested Christian secondary-school teacher in Cairo, and Sa'ad Abdoullah, who served as taxi driver. With them he traveled back and forth through the fertile area of the biblical land of Goshen, the land of Ramses (Genesis 47:11).

For his journey along the Nile Valley from Cairo to Assiut, a distance of 230 miles, Paul Perry had the wonderful chance to be accompanied by Drs. Cornelis "Kees" Hulsman, a Dutch sociologist and investigative journalist. Kees Hulsman had thoroughly studied and published on the various traditional sites throughout Egypt and was well acquainted with the local bishops, priests, shaikhs, and officials. For many years he had led numerous tours of Egyptians and non-Egyptians through the villages and towns associated with the visit of the Holy Family. His intuition and flair in combination with Paul Perry's inquiring mind have provided the story of *Jesus in Egypt*.

Finally, some readers may want to accept the challenge and follow the traditional route as outlined in this book. In these days of object-oriented travels, agencies advertise tours such as "In the Steps of St. Paul from Damascus Through Asia Minor to Greece and Italy" or "In the Steps of Moses from Cairo Through Sinai to Mt. Nebo in Jordan."

It is in this frame that people investigating different cultures may want to follow in the steps of the Holy Family, thus extending their religious horizon.

About half a century ago I used to travel along this route. In the meantime, roads and hotels have been built, and at least in the cities, many Egyptians are able to converse in English, thus making meaningful communication possible. Although a patriarchal commission of hierarchs and scholars has recently published an "official" map of the route of the Holy Family, the growth of sacred sites and legends is something dynamic that cannot be ecclesiastically controlled. Holy sites are largely based upon local oral traditions. Upon inquiry, we learn that religious, political, and economic factors have determined the route of the divine fugitives. To this day, visitors to these sites will hear of miracles of healing and unusual apparitions that are reminiscent of those recorded in the gospels. For westerners they constitute a problem of faith. To me, miracles are law-abiding events by which God accomplishes His redemptive purpose through the release of energies belonging to a higher plane than those with which I am normally familiar. Not only was this Paul Perry's experience, it will be the discovery of every person who visits the towns and villages especially blessed by God (Isaiah 19:25)!

Otto F. A. Meinardus, Ph.D., a Fellow of the Institute of Coptic Studies in Cairo and a member of the German Archaeological Society, holds a doctor of philosophy and theology from Harvard University. A past professor at the American University in Cairo and Athens College in Greece, Dr. Meinardus is the author of a number of books on the history of Christianity, including Two Thousand Years of Coptic Christianity, *published by The American University in Cairo Press.*

Prologue

The Secret Stories of Jesus

Ifelt uneasy going into the dark Cairo alley with the two strangers. I
had just met them at the Old Cathedral of St. Mark in the Azbakiya
district. I was standing in the back pews of the eighteenth-century
church admiring its incredible icons, those bright paintings that give
life to the stories of the Bible. As I moved from one icon to the next I
suddenly became aware of the two men behind me.

"Good evening," I said, stopping.

"Good evening to you, too," said the man with the mustache. "You
are American?"

"Yes," I said. It was not long after September 11, and few Americans
were traveling to the Middle East. I was conspicuous everywhere I went,
so it was no surprise that I would be singled out at a Coptic church, one
that would be off the beaten path for most American travelers anyway.

"You have come to look for Jesus?" asked Mustache.

The secret police are working overtime tonight, I thought.

"Why do you think I am looking for Jesus?" I asked.

Mustache smiled and held up his hands. "House of Jesus," he said.
"You must be here to look for Jesus."

I kept walking and looking at the icons. The two strangers stayed right with me. Mustache and his friend spoke quietly in Arabic, pacing behind me for some time as I tried to ignore their presence. Finally Mustache tapped me on the shoulder.

"Would you like to see the well of Jesus?" he asked.

"I certainly would," I said. "Did Jesus drink at this well?"

"Yes," said Mustache. "He made it, and he drank there. And it is still there. It makes women have babies. Hazem and I will take you."

"Sounds interesting," I said, assessing these rogue guides.

They were smiling, and they both seemed harmless. Not quite choirboys, I thought, but close enough to trust on a short field trip.

"Let's go," I said.

And we did. We headed out of the church and across its walled courtyard to the busy street. The "well of magic water" was less than two hundred yards away, my new friends assured me. It would be no problem getting there.

✠

I had already been in the country for two weeks, following the trail of Jesus in Egypt. It is a trail you will find nothing about in the Holy Bible. And because of that conspicuous absence of information, it represents one of the Bible's most mysterious gaps.

In the second book of Matthew, we read the story of King Herod, who is troubled when an unusual star appears in the East followed by three wise men searching for the baby "that is born king of the Jews." Herod gathers his own cabinet of wise men together and asks them where this new king has been born. They say he is in Bethlehem and quote the Old Testament prophet Micae, who wrote: "Out of thee [referring to Bethlehem] shall come a governor, that shall rule my people Israel."

Herod is obviously fearful of this newborn competition. But for some reason Herod's soldiers are unable to follow the shining star that marks the crib of Jesus. Instead he asks the wise men to return to him with information on how to find the newborn Messiah so that he too can pay his respects.

The wise men promise to return with the information Herod wants. But after delivering their precious gifts of gold, frankincense, and myrrh to the infant Jesus, an angel of the Lord appears to them in a dream and tells them not to return to Herod. Instead, they "departed into their own country another way."

With the wise men gone, Joseph is visited by an angel who divulges some harrowing information: The baby Jesus is wanted—dead or alive— by King Herod.

In Matthew 2:13 we read: "Behold, the angel of the Lord appeareth to Joseph in a dream, saying, Arise, and take the young child and his mother, and flee into Egypt, and be thou there until I bring thee word: for Herod will seek the young child to destroy him."

With that verse we are set up for what *should* be a rousing chase scene, chapter after chapter, in which the Holy Family is pursued by burly Roman soldiers with the singular goal of terminating the Holy Infant.

That chase scene doesn't happen. Instead we get this:

"When he arose, he took the young child and his mother by night, and departed into Egypt. And was there until the death of Herod: that it might be fulfilled which was spoken of the Lord by the prophet, saying, 'Out of Egypt have I called my son.'"

The next three verses tell of Herod's anger and his demented plan to kill all the children in Bethlehem "and in all the coasts thereof" who were two years of age and younger. This way he is sure to kill Jesus if he is still in the country. But Jesus is not in Judea. He is in Egypt. What is he doing there? The canonical Bible—the one we all have at home— tells us nothing. We simply have no biblical record of Jesus in Egypt.

Finally in verse 20, Joseph is visited once again by an angel, this time with good news: "Behold, an angel of the Lord appeareth in a dream to Joseph in Egypt, saying, Arise, and take the young child and his mother, and go into the land of Israel: for they are dead which sought the young child's life."

And that is it. The chase is over without us even reading about it. Jesus returns to Galilee and goes on with his amazing life.

But what did he do in Egypt? There lies one of the Bible's great mysteries.

It was my goal to solve this mystery. *What did Jesus do in Egypt?*

The question had posed itself several years earlier, when I was in Egypt working on a history film. We were filming a program on the stone temples of the Nile, those magnificent monuments to God and government that the ancient Egyptians are known for. Our days were filled with the visual imagery of these ancient buildings. Although Egypt is known primarily for its pyramids, the temples up the Nile are in their own way just as grand. Their walls and pillars are covered with hieroglyphs and paintings that tell the story of Egypt on many levels. Gods are present to tell the spiritual account, carved into the stone by master masons in scenes that make the story so alive, these static myths have almost a cinematic quality.

Surrounding the spiritual myths of Egypt are historical stories about pharaohs, great battles, even family life.

The story of ancient Egypt, from the mundane to the mysterious, is carved into the walls of her surviving temples.

As a child, I had thrived on pictures of these massive buildings with their bizarre carvings. Many nights I dreamed I was in the cities of ancient Egypt, and many days I spent hours in libraries, gazing at picture books and daydreaming about life along the Nile.

To finally see the temples firsthand was a breathtaking experience. I was not prepared for the sheer mass of the structures nor for the perfection of the stone carvings. At any of the temples I could run my hands over the hieroglyphs and feel the smooth perfection of the work of the artist who made it. Although most Egyptian art was produced by anonymous artisans, its quality and creativity on the whole is up there with that of the great artists of the Renaissance and other masters of shape and form whose work has come down through the ages.

There was another thing that intrigued me about the stone temples of the Nile. They all looked like the drawings of biblical cities that were put on the bulletin boards at Sunday school. Actually being among these temples brought those Sunday school drawings to life in my head. In fact, some temples and the streets around them have changed so little in two thousand years that seeing them would cause me to freeze in my tracks.

At the Temple of Horus in Edfu, for instance, I stumbled into a crowd of professional mourners who were wailing loudly for a recently deceased client. They were dressed in black and fully covered, and surrounded me as they passed. All that was visible was their swirling black clothing against the carved walls of the temple. The only thing I could hear was their deep and painful wailing as they accompanied a casket to the cemetery. For a moment it was like passing through a time warp and bridging two millennia in a single step.

I remember later remarking to the film's producer that for a moment I thought I had opened an illustrated Bible and fallen into one of the drawings.

Egypt is like that. Its antiquities create a wonderful environment for dreams of all kind, day or night.

It was certainly the reminder of these childhood images from Sunday school that caused me to remember a single line from a single verse in the Bible: "Out of Egypt have I called my son." *Jesus was in Egypt as a child,* I thought. *What did he learn here? And where did he travel? Did he walk these very streets? Did he seem somehow special to the Egyptians?*

These thoughts and more like them filled my mind. Although I am not a devout Christian, I am a curious one. My upbringing made me that way. My mother was Seventh-Day Adventist and my father a Southern Baptist. After World War II, my father had become so wrapped up in religion that he even got a degree from a Bible college, only to turn his back on a ministry because he had lost interest in leading the life of a preacher. Still, he didn't consider the four years spent in Bible college a waste of time. Even though both of my parents had fallen off the wagon in their religious lives, they loved to talk religion and tell Bible stories. I heard the Bible from a Seventh-Day Adventist viewpoint during the day from my mother, and from a Southern Baptist point of view at night from my father.

There are many differences between these two denominations— way too many to go into right now—but the one thing they agreed on was the power of Jesus. Several times a week I would be reminded of the miracles or teachings of Jesus.

Quotations from Jesus were delivered at the strangest times. If I made a comment about someone who looked strange to me as we passed them in the car, my mother might say, "Judge not, lest ye be judged yourself." If I looked tired, my mother might tell me to get some sleep because "the eye is the lamp of the body." When my father and I were listening to baseball on the radio and I showed pain that the Dodgers were losing, he would just shake his head and say, "O ye of little faith." And then there would be that favorite mealtime retort, "Man does not live on bread alone," which was a verbal sign for me to eat my vegetables.

Over the years, my interest in Jesus evolved from the message to the man. There was little question that the passages in the gospels attributed to him were both profound and timeless. But who was the man who said them?

Only about 10 percent of Jesus' life is covered in the scriptures. The scholars who assembled the Bible in the early centuries allowed only information from four witnesses—Matthew, Mark, Luke, and John—to tell the story of Jesus. And in doing that they omitted much about Jesus. Nowhere in the Bible, for instance, do we read a physical description of the man. And so little is known about his family life—if you rely only upon the Bible—that there is still argument about whether or not he had full brothers and sisters, or stepsiblings from a previous marriage of Joseph. Some churches still hold the belief that Mary was a lifelong virgin. And what happened to Joseph? The father of Jesus simply disappears from the Bible.

Even Jesus is elusive about his own life. "Blessed is he who takes no offense at me," he says at one point. Sometimes he would heal the sick and be done with it. Other times he tells the freshly healed that it was their faith and not his power that led to their healing. "Your faith has made you well," he says in Matthew.

Looking at Jesus as he is portrayed in the gospels is like looking at a partially completed paint-by-numbers canvas. A few of the lines are joined and some areas painted in, but for the most part you are looking at a blank canvas.

Yet through his words and his example, Jesus has been a guiding light for billions of people for over two thousand years. As Napoleon noted, "All the armies that ever marched and all the navies that ever were built, and all the parliaments that ever sat, all the kings that ever reigned, put together have not affected the life of man upon this earth as powerfully."

Perhaps because of this unseen power, I felt an almost irresistible urge to seek a more complete picture of this man. Maybe I was a modern-day doubting Thomas, the disciple who could not believe Jesus had been resurrected until he actually saw him with his own eyes and felt the wounds with his own hands. "Stop doubting and believe," Jesus told Thomas. "Blessed are those who have not seen and yet have believed." Like Thomas, I couldn't quite get over the hump. I needed more information about Jesus before I could determine for myself who the real Jesus was.

That is why, for me, the study of Jesus became an obsessive pursuit.

At first, my interest in the historical Jesus was something I could not pursue full time. To tell the truth, it was something I didn't even want to pursue full time. But being on the river Nile when the question popped into my mind—*What did Jesus do in Egypt?*—made it a subject that came to life for me. It was like suddenly being surrounded by the Bible stories of my past. It had me completely hooked.

I believed there must be evidence of what Jesus did in Egypt, for Egyptians were compulsive record keepers. Not only did they keep their own records—as is evidenced by the stories, medical cures, even building advice carved into the granite that was quarried for her great temples—but they were also the keeper of records for other cultures.

Perhaps this took place because Egypt was the crossroads of so many cultures. In the time of Jesus, for example, it was common to see Asians, Greeks, Romans, and Jews. In fact, hundreds of thousands of Jews lived freely in Egypt at the time of Jesus. Surely there were ancient records somewhere in that country of what Jesus and the Holy Family did in their years of exile.

As I sailed down the serpentine Nile on the boat we were using for filming, my mind began spinning out questions: *Where did the Holy Family spend its exile? What was baby Jesus like as an infant? Did he create miracles before the ones we read about in the Bible? Was the message of Christianity influenced by what Jesus learned here in Egypt?*

The only way I could discover the answers to these questions was to learn more about the lost years of Jesus in Egypt. And the only way I could learn about those years was to start asking questions.

Although I was in Egypt on a different project, I began talking to the locals about Jesus. At first glance, this might not seem like such a good idea. Egypt is a Muslim country, after all, and Muslims and Christians have not always gotten along. Wouldn't they resent questions about Jesus in their midst? The answer was a resounding no.

Although Muslims do not regard Jesus as the Son of God, as Christians do, they do see him as a prophet. A friend and Sufi Muslim scholar in Cairo named Shems Friedlander clarified the Muslim view of Jesus this way: "First there was the age of magic, which is represented for Muslims by Moses. Then there was the age of medical miracles, represented to us by Jesus. Muhammad is the focal point of the age of prophecy. As Muslims, we recognize all three. We just don't believe that any of them can be the Son of God in a literal sense."

From virtually every Muslim I spoke to, I received suggestions of locations up and down the Nile where the Holy Family stopped long enough for the baby Jesus to make a lasting impression.

"Go to Matariyah," said a cab driver in central Cairo. "I was born there. Jesus caused a spring to flow from the ground that is there to this day. Spiders on a tree spun a web around the Holy Family to hide them from Herod's soldiers. The tree is still there. It is like an oasis in the middle of the town."

"Go to Zeitoun," said a restaurant owner in Giza. "The Virgin Mary has appeared there many times to people of all religions. Even President Nasser saw her and admitted it to the newspapers."

"Tell Basta is the place to see," said an Egyptologist in Luxor. "This is where Jesus first made his magic known in Egypt. He caused all of the stone temples in the town to crumble. The people of the town were so angered by the destruction of their idols that they chased the Holy Family away. I have always wondered why he didn't just cause the people to crumble, too."

I recorded these sites in a notebook so I could chart them on a map later. I thought it would be interesting from a personal standpoint to produce such a map. For me it was a way of filling in that mysterious gap in the Bible into which the infant Jesus and his parents disappear into the most mysterious and often mentioned of all the lands in the scriptures.

I did not know that such a map already existed.

It wasn't until some time later, after I had returned home from Egypt, that I discovered the Holy Family trail had already been mapped by the Coptic Orthodox Church of Egypt. This mysterious Egyptian denomination of Christianity has traced the route of the Holy Family from its entrance into the country at the Sinai Desert border town of El-Arish to its turnaround at Assiut, more than two hundred miles up the river Nile. And they had created this map using oral tradition, non-canonical gospels, and the visions of church fathers from the earliest centuries of Christianity.

Most prominent of these visions are those of Theophilus. A Coptic pope from 385 to 412 C.E., Theophilus had a vision of the Virgin Mary while sleeping in a house that had been occupied by the Holy Family in Deir al-Muharraq, approximately two hundred miles south of Cairo.

During this vision the Virgin recounted many of the places the Holy Family stopped on their flight into Egypt. Theophilus learned that the Holy Family crossed into Egypt on June 1 of Jesus' second year and left three and a half years later from Deir al-Muharraq.

Oddly enough, Pope Theophilus did not write down the vision himself. Scholars who have studied the document note that the recording of the story of this vision is credited to Cyril of Alexandria, Theophilus' successor. Most scholars agree, however, that the work was probably written down by a later Coptic bishop who composed the vision as a sermon but credited the writing to Cyril.

Later the Vision of Theophilus was amended with the Homily of Zacharias, an eighth-century bishop in the Delta town of Sakha, and the vision of Bishop Cyriacus. They added many locations and stories of their own. Over the years the official Holy Family map has grown to include nearly forty sites.

Another source of stories about Jesus in Egypt are the secret gospels of Christ's infancy, also known simply as the Infancy Gospels. Like the Vision of Theophilus, these Infancy Gospels have been amended many times over the years. And because of these additions, there are many versions of these gospels. There are Infancy Gospels from Arabia and Armenia as well as ones called the Apocryphal Gospels of St. Thomas, James, and Pseudo-Matthew, and there are many Latin and Greek versions of the same.

These books have their roots in the same questions I was asking, namely, what was Jesus doing during all of those years *not* recorded in the Bible? To answer those questions, a whole new set of Christian writings sprang up. First among them were the Infancy Gospels of James and Thomas.

Exactly when these books were written is as much a mystery as who wrote them. Although they were attributed to James and Thomas, it seems clear that they were not written until after the deaths of both apostles. Most scholars feel that the Infancy Gospels were passed along orally for decades until they were finally written down. The use of the Infancy Gospel of Thomas itself can be traced as far as Irenaeus of Lyons in 185 C.E.

Like many other gospels that didn't find their way into the scriptures, the Infancy Gospels were the subject of great controversy among the Church fathers, who eventually selected the twenty-seven books that would become the New Testament.

Holding a Bible in your hand, it is easy to forget that this is not a book written by a single person, but a library of books written by various people in various lands. Some Bible scholars estimate that more than five hundred New Testament gospels were sifted through to reach the twenty-seven final books of the New Testament. It took more than three hundred years to do that sifting. Among those considered right to the end by some of these Church fathers were versions of the Infancy Gospels.

The original purpose of the Infancy Gospels was to provide the history of Mary's childhood and her eventual involvement with Joseph. The early gospels and other writings that were circulated in the very early years of Christianity left much in doubt about Mary. Some writers questioned her virginity and pointed to the fact that brothers of Jesus were mentioned in the New Testament. Others said that Mary was the child of a poor family, which implied that her virginity would have been more likely to be compromised. The more radical among the doubters even went so far as to say that Jesus was the product of a rape by a Roman soldier named Pantera.

A painting of the Virgin Mary inside a church dome at the Cairo suburb of Zeitoun commemorates the site where the Holy Virgin appeared in the late 1960s.

To fill in the events of Mary's life, the Infancy Gospel of James was written. The author of this book was probably not James, who was killed in 61 C.E., likely before this book was written. It's important to remember that the authorship of almost all of the New Testament books is in question. Although they are attributed to various apostles, such as Matthew, Mark, and John, these men most likely did not actually write the books themselves. The record of Jesus' life was passed down by word of mouth until unnamed authors finally wrote it down using the names of the various apostles. The same is true of the Infancy Gospel of James.

Since James is identified in his Infancy Gospel as being the half brother of Jesus, he is uniquely qualified to tell the family story. He does so with gusto. In this book the reader discovers that Mary's own birth to Anna and Joachim, a barren wealthy couple, is announced to the happy mother by an angel.

"You will conceive and give birth," the angel says to Anna. "And your child will be talked about all over the world."

Mary is a perfect child who can walk by the age of six months.

From the age of two she practically lives in the temple, studying the gospels and focusing on maintaining her own goodness. When she becomes a woman, marked by her menses at the age of twelve, Joseph is selected in a sort of lottery to care for her. He is described as an aging widower with children of his own, which may be interpreted as a man who is impotent.

The book goes on to describe Joseph's shock at Mary's divine pregnancy. After he returned home from a lengthy building project, he was stunned at the sight of his pregnant wife. "What prayer can I say on her behalf since I received her as a virgin from the temple of the Lord God and didn't protect her?" His lament was lengthy and even involved the thought of divorcing her "quietly."

Then an angel appeared to Joseph, telling him not to fear these events. "Don't be afraid of this girl, because the child in her is the Holy Spirit's doing. She will have a son and you will name him Jesus—the name means 'he will save his people from their sins.' "

And so it goes. Unlike the nativity story in the New Testament, the one in this Infancy Gospel has Jesus being born in a cave rather than a manger. It also describes a truly incredible event through the eyes of Joseph. He leaves the cave to search for a midwife. While he is away, the baby Jesus is born and the world stands still for everyone but Joseph, who describes the scene.

> Now I, Joseph, was walking and yet I did not walk, and I looked up to the air and saw the air in amazement. And I looked up at the vault of heaven, and saw it standing still and the birds of the heaven motionless. And I looked at the earth, and saw a dish placed there and workmen lying round it, with their hands in the dish. But those who chewed did not chew, and those who lifted up anything lifted up nothing, and those who put something to their mouths put nothing to their mouths, but all had their faces turned upwards. And sheep were being driven and yet they did not come forward, but stood still; and the shepherd raised his hand to strike them with his staff, but his hand remained up. And I looked at the flow of the river, and saw the mouths of the kids over it and they did not drink. And then all at once everything went on its course again.

In many ways, the purpose of the Infancy Gospel of James is to prove Mary's perpetual virginity. So when he does find a midwife, an apparently salty one named Salome, she immediately sets out to test the virginity of Mary *after* childbirth. It is an act that almost burns her hand off but leads to her conversion at the same time. Here is how the episode is written:

> And the midwife went in and said to Mary, "Make yourself ready, for there is no small contention concerning you." And Salome put forward her finger to test her condition. And she cried out, saying: "Woe for my wickedness and my unbelief; for I have tempted the living God; and behold, my hand falls away from me, consumed by fire!" . . . And an angel of the Lord stood [before her] and said to her: "Salome, God the Lord has heard your prayer. Stretch out your hand to the child and touch him, so will healing and joy be yours."

The Infancy Gospel of James ends with a declaration of authorship by James, who writes, "[I] am the one who wrote this account at the time when an uproar arose in Jerusalem at the death of Herod. I took myself off to the wilderness until the uproar in Jerusalem died down. There I praised the Lord God, who gave me the wisdom to write this account."

Other Infancy Gospels were assembled to answer questions people had about the childhood years of Jesus. First among these was the Infancy Gospel of Thomas. This collection of tales about the young Jesus begins when he was five and ends with the New Testament story of Jesus in the temple at age twelve. Scholars say it was written sometime between the first century and the sixth.

The Infancy Gospel of Thomas was probably the first of several gospels that focused on the lost years of Jesus.

There are stories in this gospel from Jesus' years in Egypt, although it is difficult to tell where the stories take place. It isn't until about halfway through the gospel that Jerusalem is referred to. Everything up to that point may well take place in Egypt.

In one of these stories, it is the Sabbath and the young Jesus is playing in the soft mud at the edge of a pond, shaping the clay into sparrows. A Jew sees the child playing and complains to Joseph that his son is violating the Sabbath.

Joseph and several adults walk quickly to the pond, where Joseph begins to shout at Jesus, "Why are you doing what is not permitted on the Sabbath?"

Jesus ignores his father. He claps his hands and the mud sparrows turn into real sparrows and fly away. "Be off, fly away, and remember me, you who are now alive," Jesus says to the birds.

The men with Joseph are amazed at this display of supernatural powers and report what they have seen to their leaders.

These two gospels—the Infancy Gospels of James and Thomas—became the basis for a number of Infancy Gospels. The two I became most interested in were the Arabic Gospel of the Infancy and the Gospel of Pseudo-Matthew. Both borrow heavily from the Infancy Gospels of James and Thomas. Both offer lengthy sections about the travels of Jesus in Egypt. Jerome, an early-fifth-century Church scholar, felt a certain affinity for the stories found in Pseudo-Matthew. Although he believed they contained mistakes in doctrine, he recommended that they be read for their intent. In a letter to Bishops Cromatius and Heliodorus, Jerome wrote: "[T]he sacred nativity of St. Mary was preceded by great miracles, and succeeded by the greatest; and so by those who believe that God can do these things, they can be believed and read without damaging their faith or imperiling their souls. In short, so far as I can, following the sense rather than the words of the writer, and sometimes walking in the same path."

The Infancy Gospels have had a great influence on religious art through the ages. Scenes from these secret writings can be seen in much of the great art from Europe and the Near East, especially in paintings that deal with Mary. The reason for this is simply that there is little information in the Bible on Mary for an artist to draw from. There are probably less than five hundred words written about Mary in the New Testament, even less about Joseph. In order to have something to paint about, Renaissance artists such as Giotto di Bondone had to search through the Infancy Gospels.

The Catholic Church in the Western Empire eventually banned the Infancy Gospels for the heresies they were said to contain. Most notable among these were the notions that Mary was not a virgin and that Joseph had children by an earlier marriage. Even though the existence of Joseph's children by an earlier marriage had nothing to do with Mary's virginity, it still disturbed the Church fathers. They declared the children to be maternal cousins of Jesus and not siblings at all.

Jerome, the Catholic Church official who translated the books of the

Bible from Greek and Hebrew, refused to translate the Infancy Gospels into Latin. With no Latin versions available, the Infancy Gospels were known only through secret readings by people who understood Greek.

"These books should indeed [be] purged from every Roman Catholic Church," said Pope Gelasius in 492 C.E. "And with their authors and followers of their authors, in an unbreakable chain of excommunication, eternally damned."

The Infancy Gospels thrived in the Byzantine Empire. New versions evolved through the ages and found their way into the daily religious lives of Christians in the Near and Middle East. And they were commonly accepted in the daily lives of Muslims, too. Some of the stories from the Arabic Infancy Gospels may have been used in the writing of the Holy Quran. In that holy writ are stories of the Holy Family that aren't found in the Bible, including many of Jesus in Egypt.

All of this material—visions and maps and secret gospels, archaeological discoveries, even stories handed down by word of mouth—are important because of the light they shine on one of history's central characters, Jesus.

I'm reminded of the words of Philip Yancy, a Christian author, who describes the mysteries around Jesus this way: "You can gauge the size of a ship that has passed out of sight by the huge wake it leaves behind." Would looking closely at these noncanonical sources of information allow me to see at least part of the ship?

That is what I had come to Egypt to find out.

"This is the way," said Mustache, pulling me by my arm with one hand as Hazem followed behind.

We walked down a dark and dirty street, past hole-in-the-wall newsstands and candy vendors. The street was very dark and most of the regular stores were boarded up for the night. The darkness made me nervous. Mustache and Hazem were looking larger and more sinister than they had moments ago in the cathedral.

"We must go here, this way," said Mustache, pulling me around a corner and down a dark and narrow alley.

I stopped immediately. Following strangers into an alley violated all the tenets of good sense, especially in a big city.

"Why you no go?" asked Mustache.

"We are going down an alley," I said. "I don't even go down alleys with people I know."

"Maybe," said Mustache. "But I will show you something that will give you trust."

Letting go of my arm, Mustache unbuttoned his sleeve and held his wrist up to my face. In the dim streetlight I could see a Coptic cross neatly tattooed on his wrist. He smiled as he held it up for me to see. Next to me, Hazem did the same. Now I had two smiling strangers standing in front of me, exhibiting their tattooed wrists.

"You understand now," he said. "This makes us the same. We are all looking for Jesus."

It was a good line and it worked. I rendered my arm to Mustache and we continued down the dark alley, around a corner, and down another dark alley. At different times he would pause and point at a section of wall. "Roman wall," he said, meaning that this section was left over from the time of the Roman occupation. Then we continued into the heart of darkness.

Just as my fear level began to rise again, we were passed by several women heading the other way. They were laughing and talking among themselves. We passed a small workshop where ironworkers were working in dim light to produce the brightly colored Ramadan lanterns for the holiday that was to begin in just a few days. Then we came to a courtyard that appeared to be a dead end.

"There it is," said Mustache.

Inside a building next to the courtyard was a stone well that was topped by a metal lid. It was nothing special. In fact, it was largely hidden underneath a metal staircase. This was the well of Jesus. On the wall behind it was a large and gaudy painting of the Virgin Mary. The area around her head was surrounded by flecks of silver paint that shone like mica in the desert.

I opened the lid and looked in. There was water down there, all right. And buzzing up from the surface were several dozen mosquitoes.

I closed the lid.

"This isn't supposed to be here," I said to Mustache.

He looked puzzled.

"I have a map of the trail that was followed by the Holy Family when they came to Egypt and this well is not on the map."

"I see," said Mustache. "Let us go find a monk and see what it was that the Holy Family did on this spot."

The author lifts a metal gate and gazes into the well of Jesus in the Azbakiya District in Cairo. Modern women drink from this well to increase their fertility.

Pulled along by Mustache, we went up the stairs, our feet clanging on the metal steps. As we climbed it became darker, but I was no longer afraid. Rather, I was intrigued at the discovery that had been made by this chance meeting. *What's next?* I wondered.

Several flights of stairs later I found out. Mustache tapped on a door and then entered. There, looking puzzled by our arrival, was a monk sitting at a desk. Against one wall were several chairs that were occupied by people waiting to talk to the monk about personal problems. I sat in the farthest chair and waited my turn.

The monk did not speak English, but when it was finally my turn to speak to him I received a pleasant welcome. Mustache told the monk why we had come and asked what the Holy Family had done on this location two thousand years ago.

The answer came back to me in broken English from Mustache. The monk told him that the Holy Family had been pursued by the soldiers of King Herod from the moment they left Bethlehem. By the time they reached this spot, the soldiers were no more than a day behind them and closing. That was when Mary had an idea.

"This area was all agricultural in those days, and there was a man planting melons as the Holy Family were walking past," Mustache said, translating the monk's words.

"Mary told the man of their predicament and then asked the man if he would tell the soldiers that they had come through here when he was in the midst of seeding. The man was puzzled.

" 'If I tell them you were here when I was seeding, they will know that they are only a day behind you and catch you quickly,' said the man. 'As you can see, I have just begun to seed.'

" 'I know,' said Jesus. The infant then wriggled down from his mother's lap and caused a well to spring from the ground. The water spread throughout the field, and as it did, the melons grew very quickly, right before the farmer's eyes.

" 'We don't want you to lie to the soldiers,' said Mary. 'But tell them we came through when you were seeding and they will leave you alone.'

"The next day when the soldiers came through they asked the farmer when the Holy Family had passed. When he told them it was when he was seeding, they looked at the fully grown crop and concluded that the family had come through this area at least five months earlier. They then gave up the chase and went back to Bethlehem."

"And now the water that improved the fertility of the field is drunk by women who want to have children?" I asked the monk.

"Yes, it is, and it works very well," he said confidently.

I was impressed yet puzzled. "Why have I not been able to find reference to this site in any of the source material I have gathered?" I asked.

The monk shrugged.

"Perhaps things have changed since your source material was written," he said. "The Holy Family was mysterious, and maybe all of the sites were not revealed at the same time. New ones have been found. Maybe this is a newer site."

"But if this took place two thousand years ago, and my source material is less than twenty years old, that means this site was just recently revealed," I said through Mustache.

The priest confirmed what I said with a nod.

"That is correct," he said. "God reveals things to us when he wants us to see them. There are other sites that he will reveal to us later, and those will be confirmed by priests and bishops of the church. It is the way God works. It is a thing that is hard to accept sometimes. Then the maps get redrawn, the Holy Family's route is changed, and everyone accepts what is new along with what is old."

I understood what the monk was saying: The story of Jesus in Egypt is an evolving one. Still, I must have had a puzzled look on my face because the monk continued to explain.

"Many of the stories have been written down, but many of them have been passed on by word of mouth from the time the Holy Family was here. That makes these stories even more pure and strong. That is what faith is supposed to do. It is supposed to connect people to God. It is not some kind of legal process where we try to prove if something is right or wrong. We have a different way of thinking here. It is not always just intellectual. It has much to do with faith."

Standing with the monk in a room filled with icons, I knew that I had found what I came to find: a story that was partly truth and partly fiction, a story that was based in myth, magic, and reality—the same stew of elements that has created all of the world's great religions.

"In your research you will find many things that you expect to find," said the monk. "But you will also find many things that will be a surprise to you. Some will amaze you and some might even give you awe. Some might even frighten you. That is the nature of a living belief."

As I walked back down the stairs with Mustache by my side, I thought about the beginning of my own journey to retrace the path of Jesus in Egypt, the one that started in a dusty and rough town on the border with Israel in the Sinai Desert. . . .

Part I

1. Jesus Did Not Sleep Here

June 1, in the year of our Lord 2, according to Coptic tradition.

With the wilting sun at their backs, and broiling sand at their feet, the three people and a donkey approached the western border of what was then known as Judea. They were a sad and parched lot as they made their way for Wady el-Arish, the river of Egypt.

Perhaps they felt relief as they approached the river. Crossing this muddy ribbon of water would put Judea behind them. The same could not be said of all of their problems. Soldiers would certainly follow, and the fact that the child on the donkey was wanted dead or alive by King Herod made the crossing of a border almost meaningless.

Joseph had pushed hard to get away from Bethlehem. That is what the angel who appeared in his dream had told him to do. An angry King Herod was preparing to slaughter all male children two years old and younger. The reason for this carnage was a story told to Herod by three wise men from the east. They declared that a new king had been born. The paranoid monarch saw himself as the one and only ruler of Judea. To eliminate any possible competition, Herod ordered the death of all the male children under two in Bethlehem, an event that became known as the slaughter of the innocents.

Had an angel not clued Joseph to the pending carnage, the baby Jesus would have been slain with all of the others. Now the one wanted by Herod—the one whose birth was marked by a phenomenal star in the east—was trying to escape.

With tired legs, Joseph led his family toward the border river. This muddy strip of water was the western boundary of Canaan, the place given to the people of Israel by God in the book of Numbers. In the winter, when heavy rains fell in the mountains, this rushing torrent would be impassable. But on this blazing hot day there was little water to slow their progress. The agonized travelers likely paused for a moment to drink from the brown stream, or to wash the heat and grime from their faces. They may even have found dark humor in the notion that some people in Judea considered this very bleak and barren spot to be the site of the Garden of Eden. Whatever transpired, reaching this water was a heavenly respite from the harsh desert.

Joseph looked back for a moment and then ahead. The desert in front looked the same as the treacherous desert behind. The sun was hot and beat down with such intensity that Joseph could easily have curled up beneath a bush and waited for the relief of sundown. And then there were the heat waves that rose from the pale sand and caused illusions. Several times Joseph had seen bushes in the distance that looked like people or donkeys because of the mirage effects of the desert. It may have made Joseph wonder: Were all of those incredible events that happened in the Negev Desert simply caused by heat madness and mirage? Or were those happenings real?

First there were the dragons.

According to the Gospel of Pseudo-Matthew, a book that St. Jerome attributed to the "hand of the most blessed Evangelist Matthew," the dragons came from a cave where the travelers had stopped for a rest. "Suddenly," reads the gospel,

> there came forth from the cave many dragons. . . . Then Jesus went down from the bosom of His mother, and stood on His feet before the dragons; and they adored Jesus, and thereafter retired. Then was fulfilled that which was said by David the prophet, saying: "Praise the Lord from the earth, ye dragons, ye dragons, and all ye deeps. And the young child Jesus, walking before them, commanded them to hurt no man. But Mary and Joseph were very much afraid lest the child should be hurt by the dragons." And Jesus said to them: "Do not be afraid, and do not consider me to be a little child; for I am and al-

ways have been perfect and all the beasts of the forest must need be tame before me."

The words echoed in Joseph's ears: *Do not be afraid, and do not consider me to be a little child; for I am and always have been perfect.*

How could Joseph think of Jesus as a child after that? He was a unique supernatural being. In the ensuing days, according to the book of Pseudo-Matthew, Joseph saw his holy charge perform miracle after miracle. Lions and panthers and other beasts of the desert accompanied them with respect. They showed their submission to the Holy Child by wagging their tails and bowing. And when Mary showed fear of the wild animals, Jesus engaged his mother's attention and said: "Be not afraid, Mother; for they come not to do thee harm, but they make haste to serve both thee and me."

Even the trees obeyed this infant. Several days after their journey had begun, Mary was seriously fatigued by the heat and searing sun of the desert. Seeing a palm tree, the young mother asked to rest in the shade. As she sat in the relative coolness, Mary looked up and saw that the tree was loaded with dates. She began to think about eating a piece of the moist fruit.

"I wonder that thou sayest this, when thou seest how high the palm tree is; and that thou thinkest of eating its fruit," Joseph said to her. "I am thinking more of the want of water, because the skins are now empty, and we have none wherewith to refresh ourselves and our cattle."

The baby listened to this conversation from his mother's lap. He was reported to have a "joyful countenance." The book of Pseudo-Matthew reports the scene this way:

O tree, bend thy branches, and refresh my mother with thy fruit. And immediately at these words the palm bent its top down to the very feet of the blessed Mary; and they gathered from it fruit, with which they were all refreshed. And after they had gathered all its fruit, it remained bent down, waiting the order to rise from Him who bade commanded it to stoop. Then Jesus said to it: "Raise thyself, O palm tree, and be strong, and be the companion of my trees, which are in the paradise of my Father; and open from thy roots a vein of water which has been hid in the earth, and let the waters flow, so that we may be satisfied from thee." And it rose up immediately, and at its roots there began to come forth a spring of water exceedingly clear and cool and sparkling. And when they saw the spring of water, they rejoiced with great joy, and were satisfied, themselves and all their cattle and their beasts.

As they crossed the river of Egypt and headed into the land of the pharaohs, Joseph must certainly have looked back at the boy called Jesus and at his young wife, Mary, and wondered what was ahead for them. Egypt was known as an open-minded country, one where the population was well versed in magic and supernatural powers. Still, thought Joseph, how were the people of Egypt going to take to a child mystic? One who could heal, destroy, and create with just thoughts? Would they believe that he was the Messiah, no less than the Son of God?

The day was hot and the travel was difficult. But on June 1, in the year of our Lord 2, Joseph must have felt a slight chill at what was to come in the land of the Nile.

He pressed on. The town of El-Arish was nearby.

⤙✦⤚

NOVEMBER 9, 2001

"Paul, I am sorry."

"It's okay, Ra'ed."

"It doesn't seem to be okay, Paul. You seem disappointed or maybe angry."

"I am disappointed. And maybe a little angry, too. This voyage hasn't happened as advertised."

"What do you mean? I did not advertise anything. Is that just an Americanism?"

"Yes, an Americanism. I am sorry to confuse you."

"You did not confuse me, I just did not understand. Is an Americanism something I am supposed to laugh at? Is it funny?"

"No. It is just a phrase we use a lot."

"I am glad I did not laugh, then. I did not find it funny."

"I am glad you did not laugh, too, Ra'ed. Can we not talk for a few minutes? I have to get my thoughts together."

"That is good, Paul. We will be quiet. I just want you to know that I did not know about the land mines. And I will not talk anymore to policemen or soldiers unless they speak to me first. Is that fine?"

"Yes, Ra'ed, that is very fine."

I sighed and settled back into the well-worn backseat of the Peugeot station wagon. The rough Egyptian roads had turned the black and white French vehicle into a loose assemblage of nuts and bolts. As we sped across the Sinai Desert toward the setting sun, the car owned by Sa'ad Abdoullah sounded as though it might come apart in midflight.

For a brief moment of self-pity, I saw the car as a metaphor for the day's voyage. We were rattling and rolling away from El-Arish, a dusty town near the Egyptian/Israeli border, having seen virtually nothing of what I planned to see.

Not that there was really much there to begin with.

El-Arish is the first town in Egypt that the Holy Family would have come to as they headed for the Nile. It was the first town I planned to visit as I retraced the steps of the infant Jesus and his family through the mysterious land of Egypt. In fact, El-Arish was probably a blur to the Holy Family. They passed through this dusty outpost as fast as possible. Legends say that they were concerned about being caught by Herod's pursuing soldiers and wanted to get as far away from them as they could. There might have been other reasons as well for their rush. In those days, El-Arish was called Rhinocolura, a name given to the town by Greeks who were just calling it what it was: a town for prisoners whose punishment consisted of having their noses cut off.

Although none of the Infancy Gospels or Coptic legends indicate that Jesus even did so much as sleep here, I did want to talk to the local Christians to see if there were any accounts of the Holy Family in El-Arish that had not been written down. And I wanted to see another archaeological treasure that was rumored to be there.

In the Old Testament book of Exodus, Moses tries to convince the pharaoh to let the Jews leave Egypt for the land that God had promised them. Despite two demonstrations of proof that Moses had the power of God on his side, the pharaoh refuses the request of Moses to "let my people go." To show God's power, Moses stretches his staff toward the river Nile and the water slowly turns to blood except in Goshen, where the Jews lived.

This was the first of ten plagues alleged to be unleashed on the Egyptians by God. After the bloody water came frogs, lice, wild beasts, pestilence, boils, hail, locusts, darkness, and finally, the slaying of the firstborn child of every Egyptian.

The last plague finally broke the will of the pharaoh. With his oldest son dead before him and the sounds of wailing mothers piercing the air, the pharaoh beckoned Moses and told him to leave the country.

Moses led an estimated six hundred thousand Jews out of Goshen to the shores of the Red Sea. Soon the angry pharaoh gave chase with his army. The waters parted for the Jews to cross. As the last of the followers of Moses crossed into the Sinai Desert, the pharaoh's army charged into the same canyons of water, their horses pulling hard at the heavy chariots. You know the rest of the story. God caused the waters to fall back and the powerful army disappeared beneath the waves.

It is a great story, certainly one of the central sagas of the Bible. To date, however, there is no significant archaeological proof that it took place. But there is some minor archaeological proof of the plagues. One such artifact is a black granite monolith in El-Arish found at the site of an Egyptian governor's palace, which seems to confirm the plague of darkness.

On the ebony slab is inscribed this message:

> The land was in great affliction. Evil fell on this earth.... it was a great upheaval in the residence.... Nobody left the palace during nine days, and during these nine days of upheaval there was such a tempest that neither the men nor the gods could see the faces of their next.

In addition to seeing the first stop of Jesus in Egypt, I also wanted to see this stone record of what appeared to be the ninth plague.

As it was, I would not see the mysterious granite. I would barely see El-Arish itself.

We came into the sparse and dusty town just as the noon call to prayer began to emanate from the minarets, the tall slender towers that stood like spikes next to the mosques. The call to prayer is projected from loudspeakers in the tower tops and is so loud that, as one Muslim told me, "only the deaf could deny hearing it." I expected the town to come to a halt as the faithful unrolled prayer rugs and knelt to the east, in the direction of the holy city of Mecca in Saudi Arabia. I was wrong. The town barely slowed at all when the muezzin began his nasal prayer. The people who were gathered in groups on the sidewalk continued their conversations as though nothing were taking place. Some even had a look of irritation at the auditory competition.

Still, I felt uncomfortable at continuing to drive during the call to prayer. Even though we were all Christians in the car, we were not pausing to pay our respects to another religion.

"Shouldn't we stop until the call to prayer is over?" I asked Ra'ed as we drove down the main street.

"Not unless you want to be run over," said the translator.

Our goal was to find the Coptic church, which, according to the first person we asked, was "somewhere downtown." According to the visions of Pope Theophilus in the fourth century, which first established the Holy Family trail, Jesus, Mary, and Joseph came through here in high gear, hoping to get away from Herod's pursuing soldiers as quickly as possible.

Still, I considered this an important site because it marked the point at which Jesus fulfilled the Old Testament prophecy of Isaiah 19:1, in which the prophet said: "See, the Lord rides on a swift cloud and is coming to Egypt. The idols of Egypt tremble before him, and the hearts of the Egyptians melt within them."

This is interpreted in the Coptic Church as prophesying Jesus riding into Egypt with his mother, symbolized by the "swift cloud." Seen in this way, say some religious scholars, the Copts are the only church in the world to be prophesied in the Old Testament.

Also, the prophecy is a clear attack on the pagan religion of ancient Egypt. Although there were no pharaohs when Jesus arrived, there were plenty of idols and idolatry. Festivals were still being held in honor of the various gods whose stone visages dotted the country.

In the ensuing battle between Christianity and paganism, the ancient town of Rhinocolura was the first beachhead. Egyptian Christians love to quote Hosea 11:1, which says, "Out of Egypt I have called my son." But that was later. El-Arish was where Jesus came *into* Egypt.

✠

"Where's the Coptic church?" asked Ra'ed. We had stopped in the middle of the town's main traffic circle to ask a policeman for directions. Behind us the traffic was backing up. Horns were honking furiously. The traffic cop didn't care. He stood straight and rubbed his chin for a moment. The drivers behind were in a fury by the time he leaned his head into the window.

"I don't know," he said, pointing down one of the four main streets that played off the circle. "Try down there. It might be that way."

Ra'ed smiled, but not pleasantly. "And it might not," he said as Sa'ad, our driver, hit the gas and we sped away.

Tradition says that the Coptic Orthodox Church in El-Arish marked the spot where the Holy Family paused for a few hours before continuing to Tell Basta, where Jesus' first confrontation with stone idols would take place. It was here in El-Arish that Jesus would start to gather believers, more than thirty years before he started his formal ministry. The Coptic Church believes that the visit of the Holy Family to Egypt prepared the hearts of the Egyptians to receive Jesus' message of salvation. But it was also a training ground for Jesus, a place where the manlike infant first practiced his ministry and first demonstrated his miraculous powers.

To me that made El-Arish as significant—if less dramatic—than the Red Sea was to Moses. It was the entry point for Jesus into a different kind of promised land, from which his message would eventually be spread throughout the world.

We hit the brakes and stopped in front of a bewildered man who was trying almost hopelessly to cross the street against the traffic.

"Where's the Coptic church?" asked Ra'ed in a demanding tone.

The man straightened up and looked around. Cars began piling up behind us again and with them the sound of horns. Once again, the perpetrators of this traffic jam didn't care.

"It could be down there," said the man, pointing down a different street. "I am Muslim, so I don't know where such a church might be."

Ra'ed made a flicking motion with his hand and Sa'ad hit the gas, kicking up dirt on a main street that was more dirt than pavement.

Once again I settled back into the car seat and watched the dusty town of El-Arish fly by the window. I tried to imagine what this place had been like in the time of Jesus but could not. There was too much honking and swerving to visualize an ancient town with little in it but mud buildings and criminals with hacked-off noses.

It would have been a hardscrabble place back then—heaven knows it seemed like that now—but the arrival of Jesus here signified something momentous for the Copts. It meant that they, too, were God's chosen people.

Since God called the people of Egypt "my people," in the Old Testament prophecy of Isaiah, and then sent his "only begotten son" to Egypt, the Egyptians see themselves as the first to be trusted with the safekeeping of Jesus outside of Israel.

This trust was a form of grace, wrote Coptic Pope Shenouda III in a 1981 article. "As Egypt opened its heart to Jesus and welcomed the Holy Family, so open your heart to God."

Frankly, I have serious doubts that the ancient people of Egypt opened their hearts and welcomed the Holy Family. According to the Infancy Gospels and the Coptic visions and traditions, Jesus and his parents were unwelcome virtually everywhere they went in Egypt. From town after town they were booted out. The reason was simple: Jesus was seen as a destroyer. The miracle-making infant displayed no patience for local religious traditions of stone idols and oracles. In fact, Jesus would raise the ire of Egyptian citizens by destroying their objects of worship. At times the lives of the Holy Family were threatened, with stones hurled along with death threats. But that didn't deter the infant Jesus. When the Holy Family left a town where they were not wanted, Jesus would see to it that the idol worshipers of that town suffered in one way or another. This running battle with the locals disturbed Joseph. The Infancy Gospel of Thomas tells of Joseph asking Jesus: "Why do you do such things that these people must suffer and hate us and persecute us?"

Still, Pope Shenouda interprets the constant movement of the Holy Family as a sign of their welcome. Indeed, Shenouda argues that the destruction of idols and the punishment of idol worshipers showed the Egyptians that the power of God was greater than that of their pagan gods. In short, Jesus the destroyer of idols made a lasting impression on the Egyptians. He may not have been loved by all Egyptians, at least according to the Infancy Gospels, but he was respected and in some cases feared. It was perhaps that mixture of fear and respect that made Egypt ripe for St. Mark, who came to Egypt in about 41 C.E., to spread the gospel of Christianity.

"Where is the Coptic church?" Ra'ed asked another pedestrian.

"It is that way," said the man, pointing straight ahead and giving directions. I could see a Coptic cross tattooed on his wrist, a common adornment among devout Christians.

We drove slowly down the street and then turned down a narrow alley. Garbage was strewn everywhere and stray cats were having a field day. We went about a hundred feet and then stopped in front of a junked refrigerator.

"Here it is," said Ra'ed. "Here is the Church of the Holy Virgin."

I was stunned. The entrance to the church looked more like the back entrance to a New York deli than perhaps the holiest Christian site in El-Arish.

"This is supposed to be the first site visited by Jesus in Egypt," I said to Ra'ed. "Couldn't they make the church look better?"

Ra'ed agreed. "You are correct, it does not look healthy," he said. "But the people here are very devout and it is not easy being a Christian in a town with so many Muslims. They do not have very much money because of that."

Ra'ed went on to tell me how difficult it is to be a Christian in a Muslim country. Although Egypt was once a great Christian nation, that all changed with the Arab conquest in 639–641. Christians faced increased taxation by Muslim rulers. And gradually their language disappeared, Coptic being replaced by Arabic. By the beginning of the eighth century, Arabic was the official language of the government.

Over the years, Christians in Egypt have been persecuted by a variety of rulers, even Napoleon Bonaparte, who declared himself a Muslim in 1798 when the French occupied Egypt. He didn't fool anyone; it was well known that Napoleon converted specifically to gain the favor of his new subjects. But his conversion was a blow to the Coptic Church, whose parishioners expected a renewal in both numbers and spirit when the future emperor of France took over their country.

The number of Coptic Christians continued to drop after Napoleon's reign. Now the once powerful church represents only about 5 percent of Egypt's population. After the revolution of 1952 came a call by President Nasser for religious liberty. He declared the minorities "to be like jewels, which are rare and therefore they are precious."

"It has been easier to be a Christian since then," said Ra'ed. "But there is still a lot of discrimination against us. Many people say they cannot hire us because we are Christians. The government has tried to stop discrimination but it has not helped. It is still difficult to be a Christian, especially in a small town like this that is dominated by Muslims. Nobody lets you make any money."

We went into a scruffy courtyard and waited for a priest.

I wanted to talk to a priest about the Coptic Church's version of the Holy Family map, the one that traces the nearly four-year journey of Jesus through Egypt. By reading the Infancy Gospels, it is possible to outline a fairly accurate map. In some of the gospels—as with some books of the Bible—there are actual place names to go with the stories. For the most part, though, one is left to guess as to the exact route.

The Copts, though, believe they know the exact route, not to mention the exact day on which the Holy Family crossed into Egypt. They know the Holy Family trail because of the vision of Pope Theophilus, their twenty-third pope, who reigned over the Church from 385 to 412.

It was through him, said Father Amnous, that the route of the Holy Family in Egypt became one that a pilgrim could actually follow.

"Although Jesus did not spend much time in El-Arish, we know he came through this very spot because of the vision of Theophilus," said Father Amnous.

We were sitting in the waiting room of Father Amnous' residence. When I expressed my belief that this church sat on a symbolic location, he corrected me and said that it was on the actual route itself.

"The tour of the Holy Family is known first by imitation," said Father Amnous. "Then it is known by visions."

The imitation mentioned by Father Amnous took place in ancient times, when Christian pilgrims would travel to cities and sites that they thought were associated with the Holy Family's route. Some of these were well known, such as Tell Basta, which is mentioned in the prophecies of Ezekiel in the Old Testament. Memphis was also a well-known site, as was Hermopolis. All of these sites were mentioned in the Infancy Gospels. But in the days before the Infancy Gospels were circulated among the believers, stories and place names circulated among the believers by word of mouth.

"Pilgrims would go to these well-known sites and they would hear stories about other sites. Pretty soon those sites, too, became part of the pilgrims' trail," said Father Amnous.

I pointed out that many stories about Jesus as a child are recorded in gospels that were not included in the Bible. Some of these gospels were considered contradictory to the beliefs of the scholars who put the Bible together. But others were not. They became a source of argument among those who decided what was right and what was wrong to include in the Bible. "Why aren't there more stories about Jesus in Egypt in the Bible?" I asked Father Amnous.

"When the eyewitness testimony to Jesus was written by Matthew, Mark, Luke, and John, they concentrated on the miracles, crucifixion, death, and resurrection of Jesus Christ," said Father Amnous. "It is a joyful telling that concentrates on the personality and characteristics of Jesus Christ himself. Perhaps they felt that that was enough."

Father Amnous told us about Farama, another site that the Holy Family was said to have passed through. We got directions to this site from one of the church deacons. Although this was another quick stop by the Holy Family before continuing on to the Nile, I still wanted to see it. Farama, like all the other sites I would be visiting, had an extensive and interesting history outside of its connection to Jesus. Known as Sin in the Old Testament book of Ezekiel and Pelusium by Greek and Roman cultures, this eastern outpost was called the "key to Egypt" by foreign invaders from the east. It was a busy port that served as a focal point for caravans and traders. But the Nile silted the harbor and made it worthless for sea trade, and today there are only ruins of the ancient city.

I wanted to see the dozens of archaeological digs that date to before Christ and all the way up to the seventh century. And nearby, I was hoping to see the large granite monument recording the ninth plague.

It was not to be.

On our way out to Farama we became lost, first down one long desert road and then another.

"I am afraid we are off course," said Ra'ed as Sa'ad stopped the car to consult a map.

The three of us huddled over the map, which we spread out on top of the car's hood. Down the road, maybe a mile away, an army truck was making rapid progress toward us. It billowed dust as the driver moved up through the gears to gain speed.

"I will ask these soldiers where Farama is," said Ra'ed.

"I wish you wouldn't involve the army," I said. "They are better left alone."

"It will be okay," said Ra'ed. "They are lazy. They will not ask questions."

As the truck approached, Ra'ed stepped out into the road and flagged it down. The truck stopped next to us in a storm of dust that was dragging behind it. A lieutenant dressed in the bright green of the Egyptian army got out of the passenger seat and gave us the once over. As Ra'ed started to speak, the soldier held up his hand.

"What are you doing out here?" he asked.

"We are looking for the trail of Jesus," Ra'ed said quite boldly.

The soldier eyed Ra'ed and then me. He asked if I was from Israel and when I told him no, he asked where I was from.

"This is not a place where American tourists should be right now," said the soldier. "There is border tension after September eleventh."

"Oh, he is not a typical tourist," said Ra'ed. "He is a writer. He is writing about the trail of the Holy Family."

In retrospect it seemed like a benign thing for Ra'ed to say. To the soldier, though, it meant that I was a reporter. He wanted to see my press credentials.

"Tell him I don't have any," I said. "I am writing about Jesus. He was here two thousand years ago. I am writing about history, not news."

Ra'ed translated what I said faithfully, but the soldier could not make the distinction. Then in a burst of Arabic he said something to Ra'ed that made my translator shudder.

"He has said that there are millions of land mines around here," said Ra'ed. "He said we should not even step off the road to pee. There are millions of land mines around us right here."

Somehow we had strayed into an area that was mined many years ago as protection against a possible invasion by Israel. Later I confirmed what the lieutenant had told us. A report from the International Campaign to Ban Landmines says that twenty-three million land mines are in the deserts of Egypt, a large portion of them in the desert around where we were standing. And another report, this from the Landmine Struggle Center in Cairo, said that three thousand Egyptians have been killed by land mines in the last twenty years, and five thousand injured, "including foreigners."

"This is no place for you to be," repeated the lieutenant.

We promised to return to the regional minister of tourism in El-Arish and attempt to secure press credentials. We thought that it would be easy to get the credentials and we could then return to Farama and the sites beyond. We were, of course, wrong. Given the border tensions and the fact that this man was merely a regional minister of tourism, not someone higher in the bureaucracy, it was impossible for him to issue anything but sympathy. I would have to return to Cairo to get proper press accreditation.

"Still, I don't understand why you wanted to come here anyway if you are just studying Jesus," the minister said through Ra'ed. "You have spent more time here already than the Holy Family did."

As we left his office to head back across the Sinai Desert, the minister offered the most appropriate farewell that he could under the circumstances.

"Come back sometime when you have the correct papers," he said. "Jesus did not stop here very long, but that doesn't mean that you can't."

2. Field of Fallen Idols

The tension in the car subsided about fifty miles west of El-Arish, and we started talking again. We decided not to return to the press office in Cairo. To do so would cause us to backtrack several hundred miles. I thought it would be best for us to stay on the Holy Family route. I could always go to the press office later, when our excursion through the Delta was over.

"A few days is nothing to an Egyptian bureaucrat," said Ra'ed. "If you showed up immediately, they would probably become suspicious of you. Everyone takes their time here."

The sun was dropping now. It sat like a big orange ball on the horizon, its powerful rays dampened by high clouds and a haze of sand that hung over the desert. The low sun turned the white sands of the Sinai the color of concrete. The desert became a bluish gray, marked in spots by the orange rays of the sun reflecting off the low hills.

"Let's stop and enjoy the sundown," I said.

Sa'ad pulled to the side of the road and we all got out. We stood in silence, gazing across an endless expanse of desert. The sand particles in the air reflected the light, making the atmosphere around us seem touchable. It had an eerie beauty to it, one that combined the natural and the supernatural.

A chill came over me and I reached back into the car for my jacket. When I turned back around, Ra'ed grabbed me by the arm and pointed across the desert. There, coming out of a wash, was a man leading a donkey. On the back of the donkey was a woman holding a child.

We looked at each other in stunned disbelief.

Sa'ad spoke rapidly in Arabic and Ra'ed nodded heartily.

"Yes, I agree with Sa'ad," he said to me. "This is a sign for us. It is a sign that we are on the right path."

The trio passed less than a hundred yards in front of us. They waved and we waved back. They did not slow down nor did they speak.

The woman was sitting sidesaddle on the donkey and holding the child on her forward thigh. The stride of the donkey was short and sharp, making the woman bounce up and down rapidly on the saddle. She looked like a piston in a machine.

"That must be very painful," I said to Ra'ed.

"Yes, many of these Bedouins have very bad backs," he said. "Personally I would rather be the man. He has to walk but at least his back doesn't get hammered the whole trip."

We went back to the car and soon we were flying down the highway at sixty miles per hour. Darkness fell. We were each thinking about what we had just seen.

"It looked just like the scene from the Bible," said Ra'ed.

"Yes, but a scene like that wasn't recorded in the Bible, remember?" I asked.

"You're right," said Ra'ed. "So we'll say it looked like the Vision of Theophilus. Maybe we just witnessed a part of his vision."

According to the account in the book of Pseudo-Matthew, the Holy Family had crossed from El-Arish to Tell Basta—an area in the Delta called by the gospel "the capital of Egypt"—about as quickly as we were doing right now.

Instead of following the shoreline of the Mediterranean Sea to Alexandria and then heading south, the Holy Family decided to cut across the desert. The route was much shorter, but it had its drawbacks. There were many hills and dry washes. Thieves were abundant, and the summer heat made their skin burn.

Somewhere west of El-Arish, Joseph lost his stomach for the sweltering route. He wanted to travel the long but cool way, by the Mediterranean.

"Lord, it is a boiling heat," said Joseph to his infant son. "If it please thee, let us go by the seashore, that we may be able to rest in the cities on the coast."

"Fear not, Joseph," said Jesus. "I will shorten the way for you, so that what you would have taken thirty days to go over, you shall accomplish in this one day."

And so it was, according to the book of Pseudo-Matthew. As Jesus and Joseph spoke to one another, the Holy Family accelerated to a tremendous speed. They crossed that treacherous expanse of desert as quickly as we were doing it right now in our beat-up Peugeot, only they didn't need gasoline. Before long they could "see the mountains and cities of Egypt." And then they were there, with no more back-pounding miles to cover. As if riding on the swift cloud talked about in Isaiah, the Holy Family had arrived at Tell Basta (also known as Bubastis).

Tell Basta has had a strange history, even by Egyptian standards. Four cities in the immediate vicinity have been the capital of ancient Egypt at one time or another. Tell Basta itself was the capital for a short period of time under Pharaoh Sheshonk, who ruled between 945 and 924 B.C.E.

Much of its fame is the result of it being the main center for the cult worship of the cat goddess Bastet. In honor of this feline there was an annual festival that included intoxication and promiscuous sex.

In the Bible, Tell Basta is referred to in the prophecy of Ezekiel as one of the places in Egypt that would be destroyed by God in order to break the yoke of the pharaohs. Ezekiel 30:17 reads, "The young men of Heliopolis and Bubastis will fall by the sword, and the cities themselves will go into captivity."

That particular prophecy proved to be true. Tell Basta was destroyed, possibly as late as the seventh century during the Persian conquest of Egypt.

Jesus became thirsty. Finding no water in their possessions, Mary decided to take the baby Jesus into town, leaving Joseph at the camp with all of their goods.

The voyage to town was a disaster. None of the women they encountered would give water to Mary or her child. When Mary and Jesus returned to camp they found Joseph asleep, and the golden and silver sandals of Jesus had been stolen by thieves.

Mary broke down in tears at this emotionally painful chain of events. Jesus comforted his mother and then performed another miracle. Wiping a tear from her eye, he made the sign of the cross in the dirt before them. Instantly a spring of water jetted from the ground.

After the Holy Family drank from the fresh well, described as being "sweet as honey and white as snow," Jesus blessed the water.

"Let this water help make whole and heal the souls and bodies of all those who shall drink it," said Jesus. "With the exception of the inhabitants of this town, of whom none shall be healed by it."

The next day a farmer named Klum happened on the Holy Family. They were sitting near the fields where Klum had been working. They had nothing to eat and must have amounted to a pitiful sight.

"Why are you here?" asked Klum.

"We are running from soldiers of King Herod," said Mary. "He wants to kill my child."

Klum was moved. He then invited them to his home near Tell Basta. This was an act of bravery and compassion. Not only was he willing to take in strangers, he was sheltering someone who was wanted dead or alive by one of history's most ruthless kings.

When the Holy Family arrived at Klum's house they found that his wife was paralyzed. Coptic legend offers no details of the events that followed. It says merely that Jesus healed the woman's paralysis.

A second miracle took place the next day. The First Gospel of the Infancy of Jesus Christ includes the story of the demented three-year-old son of an Egyptian priest. The gospel does not mention the name of the town where they lived, but events surrounding this healing put it in the vicinity of Tell Basta. According to the gospel, the boy "was possessed with a great multitude of devils who uttered many strange things and when the devils seized him, walked about naked with his clothes torn off, throwing stones at those whom he saw."

On this particular day, the mad child went into the inn where Mary was washing the swaddling clothes of Jesus and hanging them on a post to dry. As the gospel reads:

[T]he boy possessed with the devil took down one of them and put it upon his head. And presently the devils began to come out of his mouth, and fly away in the shape of crows and serpents. From that time the boy was healed by the power of the Lord Christ, and he began to sing praises, and give thanks to the Lord who had healed him.

When his father saw him restored to his former state of health, he said, "My son, what has happened to thee, and by what means wert thou cured?"

The son answered, "When the devils seized me, I went into the inn and there found a very handsome woman with a boy, whose swaddling clothes she had just before washed, and hanged out upon a post. One of these I took, and put it upon my head, and immediately the devils left me, and fled away."

All of the infancy sources contain a version of what happened next. It was June and shortly after the season of the cat. For a two-month period in April and May, Egyptians would descend on an island in the Nile close to Tell Basta. They came to worship Bastet, the cat goddess. Bastet represented the life-giving warmth of the sun. This festival was a time to bask in the pleasures of nature before the long hot summer arrived. It is said that more than seven hundred thousand people would descend on this area for an outdoor carnival of singing, dancing, drinking, and sex. Many hundreds of women came away from this festival pregnant, the identity of the father unknown. So common were such pregnancies that the word *bastard* may well be the cat goddess's most lasting legacy, or so say some Egyptian linguists.

Herodotus wrote about the Festival of Bastet in his *Histories, Book II*:

When the people are on their way to Bubastis [Tell Basta], they go by river, a great number in every boat, men and women together. Some of the women make noise with rattles, others play flutes all the way, while the rest of the women and the men sing and clap their hands. As they travel by river to Bubastis, whenever they come near any other town they bring their boat near the bank; then some of the women do as I have said, while some shout mockery of the women of the town; others dance, and others stand up and lift their skirts.... But when they have reached Bubastis, they make a festival with great sacrifices, and more wine is drunk at this feast than in the whole year besides.

Maybe Klum thought the young Jesus would enjoy seeing the Temple of Bastet. Loved far and wide, the temple and its grounds were set in the middle of an island in a valley, so people could sit on the surrounding hills and see the festivities. The temple itself was a square building of red granite with a magnificent shrine to the cat goddess at the center. Surrounding the statue of the goddess was an enclosure of trees—it was the only temple in Egypt with trees inside. As Herodotus said, "Other temples are greater and more costly, but none more pleasing to the eye than this."

And then there were the cats. Baby Jesus would love the cats, thought Klum. The temple was filled with well-groomed felines that were carried around in baskets by priests and fed special food. Around the temple were stone idols and monuments from the hundreds of years that the Temple of Bastet had been in existence.

Perhaps Klum took the Holy Family to the festival in heartfelt gratitude for the miraculous healing Jesus had performed on his wife. Whatever Klum's motivation was for taking them there, he was certainly not prepared for what happened.

"It doesn't look like much," I said to Ra'ed.

"You aren't there yet," he said. "It's over that hill."

Behind us was the entrance to the archaeological complex and the parking lot. From the road the entrance had seemed so cryptic that we had passed it before Ra'ed recognized it and ordered Sa'ad to stop. Once we got inside the grounds, things seemed even stranger. There was a small garden of sculptures from the pharaonic era. But other than that, this place looked like a police station. In fact, it *was* a police station of some sort. To one side was a large building with a constant stream of soldiers and police officers scurrying in and out. Toward the back of the property was a high dirt berm with the sound of gunfire coming from behind it.

"That is a shooting range for policemen," said Ra'ed. "We won't be going over there."

We continued to walk toward another hill. *This place looks like a waste of time,* I said to myself. *A total zero. All I see is scrub brush and dirt. They must have cleared this off with a road grader.*

Then we came to the hill and the entire scene changed. There in front of us was an enormous field of fallen idols. There were hundreds of them, covering perhaps a square mile. Pillars the circumference of pine trees had been toppled. Heads of stone pharaohs the size of automobiles were broken off and lying next to their own stone feet. Statues of shapely stone queens were lying on their sides. Massive steles were broken into pieces that were scattered all over the ground. Walls were crumbled, as prophesied by Ezekiel.

Near the Delta city of Zagazig is Tell Basta, a field of fallen idols surrounding a well that was dug in the first century.

And there, in the foreground, was a perfectly shaped well, its circular wall neatly fashioned from irregular bricks. I looked inside. The well was partially full of water. Floating on its surface were bits of Styrofoam cup and other rubbish.

I began to laugh at the scene in front of us.

"I did the same thing the first time I saw this," said Ra'ed.

"I can't help it," I said. "It is so true to the gospels that it's almost absurd."

I brought out my copy of the Infancy Gospels and opened it to the book of Pseudo-Matthew. "Listen to this," I said to Ra'ed, standing on the hill overlooking the ancient destruction and reading out loud.

[T]hey went into a temple which was called the capital of Egypt. And in this temple there had been set up three hundred and fifty-five idols, to each of which on its own day divine honours and sacred rites were paid. For the Egyptians belonging to the same city entered the capital, in which the priests told them how many sacrifices were offered each day, according to the honour in which the god was held.

And it came to pass, when the most blessed Mary went into the temple with the little child, that all the idols prostrated themselves on the ground, so that all of them were lying on their faces shattered and broken to pieces; and thus they plainly showed that they were nothing. Then was fulfilled that which was said by the prophet Isaiah: Behold, the Lord will come upon a swift cloud, and will enter Egypt, and all the handiwork of the Egyptians shall be moved at his presence.

Reading the Infancy Gospel at the site where the event it described had taken place was a heady feeling. It was like reading Exodus while sitting on the shores of the Red Sea, or the story of King Solomon while on the Temple Mount. I could read the words and then look up to see the place just as it was being described in the book. The story was alive in both words and scenes, even though it was two thousand years old. Being there gave life to the words.

Surely all of this really took place, I said to myself. *I am surrounded by fallen idols, just like it says in the gospel.*

I joined Ra'ed by the well.

"Yes, that is what we Copts believe happened," said Ra'ed, referring to the verses I had just read. "It has not been read to me before from that book, but it is exactly as we believe it. Jesus knocked all of these idols down with his mind."

"That was from the book of Pseudo-Matthew," I told him. "Maybe Theophilus heard the story before he had his vision."

"No, that was a vision," corrected Ra'ed. "A vision is not the same as word of mouth."

"Perhaps not," I said. "But one thing that is missing from the Infancy Gospels is any mention of this well. What is its story?"

"Oh yes, the story of the well," said Ra'ed. "The story of the well picks up where your story ends. After Jesus made the idols fall he created a well right here to convince the people that he was someone who was obeyed by nature. He just put his hand down to the ground and made the water come up to the surface. It was another miracle. But even after everything they had seen, the people still refused to believe him. They did not want to give up the cat goddess and all of their other gods. So they asked the soldiers to arrest the family."

I picked up the Gospel of Pseudo-Matthew again and opened it to the spot where I had left off.

"Yes, the coming of the soldiers is written about in this book," I said. I searched through the verses and then began to read.

Then Aphrodosius, that governor of the city, when news was brought to him, went to the temple with all his army. And the priests of the temple, when they saw Aphrodosius with all his army coming into the temple, thought that he was making haste only to see vengeance taken on those on whose account the gods had fallen down. But when he came into the temple, and saw all the gods lying prostrate on their faces, he went up to the blessed Mary, who was carrying the Lord in her bosom, and adored Him, and said to all his army and all his friends: "Unless this were the God of our gods, our gods would not have fallen on their faces before Him; nor would they be lying prostrate in His presence: wherefore they silently confess that He is their Lord. Unless we, therefore, take care to do what we have seen our gods doing, we may run the risk of His anger, and all come to destruction, even as it happened to Pharaoh king of the Egyptians, who, not believing in powers so mighty, was drowned in the sea, with all his army."

"Yes, that is interesting," said Ra'ed. "In the Coptic stories they must hide from the soldiers. It is Klum that saves them once again. He hides them in the fields until the soldiers go the other way. I like your version more. It suggests the power of Jesus much better."

We walked through this field of rubble as the antiquities guards followed us from a watchful distance. We covered much of the ancient site and did not find a single stone monument standing or intact. It looked like a stone-age junkyard. As we returned to the well I noticed that the ground was covered with broken pieces of pottery, thick jars that had been smashed to bits.

"What is this broken pottery?" I asked Ra'ed.

"That is not as old as you think," he said. "The well of Jesus is thought to be a source of luck. So women from Zagazig come here frequently with clay pots and scoop out the lucky water. After they have poured it over their heads, they smash the pots."

I picked up a couple of pieces of the pottery and examined them.

They were simple pots, made with whitish clay. The pieces broke easily when I clacked them together.

"I really don't know if they get much luck out of this water," said Ra'ed, looking down into the shallow well. "Jesus said that this well water would heal the body and soul of everyone who drank it. The only exceptions would be the people who lived in this town. He said none of them would be healed by it. I think that is a sanction that is still in place. Still it is not bad that they try."

We left the field of fallen idols and drove into the center of Zagazig. A striking town with a population of a quarter million, Zagazig is the capital of Sharqiya province. Much of it is built along an ancient branch of the Nile, a narrow canal called Bahr Mois. There one can find some of the finest examples of nineteenth-century architecture anywhere in Egypt. Most of these handsome buildings were built by the French, who used Zagazig as a staging area for the construction of the Suez Canal.

I'm sure these monuments to French architecture are worth seeing. I strained to look at them as we passed by in an endless clot of moving traffic. But touring the city was not what we had planned for the remainder of the day. We were headed for the University of Zagazig, where we would meet with Dr. Mahmoud Omar, a controversial Muslim archaeologist who has declared that the well at Tell Basta is truly the well of Jesus. He even claims he can prove it. I wanted to talk to him about that. The site we had just seen was a marvel, especially when seen in relation to the gospels. But I had a hard time believing that an archaeologist could prove the well was actually created by Jesus. And I had an even harder time believing he would make such a claim publicly.

Once we got away from the canal area, Zagazig lived up to its name, or at least the name that every foreigner thinks it has, which is "zigzag." The place became a maze of roads that cross one another in a, yes, zigzag pattern.

A municipal rat's maze is perhaps the best description, because once you have woven blindly through the city's confusing streets, begging directions from the traffic policemen and sympathetic citizens, you finally find the center of town. There you get your treat, the University of Zagazig. It is one of the largest universities in Egypt. With more than sixty thousand in attendance, the square in front of the campus literally roils with students.

As we crossed the square and headed for an outdoor teahouse to wait for Dr. Omar, I noticed that few women were veiled and even fewer wore scarves. I felt as though we were in the epicenter of an Egyptian women's movement.

"See what education does for women?" said Ra'ed. "The Taliban would never make it here in Zagazig. The women would run them out of town."

Dr. Mahmoud Omar came into the teahouse. He was dressed elegantly in a black suit, an Irish green dress shirt, and a flowered tie. He stuck out a hand that was among the softest I have ever felt and introduced himself with a simple greeting. "I am Dr. Omar."

He held his head high, so that his chin jutted forward. With his regal posture and proud gaze I first thought of him as the picture of arrogance. But I realized as we talked that he wasn't arrogant at all. Rather, he possessed the aura of a man who had been hit many times by fists of criticism, yet continued to extend his chin as a way of showing he could take a punch.

The battle he was fighting was over the authenticity of the well of Jesus. He had discovered the well in 1991. Six years later, he declared the well to be the one created by Jesus and recorded in Coptic legend. His life has not been the same since then. He said he has been "handcuffed" by the country's director of antiquities, forced to file lawsuits to maintain his rights to the archaeological site, and ridiculed by colleagues for claiming that the well was truly created by the hand of Jesus.

"My problems started right after I found the well," said Omar. "I was just out of school and had been working only a few months when I found the well. That made everyone jealous in itself. Many of these archaeologists work for twenty years and they never find anything. I found something important right away. So immediately they were jealous."

The well was an important find in itself. The style of bricks and the construction techniques used to build it fit the physical description of wells from the Roman era. But it was underneath its muddy bottom where he found artifacts that amounted to the well's real smoking gun: ancient buckets for collecting water, a pulley system for lowering the buckets, and animal bones that had been thrown into the water supply by unsanitary revelers.

Carbon-14 dating of the artifacts placed the date of the well structure at between 20 and 70 C.E. This was a first-century Roman well; there was no doubt about it.

Had Omar stopped with the declaration that he had found a first-century Roman well, he would have been on safe ground. Already the High Council of the Committee of Antiquities had agreed with the evidence that it was a Roman well.

But Omar continued to research the origin of the well and concluded that this was the well created by Jesus.

"There were a number of things that make me believe this," said Omar. "Before the time that Jesus would have been here, there were no wells in the city. After he left, it was here. And there is proof that this is not just an ordinary well. The disappearance of the ancient Egyptian religion coincides with the flourishing of the well. Once the well was created, the ancient religion fades away."

"And how about the idols? Did Jesus really knock them down?" I asked.

Omar nodded. "I think he did. The idols all fell down at the time that the Holy Family came through Tell Basta. It is no coincidence that the idols fell down, a well was created, and the ancient religion all disappeared at the same time."

Omar supported his findings with a variety of religious documents. In the Vision of Theophilus and the Homily of Zacharias he found the story of what had happened at Tell Basta. In the Bible he found confirmation that such an event was supposed to happen. The prophet Isaiah seemed to be speaking directly of Bubastis when he said, "Behold, the Lord rideth upon a swift cloud, and shall come into Egypt: and the idols shall be moved at his presence, and the heart of Egypt shall melt in the midst of it." In the Quran, the holy book of his own religion, Omar found confirmation that Jesus was sent by God to perform such miracles.

"With all of this evidence, I could only come to one conclusion," said Omar with a shrug. "I have found the well of Jesus."

When Omar revealed his find to the press, the director of antiquities stepped in. He said it was impossible to declare that the well of Jesus had been found, since there were no artifacts there that directly related to the Holy Family. He sent a telegram to the archaeologist demanding that he retract his claim. Omar refused. "If I declared this to be the well of Muhammad, you would confirm my work immediately," he said to the director. "But it's Christian, so you are denying it."

A lengthy investigation by the Supreme Council of Antiquities sided with Omar on the date of the well, placing it in the first century. But they could not agree that it was the well of Jesus. There was no physical evidence placing the Holy Infant at the site, they said.

After the findings of the council, the director of antiquities refused to allow any further money to be spent on the site. Simply put, Omar will maintain his control of the site for five years but will receive no money for further excavation. He is suing the minister of interior to regain funding. But, as with any other lawsuit in any other country, it will take time and money to reach a resolution.

I felt sorry for Omar. He had stuck his neck out for what he believed and basically got it chopped off. Still, I understood the findings of the council. There wasn't a bit of hard evidence that Jesus created this well.

When I asked Omar how he thought the court case would go, he said he was certain of a positive resolution.

"You must understand, my conclusions are grounded in science, not religion. And in the end, I think, science always wins, doesn't it?"

3. River of Faith

cience always wins. . . .

S   I thought about Dr. Omar's words later that night as I was going through my notebook.

"Do you think science always wins?" I asked Ra'ed. We were sitting in a coffeehouse on El-Talateni, the bustling main street of Ismalia, a town on the Suez Canal where we were staying. Coffeehouses are great generators of thought in the Middle East. They are where men sit in the evening and ponder the day's events. For the men at the tables next to us it was the American bombing of Afghanistan that was the topic of the day. For us it was Jesus and the theories of Dr. Omar.

"Do I think science always wins?" He repeated the question, drawing deeply on the *sheesha*, a saxophone-sized water pipe that sat on the sidewalk in front of him. "I know that is what Dr. Omar said, but I don't think it is true. There are many things in the world that are not scientific and they win."

"Like what?" I asked.

Ra'ed held his smoke for several seconds and then blew it out his nose and mouth. He looked like a dragon yet smelled like an apple tree, due to the fact that the tobacco he was smoking was soaked in apple juice to give it a fruity bouquet. When the smoke cleared he spoke.

"Love is not scientific and it wins all the time," he said. "Faith, too. Faith is not scientific. In fact, faith and science don't get along very well. They are always trying to shoot one another down. If you believe, you can't be a scientist, and if you are a scientist, you can't believe. They have a different way of looking at the world."

"So do you believe that the well at Bubastis is the well of Jesus, like Dr. Omar says it is?" I asked.

More smoke fumed from the nostrils of Ra'ed.

"Of course I do," said Ra'ed. "He is a scientist. He has looked at all of the evidence and checked it against the Church sources and he says that it is true. It is the well of Jesus, Paul."

"Other scientists don't agree with him," I said to Ra'ed, who seemed as if the *sheesha* was pulling him deeper into its relaxing spell. "Some of them say that there were many wells in the Bubastis area in the first century and that this one shouldn't be singled out. Others say that all of the idols didn't fall down during the time that Jesus was there, that they were knocked down by invaders over hundreds of years."

"Yes, and they may be scientists, too," said Ra'ed. "But he is the scientist who has looked at this the most and who has read the holy documents. He has taken all of the information—not just part of it—and decided that, yes, this is the well that was created by Jesus after he knocked the stone idols down. Why do you not believe this?"

Ra'ed's question to me was a fair one. It pointed to the differences between the Western and Middle Eastern ways of thinking, especially when it comes to the thorny subject of religion. Western researchers start by not believing something and then gather evidence until it is proven. On the other hand, religions such as the Coptic Church start by believing something until it is disproved.

It seemed to me as though Dr. Omar was caught between two disciplines. He had proven that the well at Bubastis dates to the first century, which puts it in the time of Jesus. But, at the same time, he relied upon Coptic Orthodox tradition to make the direct link to Jesus. This made Dr. Omar a man caught in the middle, stuck solidly between two competing schools of thought: religious and scientific.

He was not alone. In the previous year two Bible scholars had written a book called *Excavating Jesus* in which they discussed the ten most significant archaeological digs that proved the existence of the historical Jesus. The two scholars—John Dominic Crossan from DePaul University in Chicago and Jonathan Reed, a leading authority on first-century Palestine archaeology—sought to link the sites to locations and events mentioned in the Bible.

Their list includes the "Jesus Boat," the wooden remains of a first-century fishing boat that was found in the Sea of Galilee in 1986. Since the boat is eight-by-twenty-six feet, archaeologists conclude that it could hold thirteen people, implying that this may have been the boat from which the twelve disciples watched Jesus walk on water.

Also on their list is the apostle Peter's house, ruins of a house found underneath a Byzantine church. Ancient pilgrims called this site "the house of the chief of the apostles" but apparently did not mention Peter's name directly. In 1985, archaeologists from the Franciscan Order of the Catholic Church completed excavation of the site and declared it to be the house of the apostle Peter. They reached this conclusion because the wall of one room was covered with Christian prayers written in Aramaic, Hebrew, Greek, Latin, and Syriac.

Yet not all archaeologists see the evidence the same way. What looks like the apostle Peter's house to Catholic archaeologists may look like a common first-century house to Israeli archaeologists. It depends on who is looking at the evidence. In that sense even the best archaeology sometimes relies on faith, the faith of the archaeologist to weigh all of the facts and come to a reasonable conclusion. But in the end, as Friedrich Nietzsche said, "There are no facts, only interpretation."

I wanted a Coptic point of view on the well of Jesus.

To get one we went the next day to the Church of the Holy Virgin and St. John, one of three Coptic churches in Zagazig. Like the other two, this church lays claim to being built on the site of the house of Klum, the simple farmer who opened his house to the Holy Family and had his wife healed of her paralysis in the process.

The church at this site is a stunning example of Orthodox architecture. Built by the Greek Orthodox Church in 1925, this edifice was purchased by the Coptic Church in 1995. Constructed in the hypostyle fashion, the church contains pews arranged in rows between a hall of pillars. Massive chandeliers fill the room with a golden light and icons grace the walls, some made from silver plate. Near the altar are cylinder-shaped cases full of relics. One contains the bones of saints, including the mummified body of a child and the head of a woman.

Father Antonios, the head priest, came out to greet us. He was a pleasant man with a broad smile and fond remembrances of a vacation to the United States that took him and his family from Washington, D.C., all the way to Disney World in Florida. When he saw my alarm at seeing the mummies, he was quick to explain their origin.

"The Greeks who built this church buried these mummies underneath the altar as a form of respect," he said. "When we bought the church, we dug them up and put them where everyone could see them. They are the mummified remains of two of the martyrs of Akhmim, where Christians were persecuted in the fourth century."

I told Father Antonios why we had come to visit. I explained that I had great concerns about the veracity of Dr. Omar's claims about the well of Jesus. I recounted the particulars about how the scientists agreed it was a first-century well but could not agree with Church sources who said it was created by Jesus.

"Since you live here, you have certainly heard all of the impressions about this well," I said to the priest. "What are your feelings? Do you think it is truly the well of Jesus?"

The priest thought long and hard—so long and hard that it became obvious to me that this was not going to be a yes or no answer.

"I will tell you a true story about people who had faith and people who did not," said Father Antonios finally. "In the time of Pope Abraham (tenth century) there was an Arab caliph named al-Mu'izz who did not like Christians. Because of that, he was always trying to turn our own words back on ourselves.

"One of the ruler's underlings came to him with the Bible and said, 'We have them this time. Right here in their holy book it says that if they have faith the size of a mustard seed, they can move mountains. I don't believe that what they have said is true. But let's put them to the test. Let's make them move a mountain.'

"The Arab ruler liked that idea. So he called in the Patriarch, Pope Abraham, and asked, 'Is it true that if you have faith the size of a mustard seed that you can move mountains?'

" 'Yes, it is true,' said the pope. 'Because it is written in the Bible.'

" 'Then prove it to me,' said the ruler. 'Make this happen within three days or I will wipe out all Christians in Egypt.'

"The pope did not know what to do. So he called on the entire Church to fast and pray. In the midst of this the Virgin Mary appeared to the pope and told him that on the third day someone would come to the church where he was praying and that person would cause a mountain to be moved.

"So on the third day, while the pope and his congregation were praying faithfully, St. Simeon the Tanner came in and began to pray that the mountains of Muqattam would be moved. And indeed the mountains did move. They began to rumble and shake, and there was an upheaval.

" 'Please stop,' cried the ruler, who was in the church as the prayers were being conducted. 'If you stop the mountains from rumbling, nothing bad will happen to you. You can build churches and anything you want.' "

Father Antonios paused for effect.

"Do you understand the connection between this story and the questions about the well of Jesus?" he asked.

"That faith can be as important as science?" I said.

"Exactly," he said. "Dr. Omar has combined science and faith and has determined that the well of Jesus is where all of the idols have fallen down. So I think what he has said is true. It is the well of Jesus."

It was taking me some time, but I was beginning to see the way Copts, Muslims, and those of other beliefs integrated faith and science. To me, faith is our *unquestioning* connection with the infinite unknown. Science, on the other hand, is our determined effort to *understand* the infinite unknown. Sometimes faith and science rely upon one another, and sometimes one just hasn't figured the other one out. As George Gurdjieff, the Russian mystic, said: "A miracle is not the breaking of laws, nor is it a phenomenon outside of laws. It is laws that are incomprehensible and unknown to us, and are therefore miraculous."

My instinct at this point was to ask Father Antonios for directions to the mountains of Muqattam. There I would search for evidence that they had indeed moved in the last thousand years. That would add to the empirical evidence that, yes, faith had moved these mountains. Instead I suppressed my thought. I decided to accept on faith what the priest had told me. *Instead of disbelieving these stories until they are proven, I will believe them until they are disproven.* In a way it was like stepping into a river of faith, one that was fraught with whirlpools, swift rapids, and large animals with unknown intent. I didn't know where it would take me or where I would end up. Still, I recalled something that Father Antonios said as we were leaving: "If you are going to look at a faith, it helps to be faithful. Otherwise you can never know it from the inside."

I didn't know where it would take me, but at that point I stepped into the river of faith and let it sweep me downstream.

We spent the afternoon driving down rough country roads through even rougher country towns. Entering the settlements, we slowed to a pedestrian's pace, able to drive only as fast as the townsfolk who walked in front of us would allow. In one small village we stopped to watch a butcher slaughter a goat. As other goats looked on, the massive meat cutter lopped the head of one of their cousins and began to render it into the various salable parts. Across the muddy street a woman selling chickens from wire cages waved me over and pointed to my camera.

"She wants you to take her picture," said Ra'ed.

She smiled broadly and I clicked. Since it was digital, I was able to show her the picture on the camera's tiny screen. She laughed when she saw it and asked if I would take another, this time with her son.

As they posed, a passerby said something to her and she flicked her fingers at him like he was a pesky fly. Ra'ed watched as the man walked down the street.

"He told her she should not allow photos to be taken," said Ra'ed, keeping his eye on the man. "He said you are going to take these pic-tures back to America and show everyone how primitive Egyptians are. People in these little towns are like that. They don't trust foreigners."

We got back into the Peugeot and continued to drive. Our destina-tion was San el-Haggar, a spot that is not on the Coptic map of sites visited by the Holy Family. Nonetheless, Ra'ed insisted that the Holy Family stopped here.

"A priest in Cairo told me to stop here for sure," said Ra'ed. "There is nothing left to see, but it will give you an idea of what travel was like back in the time of Jesus."

Out the window, the business of agriculture was going on all around us. Hay fields were burning, the acrid smoke obscuring the workers who were loading vegetables into baskets and then into trucks, which would bring them to market.

"Take away the cars and you have Egypt in the time of Jesus," said Ra'ed.

One would have to take away more than that, I thought, but I understood what he meant. Farming in Egypt was largely the same then as it is now. There is no greater taskmaster than the earth, and none so under-appreciated as those who break their backs making a living from her soil. This type of work has gone on for centuries here, and in practically the same way. These people represented the silent engine of the world's oldest culture. Without their successful labors in the fertile Nile Delta there would have been no pyramids, no statues, and no modern Egypt. It was the fruits of their labor that made all advances in Egypt possible. Yet they were still picking vegetables by hand, still doing things the old way, with few advances in technology to show that they were in the twenty-first century.

It was hard to believe that this dirt-poor part of the Delta was once the most important city in Egypt. In the time of the Old Testament this was Tanis (in Hebrew, Zoan). One of the oldest cities in the world, Tanis was capital of Egypt under many pharaohs. Many believe that this was the city from which the Exodus of Moses and the Jews actually began, and thus part of the land of Goshen. Psalms 78:12 lends credence to this belief by referring to Zoan as the land where Moses "did miracles" before escaping through the Red Sea.

There are those who also believe that Tanis holds the Ark of the Covenant. The Institute for Biblical and Scientific Studies lists this city as one of three possible sites of the most precious of all biblical artifacts. They say that the Ark of the Covenant, the golden box that contained the Ten Commandments, may have been taken by Sheshonk when the gold-hungry pharaoh sacked the temples and royal palace of Jerusalem in approximately 940 B.C. The attack is recorded in 2 Chronicles 12:9, where it says, "So Shishak [Sheshonk] king of Egypt came up against Jerusalem, and took away the treasure of the house of the Lord and the treasures of the king's house; he took all: he carried away also the shields of gold which Solomon had made."

This is one of many theories as to the location of the ark. It appealed to film director Steven Spielberg in the movie *Raiders of the Lost Ark*, as Indiana Jones finds the lost ark in Tanis. It is taken from him by Nazi archaeologists who, in their hubris, dare to open the box that contains the ark and are vaporized by an army of angels for looking directly at this precious object of God.

Tanis contains a temple that is an important pharaonic site. Like so many of these sites, this temple is a hodgepodge of contributions from pharaohs throughout the ages. There is a gate built by one of the many pharaohs named Sheshonk, statues of Ramses II, walls built by Psusennes I, and several tombs containing the remains of Osorkon II, Psusennes I, and a general named Wundebawdjed.

There were beautiful scenes from the Book of the Dead and the Book of Night painted on the walls of the limestone shaft that led to one of the Sheshonk's tomb. As much as I would have liked to spend the day examining the temple and its collection of pharaonic contributions, we didn't have time. Ra'ed said we were lost.

"This is not where we want to be," said Ra'ed. "Jesus did not visit this temple, as you can see, because there are statues still standing. We are looking for something quite different."

He asked a few questions of people near the temple's entrance and then we were off again, pounding the Peugeot down a rut-filled road that ran next to the Ramses Canal, named for the pharaoh who had first built it.

Sa'ad stopped a man riding a bicycle and asked for directions. We were sent to a narrow road that ran past a mud farmhouse and into a farmer's field. The road was chained. Sa'ed honked the horn and out came a tired farmer, scratching his head as though the honk had just awakened him.

Sa'ad asked a question and the farmer pointed to a barren hill at the end of his property. We negotiated an entrance fee of one package of cigarettes and the chain came down. Then we continued on our way, down a long road deep into an agricultural area.

"Here it is," said Ra'ed.

I got out of the car and looked. There was nothing. The area we had been seeking looked like it too had been vaporized by God. The terrain looked like barren Arizona desert, except the soil was the fertile loam of the Nile. This had clearly been an area of high use in its time. There were bits of iron ore mixed in with the soil and literally thousands of pottery shards that looked like they were from many different eras in Egypt.

"I know, it looks like nothing, but it is something," said Ra'ed. "Jesus was not here in the time of the pharaohs. He was here in the time of the governors, Romans who were sent here to rule different regions of the country. To help the regions get trade, they would host travelers for free. This was one of the free lodging areas that they offered. People who had business in Tanis but could not afford to stay there would come to this spot. They could stay on the land for free. Vendors would rent them simple tents and sell food and drink. It was a good place to be if you were a traveler because it was safer to sleep where there were many people. Many thieves roamed Egypt in those days."

It was easy to see what Ra'ed was talking about. This place was shaped like a bowl, surrounded by low hills that protected against wind. From the air it must have looked like a sand trap in a golf course. Surrounding it were green fields of cotton and other crops. Yet here in the middle was a bowl of sand.

I began to thumb through my reference material. Maybe somewhere there was an allusion to this place, something I had missed. *There must be something,* I thought. *Why else would the priest in Cairo have insisted that we stop at this site?*

I found two stories that fit into the chronology of events. In the Arabic Gospel of the Infancy is a story that takes place as the Holy Family leaves Tell Basta. Concerned that the soldiers of Herod are hot on their trail, they are hurrying away when they suddenly come upon a band of thieves who are plundering several men of their baggage and clothing. It doesn't say from what vantage point the Holy Family sees these captives. Somehow, they are concealed enough that the robbers don't see them. At this point, and without explanation as to how, the Infancy Gospel tells us: "The robbers heard a great noise, like the noise of a magnificent king going out of his city with his army, and his chariots and his drums; and at this the robbers were terrified, and left all their plunder. And the captives rose up, loosed each other's bonds, recovered their baggage and went away."

The captives passed Mary and Joseph as they continued their nervous voyage on this trail. They told the holy couple what had happened and asked where the king was who had certainly ridden to their rescue. According to the Arabic Gospel of the Infancy, "Joseph answered them: He will come behind us."

This is the sort of allusion that the Infancy Gospels are filled with. People are constantly referring to a kingly presence, one of the earthly variety, only to have it confirmed that they have indeed experienced a king, but a celestial one.

A second story that fits this chronology has the Holy Family coming into another city, possibly Tanis, after leaving Tell Basta. This story is found in both the Arabic Gospel of the Infancy and the First Gospel of the Infancy of Jesus Christ, which was first translated into English in 1697 by Henry Sike, a professor of Oriental languages at Cambridge University. The story found in both gospels has the Holy Family encountering a "woman possessed with a devil, and in whom Satan, that cursed rebel, had taken up his abode."

According to the First Gospel of the Infancy:

One night, when she went to fetch water, she could neither endure her clothes on, nor to be in any house. But as often as they tied her with chains or cords, she brake them, and went out into desert places and sometimes standing where roads

crossed and in churchyards, would throw stones at men. When
St. Mary saw this woman she pitied her, whereupon Satan
presently left her, and fled away in the form of a young man,
saying, Wo to me, because of thee, Mary, and thy Son.

So the woman was delivered from her torment. But con-
sidering herself naked, she blushed, and avoided seeing any
man, and having put on her clothes, went home, and gave an
account of her case to her father and relations, who, as they
were the best of the city, entertained St. Mary and Joseph with
the greatest respect.

As I read this material to myself, Ra'ed was pacing the ground. "I
don't know why you are looking for this in your books," he said. "The
priest told me that you would not find any mention of this place. It is
part of an oral tradition. People just know Jesus was here but they don't
know what he did while he was here."

For the first time—but not the last—I was frustrated by the lack of
place names in the Bible and the Infancy Gospels. *Couldn't the people who
wrote these stories so clearly have written down where they took place?* I asked myself
as Ra'ed paced, picking up flat pieces of broken pottery and sending
them sailing through the air with a sharp flick of his arm. *Why do these
stories so often leave us speculating as to where the events occurred?*

Ra'ed began to tap his watch and I knew it was time to leave. Still, I
was perplexed. In my heart I was looking for a historical Jesus. This is a
search that has led many people down a frustrating path, given that
there are no firsthand, eyewitness accounts of Jesus to be found. Even
the gospels of Matthew, Mark, Luke, and John, according to some biblical scholars, were most likely written decades after the disciples had
passed on.

So I was leaning on geography to provide a historical look at Jesus.
I realized once again—twice in the same day—that this was probably
the wrong thing to do.

I remembered what Lotfi Sherif, an Egyptologist in Cairo, had told
me about the ancient records of historical legends. "Many times these
writings are not specific as to place. But you just have to appreciate
them for what they are. They may not give you a specific location but
they give you a sense of the adventure and spiritual promise. They help
you see what is to come. These are what built great religions. It doesn't
always matter where events took place. It just matters that they happened. These are the underpinning of faith."

Had Jesus saved the captives and healed a madwoman in this post-pharaonic campground? *Possibly*, I told myself. The chronology was right. The setting was right. Still, I breathed aloud the sigh of the un-fulfilled. I knew I couldn't have dates and times, but I at least wanted places. Geography would anchor my faith, or so I thought.

"Let's go," I said to Ra'ed. "We have a lot of ground to cover."

4. Heavenly Searchlights

By reading the Infancy Gospels it is impossible to tell the exact route of the Holy Family's voyage through Egypt. There are few place names in those ancient documents and even fewer solid hints as to where the family is at any given time. Before I left the United States I pulled out a map of Egypt and marked the route by using only the information I could glean from the five Infancy Gospels themselves. There were place names like Matariyah and Memphis that provided a sure spot for me to mark on the map. References to "the capital" were easily linked to Tell Basta (referred to then as Bubastis), because they visited a site early in the voyage that was the capital of Egypt under many pharaohs. Then there were the more cryptic references to places and geography. One reference, for example, referred to "a desert country." Where would I place a mark on a map of Egypt for that location? And then there was reference to a city "in which was the castle of a most illustrious prince." There were many potential castle sites in Egypt. Which one would I mark?

It didn't take me long to conclude that the authors of the Infancy Gospels were not concerned with the precise places where the events occurred. Like the authors of the Bible, they were more interested in the events themselves. That is a possible reason why Noah's ark has never been found and why it is still unclear where Moses crossed the Red Sea in the Exodus from Egypt. And it was the reason why I could not use the Infancy Gospels alone as a road map. Although they described fascinating events, when it came to identifying the route, the Infancy Gospels were similar to using Homer to trace the route of mighty Odysseus.

Typical of the guidance these gospels provided is the sentence in the First Gospel of the Infancy of Jesus Christ that tells where the Holy Family went when they left the Tanis area. "The next morning having received a sufficient supply of provisions for the road, they went from them, and about the evening of the day arrived at another town."

My need for place names left me very thankful to the Coptic Church. Their traditions are more specific when it comes to the Holy Family's destination. In a later version of the Homily of Zacharias, the Holy Family is said to have traveled to the town of Mostorod, a grimy and rough spot just north of Cairo. Mostorod was also known as al-Mahamma by the medieval pilgrims who visited this site in the fourteenth and fifteenth centuries. *Al-Mahamma* means "the bathing place" in Arabic, and the town is called that because it is the spot where Mary bathed Jesus and washed his clothing. It is also where the miraculous infant created another well that bubbles healing water to this day.

We parked the Peugeot across the street from the alley, by the Ismalia Canal. Getting out, I paused a moment to take in the view of the river. Garbage covered the shore and the river was an apocalyptic visage of slow-moving sludge and floating debris. It was painful to look at and didn't lend itself to the notion of being a bathing place. The stench was terrible.

"Where is the church?" I asked, scanning the buildings along the waterfront for a sign of the Coptic cross.

"It is there," said Ra'ed, pointing to an alley that disappeared between two apartment buildings.

"I hope it wasn't this dirty when the Holy Family was here," said Ra'ed, taking me by the elbow. "This is water that would have made even Jesus sick."

We crossed the street and went into the alley. The walls of the apartment buildings were crumbling in spots and a small wooden fast-food stand belched smoke as the owner cooked some kind of meat on an open charcoal fire. The alleyway was dark, despite it being midday, and it took a moment for my eyes to adjust. At the end of the alley I could see a green metal wall, its surface covered with painted stencils of Coptic crosses. Two armed policemen were sitting on a bench in front of the gate, smoking cigarettes. As we approached, one of them crushed out his smoke and stood to pull the gate open. We went inside.

Like so many of the Coptic sites that I would see, this one was an oasis of calm in the midst of a dirty and noisy city. It was a massive sand-colored church, surrounded by apartment buildings and a block wall that was maybe ten feet high. Later, when a deacon let me climb on top of the church to photograph its unique multiple-domed roof, I realized that the only nearby structure taller than the church tower was the minaret on the mosque next door. Everything else in town looked up at the Coptic cross.

A deacon named George came out of the church. He was glad to see us. One by one he shook our hands and offered us a cup of hot tea. There was no one else there at the church, and he seemed lonely. A couple of old men played baccarat at a nearby picnic table, but other than that it was a slow day.

Ra'ed and George spoke rapidly to one another, and before I knew it George had me by the arm and was pulling me toward the church.

"I have told him what you are doing and he is excited," said Ra'ed.

I knew from my study that this spot had seen a lot of action throughout history. In the time of Ramses II, about 1200 B.C.E., a pharaonic temple had been built here or nearby. If that temple was anything like other temples from the period of Ramses II, its main feature was large stone statues of the pharaoh himself, dominating a structure with hieroglyphs of gods carved into the walls.

By the time the Holy Family arrived at Mostorod, there was probably little remaining of the temple. What was still here was the crypt. It is thought that the crypt was somehow a part of the worship service in ancient Egypt. Perhaps an icon of religious importance was placed in the cave for ancient pilgrims to worship as part of the ceremony.

It was in the crypt, say local priests, that the Holy Family took temporary refuge, resting for a day or two before fleeing further from the soldiers of Herod.

There is only one story from the Infancy Gospels that may have taken place in Mostorod. It is the story of the dumb bride, recounted in both the Arabic Gospel of the Infancy and the First Gospel of the Infancy of Jesus Christ. Neither of the stories mentions Mostorod. Both refer to the healing taking place in the town after what is believed to be

Tanis. If that is true and the Coptic version of the Holy Family trail is valid, then this story did take place here:

"[O]n the evening of that day [they] arrived at another town, in which they were celebrating a marriage," reads the version in the Arabic Gospel of the Infancy.

[B]ut by the arts of accursed Satan and the work of the enchanters, the bride had become dumb and could not speak a word. And after the Lady Mary entered the town, carrying her son the Lord Christ, that dumb bride saw her, and stretched out her hands towards the Lord Christ, and drew Him to her, and took Him into her arms, and held Him close and kidded Him and leaned over Him, moving his body back and forwards. Immediately the knot of her tongue was loosened, and her ears were opened; and she gave thanks and praise to God, because He had restored her to health. And that night the inhabitants of that town exulted with joy, and thought that God and His angels had come down to them.

There they remained three days, being held in great honour, and living splendidly.

I read this story to George the deacon, who nodded knowingly. He had never heard this story, he said, but it wouldn't surprise him to know that it was true. "The people of Mostorod were said to be in awe of Jesus," said George. "Maybe that was one reason."

The main reason for the lasting reverence was inside, said George, pulling on the church door.

We went in.

The church sanctuary was stunning. Sunlight streamed through the windows in the domes like heavenly searchlights. They highlighted various features of the interior like spotlights in an art gallery. There was the iconostasis, its ornately carved wood looking rich in the bright light. There was a medieval icon painting of Mary, its surface covered with glass to keep the faithful from kissing it until the paint was loved away. There was a mother-of-pearl inlay of Mary and Joseph, sitting in what looked like an enormous egg, which I found out later was meant to symbolize resurrection.

"This way," said George, pointing to stone stairs that dissolved in darkness.

"That is the cave where the Holy Family lived," said George.

We went down the stairs.

George turned on a lone fluorescent light and the tiny crypt blazed into view. On one wall underneath the light was a picture of the Virgin Mary. Beneath it was a metal stand that was covered with the wax of old candles. The walls of the tiny crypt were an odd shade of gray, like the flat patina of pencil lead.

George spoke to Ra'ed in Arabic, and as he did, the translator took his hand from the wall and wiped it on his pant leg.

"The walls are this color because of all the people who have touched them down through the years," Ra'ed said, looking suddenly uncomfortable. "It is dirt from all of the people who have ever touched these walls."

My hands were oddly drawn to the walls. Of course they were filthy. I was careful of where I put my hands the rest of the day, until I could get to a place with hot water and soap. But I found it compelling, too, to be touching the epidermal remains of hands from ancient Egypt—perhaps even a pharaoh or Jesus himself—who had touched these stone walls in a moment of spiritual grace.

A deacon stands in front of a well inside the Church of the Virgin Mary at Mostorod, where Jesus was said to have bathed. Behind him is a cave where the Holy Family was said to have spent several days.

What were they seeking? I wondered. *And why?*

I left this gallery of DNA and went up a second set of stairs, with George and Ra'ed leading the way. There at the top of the stairs was the most perfect stone well I had ever seen, maybe four feet high. Covering it was a velvet cloth with an image of Jesus and Mary sewn to it. George removed the cloth so that I could see down into the well.

"Mary was thirsty and she needed water to wash the clothing of Jesus," said George. "So Jesus caused water to flow from this spot. It has flowed here for two thousand years. The water level has not been reduced."

He offered me a small cup of the blessed water. I did not refuse. Although the cup had probably been through as many hands as the wall, I took a swallow.

"This is healing water," said George. "Many people are healed when they drink it."

This was especially true of people afflicted with what George called "madness." By combining a walk through the cave with water from the well, a mad person was almost certain to be made whole, said George.

It was a statement of fact that I couldn't let pass. I demanded some science, or at least some case studies. "Whom have you seen being healed at this well?" I asked George.

He did not have to think for even a moment. He spoke fast and clear about healings he had seen and ones he had only heard about. His was the clear-voiced testimonial of a believer.

"There was a woman paralyzed in the legs," said George. "Her husband was not a Christian but he brought her here anyway. He asked about the healing place of the Virgin Mary. He got her down the stairs and had her stay in the cave. The priest told her to take some of the water from the well down with her. She stayed for about half an hour in the cave. She lighted seven candles and prayed. Then she came out again walking as if she was brand-new. She carried a bottle of the water home with her and drank a small amount every day for fifteen days. Then she came back again to show us that she could truly walk."

I was impressed, I said, but that was a physical healing. Did he have any tales of people being healed from madness?

"You mean haunted by the devil?" he asked. "Yes. There was a woman who came here who was definitely possessed by the devil. She looked crazy in the eyes. As soon as her family took her down into the cave, she screamed from her head. She stayed in the cave for ten minutes. Very quickly she calmed down and then she became normal. She came to the well and drank from it. She prayed to the Holy Virgin and became normal again."

As George told this story, his eyes were filled with enthusiasm.

"Doesn't it frighten you to have people come into the church who are demon-possessed?" I asked.

"No, it is exciting," he said. "When people come into this church, the Virgin Mary is here to help them. There is no one who is so bad off that the Virgin cannot help them if she wants."

Except for us, the church was completely empty. But when I asked him how many people come through each year for healings and blessings, he declared that there were at least one million pilgrims. I did the math.

"That's three thousand people per day," I said. "That couldn't be possible. There is no one here right now."

"That would seem true right now," he said. "But we have a festival every year and there are over fifty thousand people who come to receive the blessings of the Virgin Mary at that time. Today it is quiet here."

Even with such a festival, the stream of people passing through this venerated site would not amount to a million. But it didn't really matter. If tens of thousands passed through this site each year, it would feel like a million. And if only a few were healed, then word of this site would reach tens of millions. That gave the church at Mostorod a sort of cosmic presence in the minds of Egyptians.

As we left the Church of the Holy Virgin at Mostorod, I tried to express my gratitude to George by giving him a few Egyptian pounds. Most church deacons make only a small amount of money each month, and even a few extra pounds can make a huge difference in their quality of life. No matter how hard I tried, though, George would not take the money I offered him. He did not want to take money for telling us about this miracle site of Jesus.

"To witness is my job and that is payment enough," said George.

It was Ra'ed who arrived at the final solution. He took my twenty-pound note and shoved it deep into George's shirt pocket. Then, before the young deacon could react, Ra'ed closed the metal gate behind him and we walked down the dark alley that led to the street.

"Imagine that," said Ra'ed, chuckling. "An Egyptian who doesn't want to take money."

We drove out from Mostorod along the Ismalia Canal, one of the major arteries that feed water to the agricultural zone above Cairo. We were on our way to Belbeis, and the road was lined with giant eucalyptus trees that at times gave the route a picture-postcard appearance. The drive would have been relaxing, except that no car ride in Egypt is relaxing. The two-lane road was always occupied by at least three cars, some passing from behind and some from head on.

Sa'ad was as fearless as the next driver as he passed other cars on turns and missed oncoming vehicles by literally inches. I was tense as he navigated the narrow roads. I had asked him several times to stay in one lane even if it meant traveling five miles per hour slower, but he didn't seem to understand what I meant. When Ra'ed would translate my request to him, Sa'ad would look at me without an inkling of comprehension. Then he would fire off a sentence or two to Ra'ed, who would turn to me and say, "Don't worry about it."

That was what I was trying to do now. To keep my mind off the road ahead, I pulled out my copy of the Infancy Gospels and began to read out loud from the Arabic Gospel of the Infancy about the next city visited by the Holy Family.

> Thereafter, being supplied by them with provision for their journey, they went away and came to another city, in which, because it was very populous, they thought of passing the night. And there was in that city an excellent woman: and once, when she had gone to the river to bathe, lo, accursed Satan, in the form of a serpent, had leapt upon her, and twisted himself round her belly; and as often as night came on, he tyrannically tormented her. This woman, seeing the mistress the Lady Mary had the child, Lord Christ, in her bosom, was struck with a longing for Him, and said to the mistress the Lady Mary: "O mistress give me this child, that I may carry him, and kiss him." She therefore gave Him to the woman; and when He was brought to her, Satan let her go, and fled and left her, nor did the woman ever see him after that day. Wherefore all who were present praised God Most High, and that woman bestowed on them liberal gifts.

"That is an amazing story," said Ra'ed, seemingly oblivious to the Mad Hatter ride that we were participants in.

"There is more," I said, turning to the First Gospel of the Infancy of Jesus Christ. The story that I was about to read was the same one found in the Arabic Gospel. I chose this one, however, because the story was told with more color.

> On the morrow the same woman brought perfumed water to wash the Lord Jesus; and when she had washed him, she preserved the water. And there was a girl there whose body was white with a leprosy, who being sprinkled with this water, and washed, was instantly cleansed from her leprosy.
>
> The people therefore said, "Without doubt Joseph and Mary, and that boy are Gods, for they do not look like mortals."

"Have you ever heard that story?" I asked Ra'ed.

"No, I have never," he said. "But that is the kind of thing that could have happened in Belbeis."

The events of Belbeis, according to the Coptic version, were first recorded by Bishop Zacharias, the eighth-century Copt who was responsible for having established much of the Holy Family trail in the Delta. According to his homily, the Holy Family passed a funeral procession as they were coming into Belbeis. The procession of mourners and grieving family members must have been one that tugged at Jesus' heartstrings, because he stopped and took notice of them. Feeling sorry for the family, the Holy Infant raised the dead man to life. The story of the man in Belbeis so much resembles Jesus raising the son of the widow in Nain (Luke 7:11–17) that one would think they are the same if the names of the cities did not differ.

When the man came to life he was, of course, extremely grateful. According to the Homily of Zacharias, the resurrected man stood and declared: "This is the True God, the Saviour of the world, Who is born of the Blessed Virgin, Who accomplished a mystery which the human intellect cannot comprehend." Word of this miracle spread all over Belbeis, and the Holy Family was said to have become welcomed pilgrims.

We felt anything but welcomed as we drove through the tight streets of Belbeis. We were searching for the Coptic church that marked the site of the Holy Family's stay in this rough agricultural town. The streets were choked with Toyota trucks that were carrying produce in from the fields. On the sides of the dirt main street, women were beckoning from behind piles of vegetables, trying to make a sale.

"Roll up your window," said Ra'ed. "I feel bad things in this town."

There was a surliness expressed by the people as we passed, especially when they noticed that a foreigner was sitting in the backseat.

"I do not think they like you," said Ra'ed. "And they won't like me either, since I am a Christian."

There had been problems between the Copts and Muslims in Belbeis, especially since the 1850s, when the Muslims cut down the object of veneration that we had come to see, the Tree of Jesus.

As the story goes, the Holy Family rested under a tree after Jesus performed the miracle of raising the dead man. They stayed underneath this tree for three days while Mary recovered from their long voyage. The tree bore fruit for Mary to eat and Jesus caused a well to spring forth from the ground so that she could drink.

Three days later, the family pressed on. With Herod's soldiers following closely, the Holy Family could not afford to stop for long.

But the legend of the powerful little boy remained. With the boy gone, the town's people venerated the tree, declaring it a sacred spot where this special child and his family had rested.

The tree, or at least the spot where it was, remained sacred for hundreds of years. Although I could find no mention of the tree dying, it must certainly have died and reseeded itself many times over the nineteen centuries since the Holy Family was shaded underneath its branches. Finally, though, Muslims cut it down in the mid-nineteenth century to build a mosque. Some Muslims deny it, saying that the tree disappeared when the town expanded.

I didn't know whether anything still remained of the tree or if the spot was venerated in any way, by either Christians or Muslims. Even though Islam doesn't recognize Jesus as being the Son of God, it does recognize him as a prophet on a par with Moses. Was it possible that the Muslims had co-opted this site, making it one of their own?

I wanted to know.

⳩

We found St. George the Martyr Church and stopped in front of it. Built in 1932, this Coptic church was a large, squarish building with walls at least thirty feet high. From the outside this church looked like a fort. From the inside, however, it was quite different. The high walls kept the street noise to a minimum and also cut down on the amount of dust, which was substantial on the unpaved street.

The church was divided into two sections. The upper section was the main church, one modeled after a nearby nineteenth-century church that had been demolished. The lower section contained an altar from that nineteenth-century church. All of this was built on the site of a fourth-century church. No one had known the church existed when the construction started. When the workers began digging the church's foundation, a large metal cross was found and research revealed that this was the likely site of that ancient church. The metal cross was put into the foundation and the St. George the Martyr Church went up over it.

We were led upstairs by a deacon and taken down a very narrow hallway to meet Father Ghubrial. He wore a long white beard that would have made him look like Santa Claus if he weren't so thin.

Father Ghubrial amid the icons of the church of Mar Girgis in Belbeis. It was here, according to apocryphal gospels and Coptic accounts, that Jesus raised a man from the dead.

He was ill, he said, and his appearance showed it. His eyes were rimmed with red and his attempt to speak was punctuated by sniffles and a nagging cough. I offered to come back another day, as he was clearly feeling the weight of a serious cold, but he insisted we stay.

"Witnessing for Jesus is the most important thing I do," he said. "You must stay so we can talk."

As we wandered through the church, looking at the stunning icons and somewhat creepy relics, Father Ghubrial told me Coptic stories.

"When Napoleon took Egypt, his soldiers came through Belbeis and tried to cut down the holy tree for firewood," he said. "But when they started cutting the branches, the tree began to bleed. It bled all over them and left them standing in pools of blood. They became frightened and left the tree alone."

"That seems miraculous," I said.

"Yes, because it was a miracle tree," said Father Ghubrial. "Then, many years after Napoleon was gone, Muslims tried to do the same thing. It bled all over them, too. They were horrified and fled from the tree just like the soldiers had."

"That is amazing," I said. "So how did the tree finally get cut down?"

Father Ghubrial shook his head.

"I don't know what happened," he said. "About a hundred years ago some Muslims cut the tree down for firewood and it didn't bleed. If it didn't bleed, then God wanted it to be gone."

"Then where is the spot where the tree was?" I asked.

The priest looked forlorn.

"A mosque was built on top of it," he said. "This was not good and there was much anger about it from the local Christians. But the Muslims did it anyway."

"Did it cause problems?" I asked.

"Yes. There has been much unrest here between the faiths."

It seemed like a disrespectful thing for the Muslims to do, as they claimed to have great respect for Jesus. "Why would they build on top of a sacred site?" I asked.

"It was simple," he said. "They wanted to expand a mosque and they decided to build a room on top of the chopped-down tree."

But a sacred spot is still a sacred spot, he said. Despite the tons of concrete above it, the spot where the Tree of Jesus stood is still used as a prayer room for people asking God for miracles.

"Many people who pray there tell me that the room has a heavenly scent at times," said Father Ghubrial. "It is the scent from the tree. Women who want to become pregnant go there and they report a wonderful smell in the room as they pray. Those who report the perfume smell are usually the ones blessed with a child."

I told him I wanted to go to the mosque and ask the imam why they had built on a site that was sacred to the Christians.

"You can't do that," he said. "There has been a lot of trouble between us and I don't want this to make things worse."

I understood that. When it comes to such a flammable situation as religion in the Middle East, reporters can sometimes spark trouble. Still, I wanted to at least get a photograph of the site of the holy tree.

"That would not be possible," said the priest. "To tell you the truth, I cannot remember the site of the tree myself. I have not been there in many years. So I can't help with directions. And besides, it is a long way from here. No one I know goes there anymore."

Frankly, I didn't believe his response. Given what he had just told me, that women go there to pray for help with conception, I thought that he most certainly knew many people who had recently been to the site and that he knew where the site was. Still, I didn't want to pressure him. He didn't want a hornet's nest stirred up. His right to tranquility was more important than my right to know.

We spent more time touring the church and photographing the icons, and then we left. Being inside the high walls of St. George the Martyr truly did feel like being inside a fort, and now I knew why. The people inside the walls were afraid of the people outside.

✠

I thought that would be it but it wasn't. When I was finished talking to Father Ghubrial, I left the high walls of the church through the front gate and stood on the dirt street. As people walked by I nodded to them but got no response. Few tourists visit Belbeis, and even fewer Americans. Since the events of September 11 had happened only a few weeks earlier, the citizens of this out-of-the-way town could only see an American in their midst as being up to no good. No amount of smiling on my part could get them past that belief.

As I was looking aimlessly across the dusty street at the walled mosque, a young girl approached me. She was probably twelve years old. She was wearing a plaid skirt and white blouse and a white scarf and was clearly on her way home from school. She was carrying books and was beaming a broad smile. She was nervous but very expressive.

"Are you American?" she said.

"Yes, I am," I said.

"May I practice my English by talking to you?" she asked.

"Certainly," I said. "Let me start by asking you a question. Do you know where the Tree of Jesus is located?"

The smile disappeared as she thought for a moment, processing all of the words that I had barraged her with. Then she lit up again.

"The tree where Jesus sat?" she said. "You are looking at it. It is behind that wall of the mosque."

"Right there?" I asked.

"Yes, there," she said.

"Is it gone?" I asked.

"Yes," she said with great enthusiasm. "It was cut down for building the mosque. But we all remember where it was. It is an important spot."

5. *"Cunningly Devised Fables"*

As I spoke to the young girl, people began to gather. They stopped and listened. Some looked shocked. None looked happy. No one was smiling.

I noticed that Ra'ed was getting nervous and so was Sa'ad. They kept glancing nervously at the people who were stopping and saying things.

"There are many stupid people here," said Ra'ed, placing his hand on my shoulder to get my attention. "They might believe you are bad."

I continued to talk to the girl, and as I did, more children began to show up.

"I will tell the girl to leave now," said Ra'ed. "If we attract too many kids, we will draw the attention of the Islamic leaders."

He explained to the girl that she had to go, and when I protested he shook his finger at me. "We must be prudent," he said.

"But I didn't come here to be prudent," I said. "I came to look for the hidden Jesus. This girl just told me that the Tree of Jesus is right across the street, in the courtyard of that mosque. Let's go and see it. Let's talk to the imam about the tree."

"They do not want to talk about the tree at all," said Ra'ed. "Especially with an American."

The small crowd had dispersed now and the surly stream of humanity continued to pass us by, staring at me as though I had landed from another planet. Ra'ed spoke to Sa'ad and then nodded.

"Sa'ad has an idea," he said. "Don't tell them you are American. Tell them you are British."

"What good would that do?" I asked. "They are fighting in Afghanistan, too."

Ra'ed and Sa'ad huddled again. This time Ra'ed came back with a worse idea.

"Tell them you are interested in converting to Islam and then bring up the subject of the tree."

"Don't you think the imam would see right through that?" I asked.

Ra'ed nodded and then huddled again with Sa'ad.

"Please let us leave," said Ra'ed. "This town is trouble, I can feel it. Please let us go."

And so we did.

After leaving Belbeis, the Holy Family backtracked and went north to Daqadus and Samannud. These two villages lie on the eastern branch of the Nile, which splits in two just north of Cairo.

Egypt is thought of as a desert—mountains and oceans of sand that threaten to cover up all life right to the banks of the mighty river Nile. The country south of Cairo does indeed look like that. The lower four-fifths of a map of Egypt shows a thin ribbon of green on either side of the river that is surrounded by thousands of square miles of stark desert.

But the north country—downriver, since the Nile flows south to north—is a different land altogether. It is a fertile delta that has been turned into moist and rich farmland by millions of years of silt and soil from the annual flooding of the Nile. Where mountains of sand are almost always visible in the rest of Egypt, the fertile delta looks as green as the farmlands of Ohio and Michigan. It could easily be taken for them, too, if it weren't for the conflicting cultural reminders. For example there were the pigeon houses. Egyptians eat pigeons the way we in the west eat chicken. To raise them, Egyptians have enormous teepee-shaped pigeon houses made from wood and mud. I saw ones that were at least a hundred feet high. They look like a giant Plains Indian village. These pigeon houses are ubiquitous testament to the culinary popularity of a bird that most cultures have scant taste for.

And then there are the drivers. Every newspaper in the United States has daily articles about people who drive like Egyptians. They are the ones who force others off the road because they are in a hurry to get home, or the ones who are driving twice the legal limit, or, worse, the ones who use the oncoming lane to play a form of chicken as they pass the cars in their lane.

I have already mentioned this dangerous road circus before, but I mention it again because our adventure almost ended on the road to Daqadus.

I was taking notes in the backseat of the Peugeot when I noticed that Ra'ed was speaking particularly fast to Sa'ad. When I looked up there was an enormous army truck filling our windshield, its eye-level headlights being flashed on and off by its nervous driver.

Sa'ad hit the brakes firmly. A moment later, realizing the truck needed more time to clear the car they were passing, he hit the brakes harder, the tires biting into the asphalt as he swerved for the side of the road.

"That was close," said Ra'ed, piling out of the car and heading for a nearby tree to relieve himself. When he came back he had figured out a way to relate the incident to the Holy Family.

"It is good that this happened," he said, "because it will help you feel the fear that the Holy Family felt as they traveled this portion of their voyage. Remember, they were being chased by soldiers who were sent by King Herod to kill them."

Ra'ed pointed south toward Belbeis and then swept his arm in front of him until his finger pointed north.

"The Holy Family skirted the desert and went south. Then they suddenly turned and went north again," he said. "I think they were try-ing to fool the soldiers by going back to the north. They were clever but frightened. Plus they had God on their side. Without him, they would never have avoided the soldiers, that is for sure."

I felt the same way about our own avoidance of the army truck. As we climbed back into the Peugeot I asked Sa'ad to be careful. Ra'ed didn't translate what I said. "He *was* being careful," said Ra'ed. "It would have been the army truck's fault."

⛶

The church at Daqadus marks the spot where the Holy Family stopped for a day. There is no mention of Jesus coming to this spot in either the

Vision of Theophilus or in the Homily of Zacharias. Still, the site is included in the Holy Family trail because of the oral tradition that has become accepted by the Church. Since the beginning of the fourth century, local citizens and pilgrims have declared that a well on the site was created and blessed by Jesus.

Although no miracles have been attributed to the well water, many miracles have been linked to the spot itself. Queen Helena is said to have built a church here in the fourth century. She may have, or may not. There has long been a question as to whether the mother of the first Christian emperor, Constantine, ever set foot in Egypt.

To build here, locals say, a pagan temple had to be destroyed. Later, in 1288, another church was built on top of the one allegedly built by Helena. Part of an altar from a second church still remains in the one that now stands. Behind the iconostasis at the front of the existing altar is a deep hole that one can look down into and see where an altar was thought to have been.

That these churches were built one on top of the other is testimony to the importance of this specific spot to the Coptic Church, and that this church was thought to be built on the site of an ancient Egyptian temple, was testimony to the desire to literally replace pagan religion with monotheism. Coptic churches were frequently built on the exact spots where ancient Egyptians worshiped the likes of Horus, Osiris, and the dozens of other lesser gods that made up their spiritual landscape.

"Because of its closeness to the river Nile and the purity of the water that came from its wells, this spot has always been considered blessed," said Father Daoud, the priest who provided the church's historical background. "But the well of Jesus is the purest of all the wells in this area."

As soon as we arrived we were ushered into a conference room that was paneled with wood so dark that it absorbed most of the light that filtered through the windows looking out onto the cement courtyard. Father Daoud came into the room and immediately requested tea from one of the ever-efficient deacons that seemed to be always at his side.

Outside the walled compound of the church was a crush of humanity. The public market of Daqadus occupied the street in front of the church. The tiny boulevard was jammed with shoppers—Muslims were laying in a supply of food before the start of Ramadan. During that holy month, Muslims cannot eat or drink during the day. Most of them stockpile food so they can begin feasting as soon as the sun goes down.

The drive up that final road to the church had involved horn honking, loud yelling by the pedestrians, and gentle nudging with the bumper for those who were too stubborn to move of their own accord. We stepped out of the car into a cacophony of shoppers. Once we were inside the compound, though, the sound of the street was almost completely cut off by the high walls.

"When you have finished your tea, I will show you the church," said Father Daoud.

I finished as quickly as possible and followed Father Daoud across the courtyard and into the church. The main sanctuary was small. It could probably hold five hundred worshipers on a very busy day. At the front of the church was the iconostasis, a wooden screen with patterns of the cross and other religious representations inlaid in ivory and mother of pearl. It was stunning, but I had seen several similar ones already. What struck me as unique in this church was not the altar but the icons. They were the most beautiful I had seen in Egypt. Their patina made them look very old, and the techniques of the painters resembled those of Italian Renaissance artists. Unlike the Coptic art that I had seen thus far, which is largely two-dimensional, these paintings had a three-dimensional quality that brought them to life. Also, there was a definite difference in the gold leaf that is applied as the background paint in most Coptic icons. These paintings had gold leaf, too. But the paint was embossed with designs that gave them more of a spiritual quality.

It seemed a very advanced technique, especially when compared to the simpler icons in other churches. Yet when I asked questions about the origin of the paintings, Father Daoud drew a blank. "I do not know anything about the icons. They have been here a very long time, that is all I know," he said. "But I can tell you that no healings are attributed to the water. There are miracles, but the miracles that happen here are related to the icons and relics."

He took us to a glass case in the front of the church and pointed to a wooden cylinder inside. It was covered with red cloth and wrapped in a plastic zip bag.

"We have many bones of martyrs here," said Father Daoud. "Most importantly, we have the bones of St. George and the bones of the children killed by King Herod in Judea when he was looking for the baby Jesus."

He sent the deacon to an office to fetch the key. As he did, a crowd of the faithful began to gather. They knew something exciting was about to happen and they didn't want to miss it.

The deacon returned with the key and Father Daoud struggled to open the rusty lock. As he clicked it open and slipped it from the hasp, more people gathered. Now there was a knot of churchgoers standing in front of the priest, their eyes wide with anticipation.

"May we kiss it?" asked an elderly woman when he removed the relic case.

Father Daoud held it out and the chain reaction began. One after another the faithful stepped forward to kiss the case that held the bones of the infants killed by King Herod. The priest held the relic case until everyone had paid their respects and muttered a short prayer. Then he did something I did not expect. With the help of another priest, he unzipped the plastic bag and removed the relic case. Then he removed the cloth cover until he was holding the wooden case. It was a small log that had been stripped of bark and left unfinished. On the top of the log was a small door that he struggled to open. It was a balancing act that almost resulted in the relic case being dropped. But when the tiny door popped open, the sweet fragrance of incense wafted into the air. The crowd stepped forward. Inside were a handful of bone fragments. Father Daoud scooped a few of the bones out and held them in his hand.

"These were found in Israel and given to the Coptic Church," said Father Daoud.

It was a reverential moment, so I didn't ask the questions in my mind about their authenticity. Although the slaughter of the innocents is described in the Bible and depicted in sacred art, there is no solid archaeological proof that such an event took place. *How could the Coptic Church be so sure that the bones are actually the bones of these murdered children?* I thought. *Indeed, how could they be sure that the murder took place at all?*

I decided not to ask these questions. Instead I watched as the faithful streamed forward and received whatever power they could from the tiny pile of bones. I could see the tension leave the faces of parishioners as they prayed before the relic. For them this was like the opening of a sacred tomb. I knew that what I was seeing was good, and I was thankful for the chance to see it.

⳨

Before we left, Father Daoud gave us a tiny book entitled *The Shining Cloud of Daqadus.* This book, written by Bishop Philippus of al-Daqahliya, contained a short history of the Church of the Holy Virgin. Following this history there were thirty short accounts of those who had been miraculously healed while praying for divine intervention at the church. Seventeen of the miracles were related to Christians, nine to Muslims, and four to people of undisclosed religious affiliation. The book focused on some of the most amazing cures from blindness, lameness, and seemingly irreversible diseases.

Since the book was written in Arabic, I couldn't read it. But as we drove to Samannud, the next stop on the Holy Family trail, Ra'ed read of the healings with great zeal.

"Listen to this," he said, half turning so I could hear him over the road noise and honking horns. " 'During prayer time at the Church of the Holy Virgin, a woman called Soad Muhammad Arab was standing among the worshipers. Soad came from her small village to visit the Church of the Holy Virgin, as she suffered from an incurable disease. As Soad's disease became worse, she lost speech. Soad remained speechless for five days. Some people advised her to ask for the help of the Holy Virgin. Soad did have enough faith to go to the church and as soon as she stepped into the church and attended prayers, she was cured and began to speak. Soad went back to her village in full health.' "

Ra'ed emitted a low whistle, impressed with what he had read.

"Here is another one," he said, holding up the thin volume. "This one happened to a Muslim man, which shows that the power of this church extends to people of all religions. 'I, Muhammad Ahmed Ghobashy, believe in God, to whom be ascribed all perfection and majesty, and I believe in the Holy Virgin. I came to the Church of the Holy Virgin last Friday night and I called upon her to heal me from the fits of epilepsy which attack me from time to time. At the church, I found the priest praying for many people. I don't know why I had faith that if I moved toward him and he prayed for me that I would be cured. I did not hesitate, especially after I heard the priest mentioning the name of the Holy Virgin many times in his prayer. The priest prayed for me, and suddenly I went unconscious and made weird movements. I heard nothing but the priest's voice driving away the evil spirits from my body. After some time I felt comfortable and calm. I hope that it is the Holy Virgin who helped the priest in his work with me, so that I would be totally healed from my illness. I kneel to the power of the Holy Virgin for what she has done and what she will do for all the people at her church.' "

Ra'ed closed the book. "What do you think?" he asked. "There are many stories in here and many other stories about healing that are not in here. Do you believe in these healings?"

"I do," I said. I told Ra'ed about a series of books I had written that deal in large part with the healing power of spiritual experiences. "I have interviewed a number of people who have been healed by God. This happens to Christians, Muslims, Hindus, even people who say they don't believe in God. Healings happen. Like Carl Jung said: 'God is present, like it or not.' "

Ra'ed thought a moment and then nodded his head.

"Yes. I don't know who Carl Jung is, but I agree with what he says," said Ra'ed. "God is present and he is especially present in holy places like these churches."

Our next stop should have been Samannud and the Church of St. Apa Nub. It is there, says Coptic tradition, that the Holy Family spent two weeks basking in the warmth of the townspeople, who had heard rumors of this divine child. It was there that we could see another well that was blessed by Jesus and also a large granite bowl that Mary used to make bread. We could also hear the wonderful story of St. Apa Nub, who was martyred in the time of Emperor Diocletian in the third century for refusing to renounce Christianity.

That was where our next stop should have been. But it wasn't. Instead, Ra'ed thought we should return to Ismalia for the night. A scholar at American University in Cairo had told him about an evangelical minister in this Suez Canal city who claimed to have found the wheels of the chariots that chased Moses across the Red Sea. Many people have laid claim to having found archaeological hints of a historical Moses. They also claim to have found signs that the Jews actually roamed the Sinai Desert for forty years before entering the Promised Land. But all of these finds have been discredited.

"Archaeologists digging in the Sinai have found no traces of the tribes of Israel," said David Wolpe, a rabbi at the Sinai Temple in Los Angeles, in an interview in the *New York Times*. "Not one shard of pottery." Egyptologists agree, too. Most say that there is no reference in

Egyptian history to any events like the Exodus or any person like
Moses. "The Israelites were never in Egypt, did not wander in the
desert, did not conquer the land [of Israel] in a military campaign and
did not pass it on to the twelve tribes of Israel," wrote Ze'ev Herzog, an
archaeologist at Tel Aviv University, in 1999.

> Perhaps even harder to swallow is that the united monarchy
> of David and Solomon, which is described in the Bible as a re-
> gional power, was at most a small tribal kingdom. And it will
> come as an unpleasant shock to many that the early Israelite
> religion adopted monotheism only in the waning period of
> the monarchy and not at Mount Sinai.

Professor Thomas Thompson, a world authority on biblical archaeology, says that any attempt to confirm biblical stories through archaeological research is "a complete waste of time."

That is why I was so interested in Dr. Ouida. As the dean of the
Evangelical Theological Seminary of Alexandria and a senior pastor of
a large church in Ismalia, Dr. Ouida was a believer in biblical archaeology and a practitioner as well. He understood why archaeologists did
not believe in Moses—they had been looking in the wrong places.

"I have been through the Sinai Desert to all of the spots where
Moses and his people stayed," said Dr. Ouida, dragging his finger across
a map of the Sinai that he had spread on top of his desk. "I have been to
the mountain where he spoke to God—Mount Sinai—and where he
received the Ten Commandments."

"Did you find any sign of ancient settlement?" I asked.

"No," he said. "But you can go to the top of that mountain and
speak right to the face of God."

He turned for a moment and began rummaging through a stack of
papers on his credenza. The break gave me a chance to assess our meeting thus far. It was a Sunday night, and we had arrived at his church in
the middle of a sermon. Parked in the front of the church, which was
tucked into a niche between an apartment building and the Timsah
Shipbuilding Company, was a late-model BMW. The car was black and
stunning in the way that only a highly polished German car can be in
the glare of streetlights. I thought the vehicle belonged to a wealthy
parishioner. Later, to my surprise, it was Dr. Ouida who climbed into it
and zoomed away.

Dr. Ouida was thoroughly modern in other ways, too. Unlike Orthodox Coptic priests, Dr. Ouida had no beard and did not wear the dark clothing of the Orthodox clergy. He wore a reddish brown suit and a maroon tie that made him look more like a classic Baptist minister than an Eastern clergyman.

"This is a paper I wrote about the road that Moses took out of Egypt," said Dr. Ouida, dropping a hefty manuscript on the desk before him. "Most people think he took the road to the north that went out of Egypt to the east to Palestine. But he would not have done that because it was the military road and he would be afraid to run into the pharaoh's army."

"That makes sense," I said.

He pointed to a road lower on the map. "Other people think that he would have taken this middle road, but he would not have done that because it was full of Palestinian people."

"I see," I said.

"He would have taken this road, further to the south," he said. "This would have been the safe road."

The notion that everyone else had been looking in the wrong place for proof of Moses was an interesting one indeed. The land of Goshen, the triangle of land that Moses had used for a staging area for the Exodus, was not a fixed place. It had been declared to be in several different areas in the Nile Delta, including the place we were now sitting. But since no pottery shards have ever been found, or any other proof of six hundred thousand Jews amassing, the exact location remained a mystery. *Why not?* I thought. *Maybe he has found the road that Moses took. Maybe he has found proof of the Exodus.*

"If there is no record of this being the road, how did you find it?" I asked.

"We have been studying it for three or four years," said Dr. Ouida. "We did not go to the books to discover it. We went to where people were discovering the road and digging it up."

"That would be the way to do it, since this road was apparently not in the history books," I said.

"Yes, and you might ask me why we can be so sure that we found the road," he said. "And I am sure because we found the wheels of the chariots stuck in the ground. But these I do not have access to because the army took them and put them into a military museum on a military base."

"How many are there?" I asked.

Dr. Ouida shrugged.

"I did not see them," he said. "I have heard about them. Two of the people who found them began to fight with each other. They began to quarrel with each other in the newspaper *al-Ahram*. So the army took the wheels. Now I cannot see them."

"That is too bad," I said. "Those wheels could be the biggest find in archaeological history."

"Yes," said Dr. Ouida, somewhat dismissively. "But I am glad to say that the person responsible for most of the discoveries was a fanatic Muslim. He wanted to find other results to prove that the words written in the Bible were changed. And there was a committee that looked at our work. Everyone else on the committee was a Muslim. I was the only Christian. Everyone on the committee agreed that we had found the road that Moses took through the Sinai Desert on his way to the Promised Land."

I asked if I could look at the manuscript that he held under his hand. There was a map of the trail of Moses and I was curious to see the exact route. Dr. Ouida declined to let me see it.

"I want to publish it first before any stories come out about it," he said.

"If this is true, this is one of the most important finds in history," I said.

"Yes, I know," he said. "And I think this is the same route that Jesus and the Holy Family took, too. They would not have taken the military road. Jesus followed the same road as Moses across the Sinai."

Although Dr. Ouida believed that the road of Moses was also the road of Jesus, he admitted that there was no way of knowing this for sure, since none of the geographic information he had just given me was contained in the Bible.

That brought up another question. None of the stories about Jesus in Egypt was part of the canon. None of them was found in the Bible. They were found only in the visions or writings of Coptic clergymen, the Infancy Gospels, the Quran, or local legend. "How can you tell which of these stories are true?" I asked.

"That is a good question," said Dr. Ouida. "The Infancy Gospels and all of the other sources you cited are not the word of God. The word of God is the sixty-six books in the Old and New Testaments. You have to be careful with the other sources. The Jews, who wanted to damage Christianity, wrote some books that seem as though they are the word of God. But in those books you find many things that are against the word of God and try to damage Jesus.

"This is true of the Quran," said Dr. Ouida. "One of the things we hold against the Quran is that it has contradictory information in three

parts, all of which are against one another. One part is about the crucifixion of Christ. Another part is about the death of Christ, and yet another says that he was not crucified. They say that just as the Romans
came to take Jesus away, a picture came on the face of Judas so that he
looked like Jesus and they took him away instead. They say that it was
Judas and not Jesus who was crucified. It would look as though Jesus
was resurrected!"

"That's quite a claim," I said. "How do you answer that?"

"Easily," said Dr. Ouida. "I say, if they killed Judas, where is the
tomb of Judas?"

Our conversation had returned to the archaeology of religion. Finding the holy sites mentioned in the Bible was important to Dr. Ouida
because they proved the word of God. When I mentioned to him that
experts had failed to find many archaeological sites that confirm the
stories in the Bible, he said he wasn't surprised.

"Most archaeologists look for these the wrong way," he said. "When
we were tracing the route of Moses, we would talk to the local people.
The Bedouins who live in the desert would say, 'Moses passed this way,'
and when we asked how they knew, they would say, 'Because my grandfather told me and his grandfather told him.' So we rely on oral tradition to find the route."

"Was that always true?" I asked.

Dr. Ouida shrugged.

"Whether these stories did happen or did not happen, they go
along with the spirit of the word of God," he said. "If they do that, then
I believe it."

Perhaps Dr. Ouida could tell that I was confused. He had begun by
decrying sources that were not from the Bible, yet was now admitting
that he relied on oral tradition to trace the route of Moses. It seemed
contradictory to me but in some way it made sense to Dr. Ouida.

"I want you to do something for me when you get back to the hotel," said Dr. Ouida. "Do you have your word of God with you? Read
from the second book of Peter, chapter one. Read from verse sixteen to
verse twenty-one. You will understand how the disciples saw Jesus. This
word of God is the Light."

Later, when we had returned to the hotel, I took out my Bible and
turned to the verses in 2 Peter that he had referred to. Under the dim

light of the reading lamp I read the verses that Dr. Ouida had recommended. Yet, I was still confused about the Ouida method of determining spiritual correctness. The notion that something could be true even if it hadn't happened was tough to swallow, especially for someone who was trying to walk in the footsteps of the New Testament's central figure. Still, two of the verses—16 and 21—went a long way toward explaining the power of oral tradition as it relates to Jesus. They speak for themselves:

> For we have not followed cunningly devised fables, when we made known unto you the power and coming of our Lord Jesus Christ, but were eyewitnesses of His majesty. . . .
>
> For the prophecy came not in old time by the will of man: but holy men of God spake as they were moved by the Holy Ghost.

6. Sorrow into Gladness,
Mourning into Mirth

In the morning we had plans to leave Ismalia and travel as the Holy Family did, to Samannud and then on to Sakha. This simple town in the heartland of the Delta is also known as Bikha Isous, or "footprint of Jesus." As legend has it, the Holy Family arrived in this spot parched and exhausted. They looked for water but there was none.

Taking matters unto himself, the infant Jesus pressed his foot against a stone and pure water gushed forth, satisfying everyone's cravings. In addition to creating a holy stream of water, it is said, Jesus left an imprint of his foot on the stone.

The stone was placed in the baptismal pool of a monastery by monks and left there for hundreds of years. Before invaders destroyed the monastery in the thirteenth century, monks hid the stone underground beneath the front door.

The actual site of the monastery was eventually forgotten, but not the stone. As late as 1977, Coptic historian Otto Meinardus searched for but was unable to find the site of the original monastery. Still, Sakha was called by many Bikha Isous because the two names look similar in Arabic writing.

Then in 1984 construction workers found a stone in a pit of sewer water near the entrance to the modern church in Sakha. On one side was the vague imprint of something resembling a child's foot. On the opposite side of the stone were the words 1 *Allah* written in Arabic.

The workers became so excited at their find that they began drinking the sewer water it was found in. It was, after all, holy water. It is said that a man washed his face with the water and was healed of eye disease. And despite its origin, the workmen described the water as having "a beautiful odor."

I was anxious to get on the road to Sakha, as it is now known, so I could hear about the discovery of this important relic firsthand from the man who found it.

But that was not going to happen, at least not early in the morning. The night before, Ra'ed had met a woman. And not just any woman. She was unmarried, independent, and a successful businesswoman who owned a metal shop. This made her a unique woman in the Egypt that exists outside of Cairo.

He met her on the town's raucous and busy main drag, El Talateni. She was sitting on a straight-backed chair on the sidewalk in front of her metal shop, wearing a pink blouse and an abundance of eye makeup and red nail polish. She looked very strong and confident. Ra'ed said that when he first saw her she was straddling the chair "like it was a horse." In truth, this manner of sitting on a chair is very uncommon among the very conservative and modest women of Egypt. Most Middle Eastern men wouldn't approve of this attitude in a woman, especially one they planned to spend more than an hour with. But still the chic metal shop owner presented an appearance that was apparently very appealing to Ra'ed.

There on the sidewalk in front of her tiny but thriving business, Ra'ed began ingratiating himself with the woman of his dreams.

When he told her that he was accompanying an American on the Holy Family trail, she expressed an interest in meeting me. Although she was Muslim, she was still interested in Jesus, she said. Plus, there weren't many opportunities to meet Americans in Ismalia, especially now after the events of September 11. "Would it be possible to bring him by in the morning so we could talk?" she asked Ra'ed.

Now it was morning, and Ra'ed was selling me on the idea of leaving for Sakha just a little later than we had planned.

"It will not take much time," he said to me as we ate a breakfast of falafel sandwiches in a tiny outdoor restaurant across the street from the metalworks. "We will just have tea. That is all. It is a common courtesy. And since she asked us we should do it. Besides, it will be good for you to meet a woman like this, who is so free. There aren't many of them in this country."

I asked Sa'ad if he wanted to meet the woman who dared to straddle her chair. He shook his head and muttered something that caused even Ra'ed to glare at him in disgust.

"Sa'ad is afraid of her," said Ra'ed. "He thinks she is a whore because she works at a man's job. He doesn't want to go near her because he is married. Sometimes Sa'ad thinks like an old man."

I set my tea down and waved goodbye to Sa'ad. He shook his head at both of us. I don't think he expected to see us the remainder of the day. He ordered a *sheesha* from the waiter, the water pipe so popular in Egypt, and settled into his chair. I don't know what he thought was going to take place, but I could tell by the way he leaned back and drew on his pipe that he thought he was in for a long wait.

Ra'ed and I crossed the street to meet the woman named Nadia.

I was taken with her from the start. Despite the successful attempt to soften her exterior with makeup and finery, Nadia had a grip like an ironworker. She shook my hand firmly and invited us to her office at the back of the shop.

It appeared as though her specialty was ornamental iron. She had a number of iron screens with various designs stacked against the walls. Some of these were to be used for room dividers in a restaurant, she said. A couple were massive and would most likely be attached to a home's gates to make the entrance look more friendly.

There was plenty of iron stacked in racks but no workers at all in the shop.

"Business has been dead since September eleventh," she said, a smile of resignation on her face. "These Taliban went crazy and slowed it down for all the rest of us."

She told us that her husband had died eleven years earlier and left her with three children and a metal shop that she knew nothing about running.

"Life got tough for me very quickly," she said. "With my husband I had the possibility of being rich. But suddenly, without him, I had the possibility of being poor."

With no knowledge of the machinery in the shop or even how to order metal, Nadia went to work. From her late husband's employees, Nadia got a crash course in metalworking, learning to use every piece of equipment.

The notion of Nadia becoming the head of the metal business did not sit well with her husband's family. They thought her attempt to run the business was disgraceful and they tried to convince her to sell it to a man. She refused.

"No one would give me enough money," she said. "I needed enough to raise my children and last for the rest of my life. No one would pay that much."

One day an imam from the local mosque came to visit. He sat with her in her office and told her how disgraceful it was for her to be doing a man's work. She should sell the shop and stay at home, said the imam. There she could care for her children and wait for an appropriate suitor to ask for her hand in marriage.

Such a visit would wither most Egyptian women. An imam is a very powerful holy man and carries a tremendous amount of weight in the community. But Nadia, whose nickname by now was "Frozen like Iron," had a quick response.

"The Quran orders men to take care of women," said Nadia to the imam. "Here is what I need every month to live on. If you can guarantee that to me, then I will sell this business."

Nadia wrote an amount on a piece of paper and slid it across the desk to the imam. He looked at it and left. Nadia says he has never come back.

"Every once in a while the Muslims try to give me trouble, but they fear me," she said. "I can handle a man who tries to do anything wrong."

I asked her what it was like to have male employees. She just shrugged.

"Sometimes men are difficult to handle," she said. "Some men are lazy workers and won't do anything. Or I can give orders to an educated man and he won't listen just because I am a woman. That is why I prefer simple men. They listen and take orders."

It was clear that the metal shop was her castle. A drug addict came into the shop looking for a handout. She shooed him back into the street with a flick of her wrist. Another man came into the shop with the drawing of an ornamental screen he wanted for his restaurant. He treated her like an equal, shaking her hand before leaving. The man from the restaurant across the street came in balancing a tray of hot tea and sugar. She motioned for it to be placed on the edge of her desk and laughed when he mentioned that Sa'ad was still smoking and waiting for us at a sidewalk table. People around town had clearly come to accept a woman in a man's world. But, I asked, what was it like when she had to go out of the shop and into the field to work?

"It is not like you think," she said. "Men accept me and women are jealous, especially when I am out in the field with their men in places where they can't watch them. Then jealousy can run high. But the men like working with me. I can work as hard as they can and I work with them hand to hand. Most of them don't mind."

I could tell from the look on Ra'ed's face that his thoughts were turning to sex, his favorite topic. "I will ask her what she does to get lovers," he said. He began to talk very quickly and laugh nervously. I thought she would be put off by the prurient nature of the conversation but she wasn't. She actually seemed somewhat flattered by it.

"I asked her how she meets men and if she has very much sex," said Ra'ed as Nadia blushed. Then he turned to her for the answer.

"I don't have difficulty meeting men," she said. "Because I work with them I have a sense of what many men are like. When I like one I choose him out. I can use my feminine wiles to get him to me."

"Do you wish you were married again?" I asked.

"I am only forty-six, so I am young enough to marry again," she said. "I would like to marry someone who is well off so I could live a more restful life and not have to run after a living. Still, I would like to marry a man who does not try to dominate me. I have been alone long enough to know how good it feels to be free."

We sipped tea and chatted about the town and her children, all of whom were in good universities, ones that would prepare them for the fight for good jobs that was always taking place in this country of high unemployment. Then, unexpectedly, she turned on me with a bit of wrath about U.S. foreign policy.

"What you are doing in Afghanistan is stupid," she said, her eyes glowing embers about the bombing being carried out against Osama bin Laden and his al-Qaeda and Taliban followers.

"What is so stupid about it?" I asked.

"You are making a saint of Osama and killing innocent people at the same time," she said. "What you are doing is worthless. He is in deep caves. He is the only one you won't get."

"Maybe we should stop and just let them go," I said playfully. "Maybe we should let their organization grow so the Taliban would come to Egypt and take over Ismalia."

The glow of anger left Nadia's eyes and she smiled at the thought of her world being run by the Taliban.

"This would not be good," she said. "Under the Taliban I would drive them mad. I don't like veiled women and I don't like Quran fanatics. They get in the way of my relationship with God. I deal with enough fanatics now. They must die. It would be best for all of us if they did."

As we left, Nadia followed us out onto the street. Ra'ed wrote down her address and telephone number and promised to call her at the earliest opportunity. He had met Western women like Nadia, he would say later, but never an Egyptian woman. For him she was the Middle Eastern version of thoroughly modern Millie.

"I would like to know her better," he said to me as we dodged traffic on our way back across the street. Sa'ad seemed surprised to see us. He had smoked only two bowls of the apple juice-soaked tobacco and looked as though he would have been happy to smoke a third. But it was not to be. In a few minutes we were back in the Peugeot and on our way to Sakha to see the footprint of Jesus.

Once we got out of the city I pulled the three-ring binder that contained the Infancy Gospels from my backpack. I turned to a story that I had read earlier. My decision to read it now was related to Ra'ed's deep desire for Nadia.

"Listen to this story again," I said from my office in the backseat of the Peugeot. "This reminds me of you and Nadia."

Ra'ed turned and listened while I read from the pages in my binder.

" 'There was in this city a gentlewoman, who, as she went down one day to the river to bathe, behold cursed Satan leaped upon her in the form of a serpent and folded himself about her body, and every night lay upon her.' "

"This sounds good for the snake," he said. "Does it say what happened next?"

I continued to read:

> This woman seeing the Lady St. Mary, and the Lord Christ the infant in her bosom, asked the Lady St. Mary, that she would give her the child to kiss, and carry in her arms. When she had consented, and as soon as the woman had moved the child, Satan left her, and fled away, nor did the woman ever afterwards see him. Hereupon all the neighbors praised the Supreme God, and the woman rewarded them with ample beneficence.

Ra'ed was silent for a moment.

"What is that story from?" he asked.

"It is from the First Gospel of the Infancy of Jesus Christ," I said.

"Those Infancy Gospel stories are very strange," he said. "But maybe not. Things were stranger back in those days. Not so many strange things like that happen now."

However, Ra'ed's assertion was not true. Strange things still happen. Sakha was proof of that.

We were met at the gate by a deacon and a priest, Father Mattias. He took us into the church, bypassing the glass case that held the footprint of Jesus, to show us the bones of Severus, a sixth-century pope of Antioch. This wooden container of bones was clearly the priest's pride and joy. Like all church relics, these were kept in a red velvet bag and stored in a glass case near the altar. Father Mattias told us that these bones had been found during the church restoration twenty-five years earlier. They were taken before a committee of bishops, who deemed them the bones of Pope Severus. Like all relics, his bones were divided and sent to churches throughout the Coptic kingdom. But the bones that rest here are perhaps the most important, said the priest, since this was the town in which he chose to live out the last years of his life.

"His sainthood was certainly something to be questioned," said Ra'ed, speaking to me in English as the priest smiled, not knowing what was being said. "He went to Alexandria and ordered monks to kill all Arians and other people who were not of the right 'belief.' Good saint, right?"

I smiled at the notion of such a man being considered a saint and the priest smiled at what he thought was my appreciation of the saint. Everyone was happy.

"This is also the town where St. Agathon the Stylite lived," Father Mattias said. "He was Egypt's only Stylite saint."

Stylites are among the most bizarre of Christian ascetics. Unlike hermits, who live mostly in mountain caves and deny themselves earthly pleasure in order to connect more closely with God, Stylites lived on pillars to get closer to God. They relied upon the kindness of strangers to feed them and provide water.

Although it seems as though living atop a pillar would be a life-shortening experience, such was not the case with St. Agathon. According to Father Mattias, he lived a total of a hundred years. The first forty were spent living a normal life. The next ten were spent as a hermit in the desert. His final fifty were spent on top of the pillar.

"He was a very great man," said the priest.

"Yes, and weathered and sun-stroked," I said.

The priest laughed. It would be hard not to find at least some dark humor in the Stylite way of life.

Father Mattias took us to another relic case, this one sitting next to the case that held the supposed footprint of Jesus. In this case were bones of Bishop Zacharias of Sakha, one of the church fathers who gets credit for mapping the route of the Holy Family in the eighth century. Zacharias, a saint, was revered for his scholarship and eloquence in both writing and speaking. Somehow, though, people had forgotten where they buried his body.

"Then, when the church was being renovated twenty-five years ago, we found his bones beneath the church," said the priest. "It was a blessed event. We were able to recover the bones of one of our greatest saints."

Ra'ed had a sour look on his face as he translated the words of the priest. I could tell there was more to this story than the priest was letting on.

"What else can you tell me about these bones?" I asked Ra'ed.

"You won't hear this story from the priest," said Ra'ed. "It is true that they dug up the bones twenty-five years ago, when they were digging under the church. But no one really knew to whom they belonged. They were just some bones with a cross on top of them. Then one night a person in the church had a dream that these were the bones of Bishop Zacharias and it became so. Since then they have been worshiped as such. It is very unscientific."

I couldn't argue with that. It seemed as though much of what I had seen thus far did not stand up to Western standards of scientific proof. It was clear that "scientific proof" meant something entirely different when it came to the Coptic Orthodox Church. Western archaeologists would require scientific proof before declaring these bones the last remains of an important saint like Zacharias. Once again, faith carries as much weight in Coptic archaeology as evidence in determining the authenticity of a site, an artifact, or bones. Dreams, visions, or even just "feelings" about an object can be considered sufficient evidence when declaring its provenance.

This was evident when we came to view the footprint of Jesus, which was sitting in an unassuming glass case next to the bones of St. Zacharias. Here, in a place that he had obviously occupied many times before, was Halim Mikha'il. In April 1984, he had been watching workers dig the sewer line to the church. When one of the workers found the stone, it was Halim who jumped into the water and declared it the lost stone with the footprint of Jesus.

I wanted to hear the story from his own lips, but Halim was reluctant to talk. Some people in the town had expressed feelings that Halim took too much credit for the find. They pointed out that someone else had actually found the stone. All Halim did was recognize it for what it was, the footprint of Jesus.

So Halim had decided to talk very little about finding the stone. He would not open himself to more community criticism.

Thinking he was just pouting, I decided to flatter him.

I mentioned that the Rosetta Stone had been found by workmen who had no idea of the importance of their discovery. It wasn't until the French archaeologist Jean-François Champollion was given the stone that it was found to be the key to understanding the ancient Egyptian language.

Halim warmed to that idea. Slowly he began telling me of his own discovery. Before long he was recalling it with great animation.

"I was supervising the workmen as they dug through the sewer water," said Halim. "As they dug, one of the men began to uncover a stone that was on top of another stone. The stone on top was the fancy part of a column. I became very excited when I saw this because I knew that when the monks buried the stone to hide it they placed part of a column on top of it to mark it. The stone was brought out and I looked at it. It looked just like it does today. There was a depression on one side that people claim is a footprint and on the other is written 1 Allah in Arabic.

"I jumped into the water and said, 'This is the footprint of Jesus!' Then I began to drink the water because it was holy water."

I made a face at the thought of him drinking sewer water, but Halim assured me it was all right.

"This was holy water," he said. "It smelled heavenly. It did not smell bad at all."

The way Halim described it, the men began splashing and playing like children in the water. One of the men washed his face with the water and was healed of an undisclosed eye disease that was plaguing him.

"It was a very holy moment," he said.

Uncertain that this was truly the footprint of Jesus, the two priests who were serving at the church decided to seek out the Church's highest authority. They took the stone to Pope Shenouda, who was at that time under house arrest in the Monastery of St. Bishoi. The pope performed three liturgies over the stone and then announced that this was truly the footprint of Jesus.

Halim Mikha'il stands next to the stone that many believe contains the footprint of Jesus. Found by Mikha'il at a construction site in 1984, it is displayed at the Church of the Holy Virgin at Sakha in the Delta.

"No further confirmation is necessary as far as we are concerned," declared Father Mattias. "Thousands of people come to see the footprint on the stone. What more is needed than that? Believers cannot be fooled."

"We have traveled out of order," said Ra'ed after we left Sakha.

"What do you mean?" I asked.

"The record says that the Holy Family went first through Samannud and then through Sakha," he said. "It is a minor error but still an error."

I thanked him for telling me, but I felt as though it didn't matter very much. The route of the Holy Family through the Delta seemed at times to be a roundabout route to nowhere. After crossing the Sinai they went south only to loop back north, then west, where they looped back to the south and headed for Cairo. It was an evasive route, which made sense since they were trying to flee from the soldiers of King Herod.

But it was also a route that had been changed many times over the years. The first account of the Holy Family's journey came from the Vision of Theophilus, which was recorded to have taken place in Deir al-Muharraq. That original itinerary includes only three locations, Tell Basta in the north and Ashmunayn and Deir al-Muharraq in the south. The Homily of Zacharias, the next official account of the Holy Family's voyage, adds six additional sites to those in the Vision of Theophilus. Since then, the number of sites on the route has grown because of visions, homilies, oral tradition, and the accounts of travelers from other countries. The official list now consists of more than thirty sites and it is still growing.

Later, I would get a chance to talk about this with the bishop who was the head of the committee working to establish the official route of the Holy Family. For now, though, we were pushing on, making our way to Samannud.

I searched for possible references to a place like Samannud in the Infancy Gospels and found two. These stories take place before the family went to the edge of the western desert, a definite geographic marker. Both stories mention a place where they spent nearly two weeks. Since the Coptic record has them spending between fourteen and seventeen days in Samannud, I thought it was possible that the Infancy Gospel stories refer to this once-important city.

"Here are some stories from the Infancy Gospels that most likely took place in Samannud," I said to Ra'ed. I began to read one about curing impotence from the Arabic Gospel of the Infancy.

Coming thereafter to another city, they wished to spend the night in it. They turned aside, therefore, to the house of a man newly married, but who, under the influence of witchcraft, was not able to enjoy his wife, and when they had spent that night with him, his bond was loosed. And at daybreak, when they were girding themselves for their journey, the bridegroom would not let them go, and prepared for them a great banquet.

Ra'ed looked at me and smiled.

"He was involved in healings of all kinds," he said.

"Yes, he was," I said. "But listen to this one. This is one of the most fantastic healing stories I have ever heard."

I opened the First Infancy Gospel of Jesus Christ to read of a man who had been turned into a mule by a jealous suitor. The same story appears in the Arabic Gospel of the Infancy. Stories like these were not uncommon in ancient Egypt. It was possible to purchase magic spells for all kinds of purposes in the Egypt that Jesus visited. A short list of the incantations includes methods of getting rid of evil spirits, protecting against scorpions, eliminating the collection of water in the eyes, "warding off the wind of sickness," and, yes, turning a person's face into that of a mule.

As I began to read, Ra'ed at first looked incredulous. Then he began to settle down and accept what he was hearing.

[G]oing forward on the morrow, they came to another city, and saw three women going from a certain grave with great weeping. When St. Mary saw them she spake to the girl who was their companion, saying, "Go and inquire of them, what is the matter with them and what misfortune has befallen them?"

When the girl asked them they made her no answer, but asked her again, "Who are ye and where are ye going? For the day is far spent, and the night is at hand."

"We are travelers," saith the girl, "and are seeking for an inn to lodge at."

They replied, "Go along with us, and lodge with us."

They then followed them and were introduced into a new house, well furnished with all sorts of furniture. It was now wintertime and the girl went into the parlour where these women were and found them weeping and lamenting, as before. By them stood a mule covered over with silk, and an ebony collar hanging down from his neck, whom they kissed, and were feeding. But when the girl said, "How handsome, ladies, that mule is!" they replied with tears, and said, "This mule, which you see, was our brother, born of this same mother as we. For when our father died, and left us a very large estate, and we had only this brother, and we endeavoured to procure him a suitable match, and thought he should be married as other men, some giddy and jealous woman bewitched him without our knowledge. And we, one night, a little before day, while the doors of the house were all fast shut, saw that our brother was changed into a mule, such as you have now seen him.

"And we, in the melancholy condition in which you see us, having no father to comfort us, have applied to all the wise men, magicians, and diviners in the world, but they have been of no service to us. As often therefore as we find ourselves oppressed with grief, we rise and go with this our mother to our father's tomb, where, when we have cried sufficiently we return home."

When the girl had heard this, she said, "Take courage, and ease your fears, for you have a remedy for your afflictions near at hand, even among you and in the midst of your house, for I was also leprous but when I saw this woman and this little infant with her, whose name is Jesus, I sprinkled my body with the water with which his mother had washed him, and I was presently made well. And I am also certain that he is also capable of relieving you under your distress."

I stopped reading for a moment and let the words soak in with Ra'ed. There was silence in the car as he thought about the scene that had been presented to him by my reading of the gospel.

"I can see all of this in my head, and it looks like a fairy tale," he said. "What happens finally?"

I continued reading:

"Wherefore, arise, go to my mistress, Mary, and when you have brought her into your own parlour, disclose to her the secret, at the same time, earnestly beseeching her to compassionate your case."

As soon as the women had heard the girl's discourse, they hastened away to the Lady St. Mary, introduced themselves to her, and sitting down before her, they wept. And said, "O our Lady St. Mary, pity your handmaids, for we have no head of our family; no one older than us; no father or brother to go in and out before us. But this mule, which you see, was our brother, which some woman by witchcraft have brought into this condition which you see: we therefore entreat you to com-passionate us."

Hereupon St. Mary was grieved at their case, and taking the Lord Jesus, put him upon the back of the mule. And said to her son, "O Jesus Christ, restore [or heal] according to thy extraordinary power this mule, and grant him to have again the shape of a man and a rational creature, as he had formerly."

This was scarce said by the Lady St. Mary, but the mule immediately passed into a human form, and became a young man without any deformity. Then he and his mother and the sisters worshipped the Lady St. Mary, and lifting the child upon their heads, they kissed him, and said, "Blessed is thy mother, O Jesus, O Saviour of the world! Blessed are the eyes which are so happy as to see thee."

Then both the sisters told their mother, saying, "Of a truth our brother is restored to his former shape by the help of the Lord Jesus Christ, and the kindness of that girl, who told us of Mary and her son. And inasmuch as our brother is unmarried, it is fit that we marry him to this girl their servant."

When they consulted Mary in this matter, and she had given her consent, they made a splendid wedding for this girl. And so their sorrow being turned into gladness, and their mourning into mirth, they began to rejoice and to make merry, and sing, being dressed in their richest attire, with bracelets.

Afterwards they glorified and praised God, saying, "O Jesus son of David who changest sorrow into gladness, and mourning into mirth!"

After this Joseph and Mary tarried there ten days, then went away, having received great respect from those people who, when they took their leave of them, and returned home, cried, but especially the girl.

I closed my binder and we rode in silence for a couple of minutes. Then Ra'ed offered a short version of the story to Sa'ad in Arabic. He listened seriously to the story and then looked back at me and nodded. He said a few words to Ra'ed and then Ra'ed translated.

"Where did this take place?" he asked.

"I am not sure exactly," I said. "I know it happened after Bubastis and before they came to the desert. And since the Infancy Gospels say that they stayed for ten days and were received with great respect, I can only guess that it was somewhere in this area, probably in Samannud. The Coptic tradition says that the Holy Family stayed there for at least two weeks and that they were well received. So it seems most likely that this story took place in Samannud."

"I would agree," said Ra'ed. "I have never heard this story before but I found it very interesting. That Jesus can turn a mule into a man shows how powerful he truly is."

7. Miracles Are Forever

The priest at Samannud listened patiently as I told the mule story to him and then shook his head when I asked him if the story was a familiar one.

"I have never heard that story but it would not surprise me if it happened," he said. "The Holy Family was here for seventeen days and Jesus worked many miracles. So it would not surprise me if he did one like the one you have just spoken of."

I told him that I had read the story in the First Gospel of the Infancy of Jesus and he nodded wisely. "Those are not accepted in our church, so we do not read them. But it sounds reasonable, so it could be true."

The priest had met us at the gate of the Church of St. Apa Nub. His name was Father Johanna. He was a dignified man with a bushy gray beard and kind eyes that could relax even the most penitent sinner. He seemed genuinely glad to see us. This was an important site on the Holy Family trail, he told us. According to Coptic tradition, the Holy Family arrived here after crossing the Damietta branch of the Nile by ferry. Samannud, which was called Sebennytos or Zeb-nuter in those days, had been an important production site for pharaonic sculpture. Even though such sculpture had not been produced for many decades when the Holy Family arrived, they must have passed through a veritable sea of stone gods on their way to the main part of town.

There, according to the priest, Jesus saw a pharaonic temple, one dedicated Horus-Ahar, fighting Horus. Just why this god from Upper Egypt was venerated here in the Delta is not clear, but Father Johanna assured us that it was a temple dedicated to the lance-bearing Horus that the Holy Family saw when they arrived in central Samannud.

"Jesus did not go into the temple," said Father Johanna. "He just called for it to be destroyed and it was. It collapsed right here on this spot."

The spot he referred to was the new church, built on the site of the old church 180 years ago. The old church, according to the priest, dated back 500 years. That meant that beneath us were the remains of an ancient church and a pharaonic temple. We were standing, literally, on a fount of religious history.

"The people of Samannud must have been angry when Jesus destroyed the temple," I said.

"No, no, not at all," Father Johanna insisted. "They knew that he was a divine being and they loved him right away. They loved him because he performed a miracle with their well."

Father Johanna explained that the well in the city had nearly run dry and the people of the town were becoming desperate for clean drinking water. When the Holy Family arrived, Jesus realized that the people needed water and he caused the water to rise. Then he blessed it so it would heal everyone.

"That is why they loved him," said Father Johanna, smiling with an accepting benevolence. "They saw him perform a miracle as soon as he arrived."

"That must have been quite a shock," I said to the priest. "Here was this little two-year-old performing a miracle—"

"He *looked* like a two-year-old but his thoughts were not a child's," interrupted the priest. "They were not even of a grown man. They were the thoughts of God. He was both divine *and* human."

After destroying the temple, Jesus and his parents were welcomed into the town. The divine infant performed many other miracles, although the priest said there was no record of them. The mule miracle could certainly have been one of them, he offered.

"By the end of their stay, Jesus loved Samannud so much that he blessed this town," said Father Johanna. "Then he promised his mother that someday there would be a church on this spot in her name—the Holy Virgin—and his name."

This became a point of discussion in the Coptic Church. Naming the church after the Holy Virgin would be just fine as far as the Church hierarchy was concerned, but naming it after Jesus Christ would not be good, since all churches are automatically for God. Would naming this church for Jesus Christ make it seem more godly than all the other churches in Egypt? The Church hierarchy thought so.

"That was why this church was originally named the Church of the Virgin Mary," said the priest.

"But now the church is named for St. Apa Nub," I pointed out. "Why the name change?"

"Because Apa Nub was the greatest miracle that Jesus performed," said the priest.

Since Apa Nub lived three centuries after Jesus was here, I was puzzled by what Father Johanna had said. Before I could ask the priest to explain such a far-removed miracle, he had lengthened his stride and was headed into the church, beckoning me to follow.

Icons of the sainted Apa Nub were everywhere. Images of a dark-haired little boy kneeling in prayer could be seen in every nook of the church. Large paintings of the little saint hung on the walls, his head surrounded by three cherubic angels, each carrying a halo. On the walls where pictures weren't hung, Apa Nub was literally the wall, his praying image carved from the wood that paneled the lower third of the church interior. There was no mistaking that this was the church dedicated to a saintly child.

The priest was excitedly giving us a tour of his unearthly treasures. "Here we have the remains of Apa Nub," he said, resting his hand on a small glass case with a red-velvet-covered box of bone chips inside. "In this relic case we have the bones of St. George of Egypt. Here we have Pope Butrous, one of the last popes in the time of the martyrs. Then there are the remains of eight thousand martyrs, all children who were killed by the Roman emperor Diocletian for refusing to give up Christianity."

I have always felt that there were two ways to look at relics. The skeptic would consider them to be mere bags of bones, chips of human calcium that were revered far beyond their value and used as a cynical means of manipulation. Believers, on the other hand, see relics as venerated objects that connect them with the roots of their religious past. For them a relic can provide meaning, mystery, comfort, and reverence, all at once.

As I watched members of the congregation offer prayers to the remains of the saints, kissing the glass case and sometimes sliding in notes for special prayers, I saw that for these people they were a means of direct connection with the divine.

Parishioners brought their problems to these hallowed remains. They came asking for divine intervention and always seemed to leave feeling better. Seeing them reminded me of something I had heard as a child: "The value of persistent prayer is not that He will hear us, but that we will finally hear Him." As I looked at the parishioners praying over the relics and asking for blessings from the saints, I couldn't help but feel that they had connected with God and that the connection was good.

"I will take you to the well of Jesus now," said the priest, walking out another door that took us across a small courtyard. He headed toward a well that was surrounded by more icons of the pious Apa Nub, though none of Jesus or the Holy Family.

"There are no icons of Jesus," I said to the priest. "Are you sure this isn't the well of Apa Nub?"

"Oh, I am certain," said the priest seriously. "This is the well of Jesus. You can even look inside."

He opened the well's wooden lid and stood back so I could look in and see myself looking back in the still pool of water fifteen feet down. It was the cleanest well of Jesus I had seen thus far on my trip. Still, I was reluctant to drink from the bottle of water that Father Johanna filled for me from a spigot that was next to the well underneath a simple painting of Apa Nub.

"Go ahead and drink it," said Ra'ed, smiling faintly at my obvious microbe phobia. "The priest is saying that the Holy Family drank of this water, so it is good if holy visitors drink of it, too. To drink of it is *baraka* (blessing). Of course, to drink of the well without the filter might not be such a blessing."

I was trapped. The priest handed me the bottle of water and I gulped down half of the holy offering. The only blessing I asked for at this point was that I would not be made ill from some unholy bugs that might have made it into the water.

Father Johanna was pleased that I had imbibed the holy water. He led me immediately to a large granite bowl that was enshrined in what resembled a glass telephone booth. The glass on the front of the booth had a hole cut in it. It could easily have passed for a ticket booth if it weren't for that big stone bowl in the middle. It looked like a primitive cereal bowl for a giant.

"That is the bowl used by the Virgin Mary to bake bread for the Holy Family while they were here," said the priest.

"How do you know it's the bowl of the Holy Family?" I asked. "Is there something on it that says it was owned by the Holy Family?"

The priest was not angered by the query but I think he was surprised that such a question would be asked.

"We know it is the bowl because it has always been the bowl," he said. "It is the bowl that has been handed down through history."

This was not the sort of argument that would stand up in the West, but, as I kept learning, it was the one that had always worked for the Coptic Church. An artifact was holy if Church fathers deemed it holy.

We watched as a woman reached through the glass hole and dipped her hand into the water. Then she brought the water out and touched it to her forehead. The priest smiled when he saw her do that.

"That is not holy water in the bowl," said Ra'ed, translating the priest's words. "That is just regular water. But he says you can still receive a blessing from that water. If you think it is blessed, it is blessed."

"So if it's not holy water, why is there any water in the bowl at all?" I asked.

Ra'ed knew the answer without asking the priest.

"People put money in the bowl as an offering if there is no water in it," he said. "Then less honest people come along and steal that money. The temptation of an unguarded money supply is too great for many Egyptians. They put water in the bowl so no one will put money in."

✢

As we returned to the sanctuary, I finally admitted to Father Johanna that I still did not understand why Apa Nub's name had been added to the name of the church. I also had to acknowledge—blushingly, I might add—that I did not know who Apa Nub was.

"He was the greatest miracle that Jesus performed while he was here," the priest repeated. "It was Jesus who came to Apa Nub and allowed him to endure the pain of martyrdom."

We sat on one of the church pews as the priest began telling me the story of this young yet formidable saint.

"Apa Nub came here from another town in the years of the Roman emperor Diocletian," he said, referring to the Roman who ruled in the years 284–305. "Diocletian killed many Christians. Right here on this spot he killed eight thousand children for refusing to bow down before the Roman idols.

"One of these children," said the priest, "was Apa Nub."

When he had first arrived here, Apa Nub was alone since both of his parents had died. Yet he found God and became a Christian. He went to the regional Roman governor and spoke to him about his Christian faith. The governor said that Apa Nub had to give up his faith in Jesus, but the boy refused. "I believe in Jesus too much," he declared to the governor.

The governor did not want to kill the boy. Rather, he wanted to torture some sense into him. He ordered that the boy be taken to a ship on the Nile, where he was tied upside down to a mast. The ship sailed with young Apa Nub seeing the world upside down until the ship reached Atfih, about forty miles away.

"By then the Romans thought that the pain of this voyage would make him renounce Jesus," said the priest. "But when he was taken to the governor of Atfih, he made the sign of the cross. Despite his suffering, he would not turn his back on Jesus."

The governor of Atfih did not want to kill Apa Nub, either. He put him back on the boat and sent him to the governor of Alexandria.

"That governor was not so kind as the other two governors," said the priest. "And I don't mean to say that they were kind. But the governor of Alexandria was a very bad man. He gave Apa Nub another chance to renounce Christianity and when he refused he rewarded the young boy with martyrdom."

Which means, of course, that the governor killed him. Or as the priest stated it, "This was when he received his crown of martyrdom."

Somehow his body was identified and returned to his hometown of Nahisah and then eventually to Samannud, where it was buried.

"That is how we were able to get the bones of Apa Nub for the relics," said the priest. "They were returned to this town."

Once again my Western skepticism reared its head. How was it that the Coptic Church could track the bones of one boy who refused to renounce his religion to Roman authority when there were eight thousand children buried in the same spot? I was puzzled. I asked the priest if such accurate bone keeping was possible. He assured me that it was. In fact, he said, he had proof.

"Many children who come here actually see Apa Nub," he said. I looked at the priest with skepticism, though I had heard this claim before. Otto Meinardus, the noted authority on Coptic theology, wrote in his book, *Two Thousand Years of Coptic Christianity*, "Local Christians report that every so often Apa Nub steps out of his icon to play with the children."

"Do you believe that children see him?" I asked.

"Oh yes," said the priest. "That wheelchair is proof of one such sighting."

He motioned to an old wheelchair that was sitting in a window. He said it had been there for at least fifteen years, left by a young girl who was paralyzed by polio and was wheeled into the church by her mother. After praying to Apa Nub, she walked out, never to need the chair again.

"This child had polio. Her mother had carried her into the church many times and prayed for healing," said Father Johanna. "The last time she came she was in this wheelchair. She was here for a few moments and suddenly she began walking. She walked all around the church and then walked out and left the chair."

"Did she see Apa Nub?" I asked.

"I do not know," said Father Johanna. "I do know that she has given thanks to God that St. Apa Nub was able to give healing to her."

Many such miracles are recorded at Samannud. In one case, said Father Johanna, a young girl who came to the church was "full of devils."

"She was not Christian but we prayed for her anyway," said Father Johanna. "I read the Psalms of St. David to her. As I did this she began to cry and cry for a long time. And then the devils came out of her."

"Is she still without devils?" I asked.

"I believe so, but there is a problem," said the priest. "Because she is not a Christian the devils may come to her again. But Christians who are healed are healed forever."

"Sounds like there is a lot of psychology involved in these healings," I said.

"No, no, not psychology," said Father Johanna. "Especially not for Christians. If there is psychology involved, the healing will only be temporary. Miracles are forever."

We left Samannud and headed for the Convent of St. Dimyana, twenty miles away.

As we got close to the convent, it reminded me of Fort Apache, in the movie of the same name starring John Wayne, for this is a community of religious women who live in a compound surrounded by a twenty-foot wall posted with armed guards. Located on the edge of the town of Dimyana, the convent is in "the wilderness of Bilqas," a former salt marsh.

Driving through the town, I had a hard time believing that there was any reason for the nuns to be worried. This was, after all, just another mud village dedicated to agriculture and simple commerce like bakeries, auto repair garages, clothing stores, and butcher shops. But underneath the calm exterior, said Ra'ed, is a seething cauldron of tension.

"There was a big battle here between Muslims and Christians in 1996," said Ra'ed. "You might want to close your window going through town. Some of these people aren't so nice."

"What happened?" I asked.

"It doesn't seem like much but it exploded into a big deal," said Ra'ed. "Two traders got into a dispute over a small amount of money. Before long people started choosing sides and before long there was a war between Muslims and Christians. A lot of people were killed before the police showed up."

The newspapers said that a number of people died in street riots that involved individuals shooting guns as well as throwing rocks and sticks. Within a day the Al-Amn Al-Markazi, the notorious Egyptian riot police, arrived in their black gear and formed a line in front of the convent to keep the angry populace out. One of the church deacons told us later that he was spotted on the main street by a gang of angry Muslims and chased into a storage room. There he barricaded himself inside and watched in horror as the crowd proceeded to splinter the door. Had the Al-Amn Al-Markazi not arrived to rescue him, he felt he would have become a certain martyr.

Martyrs are common in the Monastery of St. Dimyana. St. Dimyana herself is buried in the middle of the church surrounded by forty virgins in the pattern of the cross. All were murdered by Diocletian for refusing to renounce their faith in Jesus Christ.

Dimyana was selected as the focal point of the martyred virgins because her father was the governor of the region. He had led her to Christianity and away from pagan idol worship. When the emperor

heard that one of his loyal bureaucrats had become a Christian, he ordered him to stop worshiping Christ. Dimyana's father was frightened
by the emperor's order, and promised that he would immediately return to the old religion. His daughter was shocked.

"How could you do this, Father?" Dimyana asked. "How could you
worship statues? You taught me everything about Jesus."

Ashamed, Dimyana's father went to Rome and denounced the Roman religion. The emperor killed him immediately and then sent a
hundred soldiers to convert or kill Dimyana.

Conversion was not a subtle art in those days. Dimyana was tortured severely. Medieval sources say that she was dragged by horses
through the streets, cut with swords, even tied between steeds and pulled
until her joints popped. Still she did not renounce her new faith. After
each torture she announced seeing a vision of the Virgin Mary, which
helped ease her pain.

Finally the commander slit her throat and let her bleed to death.
She was buried along with the forty virgins who stood steadfast against
the soldiers. History has it that ninety-five of the one hundred soldiers
sent by the emperor ended up converting to Christianity. They were
killed also.

It is also reported in Coptic legend that Helena, the mother of Emperor Constantine, heard this story and came here about one hundred
years after Dimyana's death with Pope Alexander to bury Dimyana and
the forty virgins. But there is no historical record of Helena ever coming to Egypt.

Although there is no written record of the Holy Family ever coming to Dimyana, local oral tradition says that they did. This area is
blessed, say the people who live here. And blessed ground is always a
sign that the Holy Family at least passed through.

We were now joined by a deacon, Joseph Nagy. Nagy was a handsome man who looked a little like Clark Gable and had the bright, almost electric eyes of a true believer. Because this ground was blessed, it
had seen many great miracles, he said.

"During the dark days of the Arab conquest a caliph [a Muslim
ruler] became angry because the Nile had flooded and covered this entire area with water," he said. "The caliph told the pope that all of the
Christians in this area would be killed unless the pope made the water
recede. And so the pope did. He had the people chant for three days—
'Give us your grace'—and the water receded. Then the caliph was silent
because he knew the power of Christianity."

Behind Deacon Nagy, inside the walls of the convent, someone else was learning the power of Christianity. Father Hedra, one of the convent's priests, was shouting hard and gesturing at a man who was squirming in his *galabíya*, the loose traditional garb of Egypt. The shouting went on for what seemed to be several minutes. He walked around the man, upbraiding him, as parishioners watched in a sort of restrained glee.

A small crowd had gathered and we joined them as the priest continued to unload his wrath. He was aware that his anger had attracted an audience, and he played to that audience by becoming more theatrical, even waving his fists at times. His bearded face was bright red and seemed ready to burst.

The man in the blue *galabíya* was blushing so brightly that I thought he might start hemorrhaging through his skin.

"He is talking so fast that I can hardly translate," said Ra'ed. "But this man is a plainclothes security man. He came into church during the church service and arrested someone. To do something like that during Holy Mass is not good. But it also shows that this man does not respect the house of the Lord and the power of the priest. I think the father is making him respect his power right now."

Finally the priest stopped. I thought he was going to kick dirt on the plainclothes policeman as he walked away but he didn't. He just turned his back on the man and approached me.

"It is good to see you," he said in Arabic as a timid Ra'ed translated.

I wanted to talk him about the Holy Family in Dimyana but he said there was little to talk about. "They merely passed through here," he said. "There is little to say about Jesus in Dimyana."

Still, he implied that it was even the brief passing of the Holy Family that gave young Dimyana and the forty virgins the strength to resist the pain of torture and thereby resist renouncing Christianity.

And it is the combination of these things—the Holy Family and Dimyana and the forty virgins—that makes this a church where people come for healings.

"There are many miracles that happen here at Dimyana," declared the priest. "When people ask for proof of God I always laugh and say that proof is everywhere. But it is especially true of the miracles of St. Dimyana."

The priest sent Deacon Nagy to get a book from his office. He returned with *The Miracles and Appearances of the Virtuous Martyr St. Dimyana*. As Ra'ed read, I listened.

"Here is a short one entitled 'Giving Birth After Twenty-five Years of Sterility,' " he said.

Ghali Iskander, a merchant from Port Said, was married to a hard-minded woman. He has been a member in the Association for Burial of the Dead. The couple has been married for twenty-five years without having any children. Their friends advised them to visit the Monastery of St. Dimyana and St. Dimyana will ask God to give them children.

The wife did not believe in the intercession of saints and was against this advice. She kept fabricating arguments in order not to make this visit. She kept claiming that she was sick and suffered from headaches. The husband was determined to make the visit, and they did visit the Monastery of St. Dimyana. In the same year, God gave them a child after twenty-five years of marriage. It was a great joy.

"That's okay but I'm not fond of miraculous pregnancy stories," I said to Ra'ed. "For some reason they don't seem miraculous enough to me."

"I understand," said Ra'ed. "Only virgin birth seems a miracle from my point of view."

He thumbed through the book of miracle case studies and came to one that he thought I would like better.

"Here is one for you," he said. "This is from Mrs. Shelans Fadel Saleeb. She says:

In the past twenty years I have suffered from a high blood sugar level. This disease affected my retina and caused an edema. I was not able to see anything beyond one meter. For example, I was not able to see the stairs when I was climbing them. Moreover I was seeing everything double, which caused me much annoyance.

Dr. Abdel Latef Sayam gave me a report describing my case. Dr. Sayam and Dr. Rifaat Nazmy from Dumiat emphasized I quickly, within fifteen days maximum, needed a laser therapy. I was given a card to enter the hospital and make the laser therapy in the quickest time possible. I was so upset and afraid.

I asked for the intercession and prayers of St. Dimyana

because I know that her intercession is quite acceptable to the Lord. I made a vow that I would devote my eyes to St. Dimyana if she would heal me. Directly after this, I went to the Church of the Holy Virgin in Dumiat. It happened that Bishop Bishoi was at the church that day. Bishop Bishoi put an altar curtain, on which a picture of St. Dimyana was drawn, on my eyes. At that moment, I asked for her prayers for me and repeated my vow.

One day after, I felt that my eyes became quite normal and that I was totally healed without any laser therapy or medication. Because I wanted to be certain I went to Dr. Khaled Eyada in Cairo, who emphasized that my eyes were sound and my visual acuity was good. He gave me a report mentioning these facts.

I became sure that this is the blessing of St. Dimyana, whom I had asked for her intercession and prayers. It is also the prayers of Bishop Bishoi that allowed this miracle to take place. Today, I can see everything clear and I practice needlework.

"That sounds much more like a miracle to me," I said. "Sounds like she had diabetic retinopathy, which isn't likely to reverse overnight, especially if it's so severe that laser therapy is required."

"Yes, I would agree," said Ra'ed. He looked quite sincere. "Making people have babies is maybe not so impressive. But curing blindness is the sort of miracle that makes us all believe."

Later that night after dinner I had a chance to speak further with Father Hedra about the healing miracles of St. Dimyana. I told him about the increasing amount of research coming out of American institutions about the power of prayer to heal. Dr. Larry Dossey, one of the leading researchers in this field, calls prayer and miracles "nonlocal healing"—the Western way of saying that a person was healed supernaturally.

Modern medical research no longer ignores these miracles, I said. In fact, medical journals are filled with studies in which doctors in white coats try to create miracles in laboratory settings so that they can replicate them. Amazingly, they have created miracle healings and replicated them several times.

I recounted an experiment in which members of a church congregation in San Francisco were assigned seriously ill heart patients to pray for. They did not know these patients and the patients did not know they were being prayed for. Yet by the end of the study, the patients who were prayed for got well faster and better than those who were not. This study was replicated three times in different parts of the United States and each time the "nonlocal healing" of prayer was found to make a significant improvement in the health of heart surgery patients.

"Then you have miracles, too," Father Hedra said. "You like to prove your miracles and we like to accept ours. But there are miracles from God all over the world."

Still, said Father Hedra, the Monastery of St. Dimyana holds a special place in the world of miracles. Perhaps it is the power of St. Dimyana and her unique story of martyrdom that appeals to people of all religions. Even as the armed guards keep their vigil at the front gate and deacons, nuns, and church workers relax in the courtyard after their day's work, Father Hedra told me that many Muslims come to the convent to study the nature of Jesus.

"They may have a different view of our Lord, but they honor him just the same," he said. "They come here to get information from the church that honors him the most."

8. Lightened by Piety

The Holy Family probably spent thirty minutes in Dimyana, just the time it took them to walk through this swampy area on their way to the desert to the west.

We spent the night.

We stayed in guest rooms that overlooked a deep green field. Most of the year these fields are dedicated to agriculture. But between May 5 and May 20, as many as a hundred thousand pilgrims or more come to the monastery and pitch tents in these very fields. Merchants come, too, setting up a makeshift bazaar in which they sell clothing, jewelry, perfume, incense, and crosses, many imported from Jerusalem.

The purpose of this religious gathering, or *mulid*, as many Copts refer to it, is to celebrate the date of May 21, which was when St. Helena is said to have dedicated the church. Another such *mulid* is held January 20, the day of martyrdom for St. Dimyana.

"It is quite an unbelievable sight," said the priest after we had completed breakfast and joined him in the courtyard. "There are thousands of people walking through here receiving blessings from the saint. Many are women who want to become pregnant. Dimyana is especially good at making women bear fruit."

"Having children seems to be very important here," I said to Ra'ed.

"Yes. People here like to have many children so they will be taken care of in their old age," said Ra'ed. "It is the Egyptian version of social security."

"Do you have anything like these *mulids* in America?" asked the priest.

The closest companion I could come up with was a rock music festival such as Woodstock, or the bizarre Burning Man Festival in Nevada. Frankly, I couldn't imagine many Americans camping for several days to pay their respects to any saint.

"Perhaps your country is not old enough yet," said the priest. "Things that are old are worshiped more than things that are new."

That could easily be part of the reason. Behind me were the four churches of Dimyana, the oldest built one thousand years before Columbus discovered America. There is something about such age that inspires reverence.

Called the First Church of St. Dimyana, it was built by Pope John I in 496. At some point a flood filled the church with mud and silt and covered the grave of the saint and her forty virgins for more than seventy years. The church itself was believed to have been destroyed by decades of erosion caused by the flood.

Some twenty years ago, the nuns of the convent prayed that St. Dimyana would give them a sign indicating where that first church was buried. Such a sign came in the form of a dove. Several nuns saw a dove land on a spot near the Second Church of St. Dimyana and disappear into a hole in the ground. Workmen began to dig and soon they discovered an ancient brick dome. Dirt was cleared from inside the dome to reveal a magnificent painting of Jesus sitting on a heavenly throne.

Now this ancient church is cleared of the dirt and silt that was deposited there by the flood. It is a remarkably well-preserved structure with an altar stone still intact beneath the dome painting of Jesus from the church built on top. The sanctuary has no roof and the plaster that most certainly covered the walls is gone, but the structure itself has held up nicely. This is most likely due to the mud that filled the church and protected the bricks and wood for so many centuries.

Metropolitan Yuhanna of Burullus built the Second Church of St. Dimyana. He camped near this spot in the late nineteenth century and had a vision of St. Dimyana in which the young girl declared that a church should be built in her honor. The church has been described by Coptic historians as being "unspectacular" with the exception of the prayer chamber. It is here, beneath a mound of earth covered by cement, that St. Dimyana and the forty virgins lie.

This revered spot is surrounded by a Plexiglas wall to keep the faithful at bay. A cement arch over the entire gravesite declares in both English and Arabic that this is "the tomb of St. Demiana [Dimyana] & the forty Virgin Martyrs."

Flowers, crosses, and articles of clothing have been thrown over the partition as votive offerings. Folded notes have been tossed onto the site to ask the saint for specific prayers. There is a constant stream of visitors to this holy burial mound, asking for favors.

Two more modern churches are adjacent to the Second Church of St. Dimyana. One of those, currently under restoration, has spectacular stained-glass windows that tell many Bible stories as well as some that aren't in the Bible, like the story of the Holy Family's voyage into Egypt.

Father Hedra was very proud of this new church and the "windows that tell stories." He took us into the church beneath scaffolding where workers plastered the walls at an Egyptian pace, which amounted to ten minutes of work and thirty minutes of talk. At one point, in the midst of telling us about one window that depicts Jesus turning water into wine, he suddenly lashed out at three plasterers across the church who were talking too loudly. He wanted them to quit talking and work, he said. Reluctantly they did—at least until we left the church.

By late morning we left the Monastery of St. Dimyana. So we wouldn't forget the saint, Father Hedra gave us pens adorned with an image of St. Dimyana and the forty virgins. He also gave us a key chain featuring a simple image of the Virgin Mary.

I thanked the priest and said that these holy items made me feel as though I was loaded down with piety. He corrected me.

"You are not loaded down by piety," he said. "You are lightened by it."

And so we left the Monastery of St. Dimyana, lightened by piety, ready to face the road to the stark and vast western desert.

Driving through the verdant Delta toward the western desert is like approaching the opposite of a mirage. Instead of seeing the false comfort of water in the distance, you see only the harsh reality of mile after mile of sand.

The Copts say that after leaving the Monastery of St. Dimyana, the Holy Family hired a boat and sailed south on the western branch of the

Nile. At the southern end of an area now known as Liberation Province, they left the boat and continued their journey on foot. Here they looped away from the Nile and stood at the edge of the desert. According to all sources, the place they saw was a brackish salt lake called Wady el-Natrun.

In the late summer, when the water had evaporated, large deposits of *natrun* were left behind. This chemical compound, consisting of sodium carbonate, sulfate, and sodium chloride, was collected by merchants and sold to the morticians of ancient Egypt. They used it in the process of mummification to preserve the organs of the deceased.

In the second century, a Christian led a group of seventy holy men to this desert region to fast and pray. Their numbers grew to as many as five thousand, living in reed houses and caves as they fasted, prayed, and struggled to become closer to God.

Why did they choose to live the ascetic life in the harshness of the desert instead of the comfort of the fertile Delta? In part it was to get away from civilization so they could be alone with God. But historians also say that hermits chose the starkest desert possible so they could struggle against Satan in his own territory. Wady el-Natrun was known to the locals as "the home of demons and evil spirits." It is such a desert in Egypt that many hermits thought St. Paul was referring to in Ephesians 6:12 when he wrote: "Our battle is not against human forces, but against the principalities and powers, the rulers of this world of darkness, the evil spirits in regions above."

Many stories came from these spiritual battlefields. Among the most famous are those of St. Anthony of Egypt, the father of monasticism. He moved to these deserts in the late third century. It is here, according to St. Athanasius, his biographer and contemporary, that he fought many battles with Satan. St. Anthony was tempted body and soul by the devil, and when temptation did not work, he was beaten almost to death by his supernatural foe. It was an ordeal similar to the one Jesus faced when he too went to the wilderness. But instead of lasting forty days and nights, as Jesus' did, St. Anthony's battle with Beelzebub lasted many years. Finally Satan gave up. Yet, despite the victory, St. Anthony felt abandoned by God.

"Why were you not here to help me?" he asked God.

"Anthony, I was here the whole time," said God. "I stood by you and watched your combat; and because you have manfully withstood your enemies, I will always protect you, and render your name famous throughout the earth."

St. Anthony went on to found many monasteries, which in those days were loosely organized colonies of hermits. He would travel among these monasteries, inspiring his fellow hermits with his own stories of battling Satan. Today we might think of his message as having a Zen quality to it. "Do every action as if it were the last in your lives," he would tell the gathered ascetics. Other words of wisdom include "The devil dreads fasting, prayer, humility and good works" and "If prayer becomes too difficult, turn for a while to manual labor." According to St. Athanasius, St. Anthony died at the age of 105 without ever being sick or suffering poor vision or even losing a tooth.

Historians estimate that as many as fifty monasteries dotted the area of Wady el-Natrun by the year 1000. Many of these were surrounded by high walls as defense against frequent attacks by the tribes that roamed the desert.

Churches were plundered, monks were slain, but still the monks stayed. Their chosen role in life was to fight the powers of darkness, be they physical or metaphysical. That was their God-given burden.

Wady el-Natrun is home to four functioning monasteries now. One of those, the Monastery of St. Macarius, is an intellectual center that has been the spawning ground for at least twenty-nine Coptic Patriarchs. More than a hundred monks make up the population of this important monastery, the vast majority of which are college-educated intellectuals who produce the monthly magazine *St. Mark* on their fairly modern printing press. A special crypt houses what are believed to be the remains of St. John the Baptist.

A farm is cultivated nearby on two thousand acres of land donated in 1978 by the late president Anwar Sadat. More than four hundred workers help the Coptic monks work this land and raise farm animals such as cows and goats.

In a land condemned once by the people of Egypt as "the home of demons and evil spirits," a place where the battle of good against evil was waged by praying hermits in caves, it appears as though good has won. But that is the way it was destined to be. For according to Coptic belief, the Holy Family stopped to drink from a well of fresh water on the edge of this desert. While they were resting beneath a tree, two lions approached them. Mary became frightened by the beasts, but young Jesus was not concerned. With a dismissive wave of his hand he told the lions to leave. Without hesitation they obeyed, bowing their heads and walking away.

Mary was relieved, but her son spoke prophetically.

"O Mother, in this vast desert there will live many spiritual fighters, male and female, who will serve God like angels and will mention your name with great reverence. For their safety, from now on, no fierce animals nor mischievous insect shall be allowed to live in the area."

We got out of the car and looked out at a desert that has probably changed little in two thousand years. It was stark and bleak and fathomless, and reminded me of why it is that Egypt has never been conquered by a force coming from the west across these endless dunes.

"What happened here?" asked Ra'ed as I opened my copy of the Infancy Gospels and began search for the appropriate passages.

"One of the most amazing things that happened to Jesus in Egypt happened right here," I said. "According to the Infancy Gospels, he met the two thieves who would eventually hang on crosses on either side of him when he was crucified in Jerusalem."

"Is such a thing possible?" asked Ra'ed. "That would mean that Jesus knew the end from the beginning."

Ra'ed had hit it right on the head. As the most divine of beings, Jesus knew how his own life would end, even as an infant. He knew his alpha from omega.

The First Gospel of the Infancy of Jesus Christ contains the oldest version of this desert story. But the most colorful is in the Arabic Gospel of the Infancy, an account of the infancy of Jesus that evolved from the First Gospel of the Infancy of Jesus Christ as Christianity spread from Syria onto the Arab peninsula. Earliest examples of this work go back to the fifth century and are called the Arabic Gospel of the Infancy because they were translated into Arabic from Syriac. It is believed that this book is the source of many of the Holy Family stories found in the Quran.

It is the book I read from as we stood on the edge of the desert.

" 'They came to a desert; and hearing that it was infested by robbers, Joseph and the Lady Mary resolved to cross this region by night,' " I read.

But as they go along, behold, they see two robbers lying in the way, and along with them a great number of robbers, who were their associates, sleeping.

Now those two robbers, into whose hands they had fallen,

were Titus, an Egyptian, and Dumachus, a Syrian. Titus therefore said to Dumachus: "I beseech thee to let these persons go
freely, and so that our comrades may not see them."

And as Dumachus refused, Titus said to him again: "Take
to thyself forty drachmas from me, and hold this as a pledge."
At the same time he held out to him the belt which he had
about his waist, to keep him from opening his mouth or
speaking. And the Lady Mary, seeing that the robber had
done them a kindness, said to him: "The Lord God will sustain thee by His right hand, and will grant thee remission of
thy sins."

And the Lord Jesus answered, and said to His mother:
"Thirty years hence, O my mother, the Jews will crucify me at
Jerusalem, and these two robbers will be raised upon the cross
along with me, Titus on my right hand and Dumachus on my
left; and after that day Titus shall go before me into Paradise."

And she said: "God keep this from thee, my son."

I put the Infancy Gospels away and opened the King James Version of the Bible to the story of the crucifixion in St. Luke. Of the four
accounts of the crucifixion in the New Testament, the one in Luke contains the most information about the thieves who were hung on the
cross next to Jesus. I read these verses now to see if the thieves were
named and if there was any indication that they had met before. One
of the criminals hung on crosses on either side of Jesus says, "If thou be
Christ, save thyself and us." The criminal on the other side disagrees
with his partner in crime.

But the other answering rebuked him, saying, "Dost not thou
fear God, seeing thou art in the same condemnation?

"And we indeed justly; for we receive the due reward of
our deeds: but this man hath done nothing amiss."

And he said unto Jesus, "Lord, remember me when thou
comest into thy kingdom."

And Jesus said unto him, "Verily I say unto thee, Today
shalt thou be with me in paradise."

I closed the Bible and looked to Ra'ed for comment.

"The thieves were not named in the Bible," said Ra'ed. "So the encounter Jesus had with them here on this spot puts a name to them."

"That is one way to look at it," I said.

"What is another?" asked Ra'ed.

"That the encounter in the desert never took place because no one acted as though they had ever met the other," I said. "Don't you think that at the hour of their deaths they would have said something about their chance meeting in the desert thirty years earlier?"

Ra'ed shook his head.

"These criminals would maybe not have remembered meeting Jesus so many years earlier. And they would not have recognized him. He was only about three years old when they first met," he said. "And Jesus had a lot on his mind that day. If that story you read is true, maybe he just neglected to mention that they had all met before."

That explanation was good enough for me.

"Sa'ad wants to know if we can leave," said Ra'ed. "The desert road back to Cairo is not so good at night. There are many accidents and he does not want to be one."

Any road that would frighten Sa'ad was certainly one that would frighten me. I took one last look at the deep and mysterious western desert and then climbed back into the car for the drive back to Cairo.

As the sun faded I tried to imagine what it would have been like to live as a hermit hundreds of years ago in Wady el-Natrun. They would spend their days and nights reading holy scriptures and praying for a greater closeness to God. The days would bake them with the unfettered rays of the sun while the night chilled them quickly as the desert heat radiated skyward from the porous sand. Animals lurked around the caves, sensing the life and food that was inside these homes of stone. And then there were mysterious noises heard and supernatural beings seen. Were these phantasms manufactured by the lonely minds of these hermits or did they truly exist?

These early hermits were brave people, I thought, as the desert faded to darkness. They had come here to get closer to God, but they were also spiritual warriors fighting the forces of evil on Satan's home turf. And they were fighting them with no weapons except prayer, a solitary life of contemplation, and rigorous discipline.

In the name of God they lived their lives in almost total silence. But they were happy with that life. After all, silence is a form of communication, too.

Still, I had difficulty understanding the force of God that kept them in such unpleasant surroundings. Some of these hermits may have been mad and were driven to social isolation by their own mental disorder. But for the most part hermits were well educated and intelligent. Why, I wondered, had they taken their religious beliefs to such extremes?

The answer was made clear to me much later in my voyage, when a monk at another monastery attempted to explain the hermitic life through a story that was common among the hermits of Egypt.

"A man wanted to become a hermit, so he visited the hermitage of a holy man in the deserts of El-Natrun," he said. The young man wanted to become a hermit but he was afraid that his beliefs would not be strong enough to last longer than a few years.

"Why is it that people who come to the desert to be hermits leave after a year or two and others stay faithful to their intent and remain hermits for a lifetime?" he asked.

The old man thought a moment. Finally he said, "Without a vision, people cannot keep their faith."

"I don't understand," said the young man.

"I can see that," said the old hermit. "I will explain it with a story. One day I was sitting here with my dog. Suddenly, a rabbit ran in front of us and raced out into the desert. My dog saw the rabbit and began to run after it very hard. He barked as he ran and that attracted other dogs. Soon there was a long line of dogs running across the desert.

"Soon the dogs became tired. They began to slow down and stop. Eventually the only dog that was still chasing the rabbit was my dog. He did not stop for a long time. In fact, I thought I was going to lose him to the chase."

The old hermit sat back and was silent for a while.

"That is the answer to my question?" said the young man.

"It is the answer," said the old hermit. "The other dogs stopped chasing the rabbit because they had never *seen* the rabbit. My dog had seen the rabbit and therefore he had the passion to continue the chase. He had a vision of what would happen when he caught that rabbit. It was that vision that gave him longevity."

It was the same vision that gave all hermits the endurance to carry on with their faith, said the monk. "First it was the vision of Jesus that hermits should inhabit this special desert. But it was the vision of each of these hermits individually that kept them here, anchored to their faith. If they did not have that vision, they could not continue with their vows of the hermitic life."

He then recited something he had once heard that helped explain the purpose behind the hermitic life.

A man will despise all things present as being transitory when he has securely fixed the gaze of his mind on those things which are immovable and eternal. Already he enjoys, in contemplation, the blessedness of his future life. It is as when one desires to strike some mighty prize—the prize is virtue—which is far off on high, and seems but a small mark to shoot at. The archer strains his eyesight while he aims at it, for he knows how great are the glory and rewards which await his hitting it. He turns his eyes away from everything, and will not look save thither where the reward is placed. He knows that he would surely lose the prize if his strained sight were turned away from the mark even a very little.

Another hermit named Alladius was even more succinct as to his reasons for becoming (and remaining) a hermit: "Except a man say in his heart, 'I and God are alone in the world,' he will not find peace."

We returned to Cairo and parted ways. Ra'ed went back to teaching English in his secondary school. Sa'ad returned to driving his cab in Cairo. He seemed very glad to be back in the big city. He had missed his family while he was on the road but he was also glad to be far away from Nadia. He didn't like women like her, he said with a sincere smile. They made him very, very nervous. "I had a dream of her driving a cab," he told me. "Her car was always full of people."

I went back to the Sonesta Hotel, where I planned to spend at least a day organizing my notes and thoughts before continuing with my journey on the Holy Family trail. The voyage so far had been a spectacular one. I had been awestruck by the naked desert and understood the great difficulties faced by the Holy Family as they crossed the Sinai's horrible beauty. I now understood that just the proximity of the Holy Family to many of the sites made them sacred, able to impart healing powers when modern medicine had failed.

But I had a nagging question in my mind: How could I be sure that what I was following was truly the Holy Family trail? After all, the trail was not based on a route found in the Holy Bible. It was not even based on ancient maps created by early Christian pilgrims. Rather, the Holy Family trail has been cobbled together over the centuries from a variety of sources, including oral traditions, sermons by bishops, histories of saints, Infancy Gospels, and, most mysterious of all, visions.

It wasn't even until 1999 that the Church brought together a committee of bishops to create an official map of the Holy Family trail so they could have one ready for the second millennium. Yet even now the map keeps changing. Local traditions, newly found evidence, and even modern visions have added sites that are not on the officially sanctioned map. Faith is clearly in flux here. And although some of these sites seem to genuinely belong on the Holy Family map, priests in other spots appear to have commercial or political interests in mind when they insist that their church be a part of the Holy Family trail.

What assurance could I have that the Holy Family trail was more than just a myth? Were the sources it was derived from more than just legends and wishful thinking?

I decided to formulate a few questions that I had about the traditions of the Holy Family trail and ask these questions of experts in the field of biblical documents and historical study. I did not want these experts to be clergymen. Rather, I wanted to talk with scholars.

The reason for seeking out an academic point of view was one of objectivity. The religious authorities on the trail ahead of me would be bishops and priests, men who would surely believe that oral tradition was at least somewhat sacred and that the vision of a patriarch was divine. But here in Cairo I could talk to academicians whose answers would not have to be in line with any church's viewpoint. To my Western way of thinking, their answers would weigh dogma against fact to derive the kind of opinion that could stand up in court. At least a Western court.

I formulated a few simple questions and went in search of the scholars who could answer them.

HOW RELIABLE IS ORAL TRADITION?

The bulk of the accounts of Jesus in Egypt come to us from oral tradition, but so do the gospels of the New Testament. Most biblical scholars believe that at least forty years separate the death of Jesus from the writing of the first gospel or "good news" which was attributed to Mark. Then by many accounts, Matthew's gospel was written fifteen years later, followed by Luke's another fifteen years after that. The final book was the Gospel of John, which was written sometime between 90 and 100 C.E. It is possible, say many scholars, that none of these books was written by the disciple it is attributed to. Their true authors are all unknown.

Scholars say that attributing written works to famous people was a common practice in the ancient world. Indeed, many of the infancy stories I was using in Egypt were said to have come from such disciples as Matthew, Thomas, and James. Others sites on the Holy Family trail were added as a result of oral traditions that had circulated in Egypt, some for hundreds of years until they had finally been recorded and accepted by the Coptic Church.

Did the fact that they had finally been accepted by an official church make them truth? In short, when can an oral tradition be accepted as truth?

To explore this question I spoke in Cairo to Stephen Davis, a former professor of New Testament and early Church history at the Evangelical Theological Seminary in Cairo, and now a professor of religious history at Yale.

Davis is a tall, reed-thin scholar with a thick head of blondish hair and a thoughtful demeanor. The question "When is oral tradition true and when is it false?" caused him to pause for a moment while he processed the answer.

"It is always not true," he said. "Anytime you write a narrative or tell a story you are selecting information. Plus, the oldest written evidence for a visit by the Holy Family to a specific place is from the fifth century. That leaves a five-hundred-year gap between when things happened and when the first record of a tradition was written down. A Western scholar who said that Jesus Christ was actually here would be hanging himself out to dry. Why? Because Western scholarship does not value oral tradition as a source.

"But it's different here in the East. Oral tradition holds equal weight—sometimes even greater weight—because of the religious authority behind it. If a religious authority in the Church says that an oral tradition is true, then it is true. To a Western scholar, religious authority means nothing and written sources mean everything. For the Copts it can be the other way around.

"So [as a Western scholar] you can do the necessary research and most likely conclude that there is no history to back up the Holy Family trail in Egypt, only oral tradition. And then you wipe your hands and say, 'That's great.' After that, it becomes a matter of persuasiveness."

⳨

My next question related to the Vision of Theophilus, the Patriarch of Alexandria from 385 to 412. In his vision, Theophilus said he spoke to the Virgin Mary and she told him about the voyage of the Holy Family into Egypt. It was through Theophilus' vision that the Holy Family trail first gained popular acceptance. My question was an obvious one:

WHEN IS A VISION TRULY A VISION AND WHEN IS IT JUST A VIVID DREAM?

For an answer I went to the Center for Patristic Studies, an academic think tank dedicated to the study of the works of the early fathers of the Coptic Church. Located in Cairo, the center has none of the icon paintings or elaborate religious ornamentation I had come to expect at other Coptic buildings. Instead it is housed in a steel and glass office building. Their offices had a few photos of Coptic clergy gathering for academic sessions but other than that it looked as stark as the office of an insurance broker in Brooklyn.

I met with Dr. Joseph Faltas, the center's assistant director. Faltas is a slender man with the intense, gaunt look of someone who spends a lot of time reading documents very carefully for their truest meaning. He simply shrugged when I asked him the question.

"When is a vision a vision and when is it just a dream?" he repeated. "That is very difficult to answer. Indeed, that is *very* difficult to answer. Even for us today, from our own personal experiences, you cannot be sure. Sometimes you might have a vision and part of it comes true and part of it does not. Does that make the part that does not come true a dream? I don't know."

"Then how did the Church deal with visions in ancient times?" I asked. "Was there a committee of bishops that decided whether a vision was true or not?"

"No," he said. "The Church fathers were concerned with the doctrine of the Church. They did not have a prescription for when a vision was real or a dream. They were concerned with doctrine, the dogma of the Church."

"Theophilus' vision is not considered dogma?" I asked.

"No, the vision is not considered dogma," said Dr. Faltas. "Some even call it Coptic folklore. That would make it a form of oral tradition." Then he offered an example. "For instance, the sign of the cross is an example of oral tradition."

"It is?" I asked.

"Yes. We cannot find it in any of the scriptures," he said. "There is reference to the cross in the Bible but not what it looks like. So the one that is used by the Church is oral tradition. Because it cannot be found in the scriptures it is oral tradition."

"So you think that the Vision of Theophilus may have been oral tradition and not a vision at all?" I asked.

"It is possible," said Dr. Faltas. "Whatever the case, Theophilus did not write it down himself, or so it seems. The vision may have taken place in the fourth century but it was written down by someone else, maybe someone in the eleventh century. Bishop Cyriacus, possibly."

"So it was written by someone else many centuries later and attributed to Theophilus? Was that a common thing to do?"

Dr. Faltas nodded.

"It was common, even at the time of the great fathers," he said. "For instance, we know from history that many of the writings of St. Athanasius were not authored by him. They were written at a later time and attributed to him. So Theophilus probably spoke about the vision and then it was passed down through the centuries until it became a written text. It may seem strange now, but that is the way things were done then."

I must have looked puzzled or distressed because Dr. Faltas leaned forward for emphasis and repeated himself.

"It is just the way things were done then."

Gospels not written by their authors . . . visions recorded seven hundred years after the fact . . . oral traditions that carry more weight than the written word . . . my Western mind was boggled. Was I following a complete fiction in this voyage up the Nile? Was there actual proof anywhere that Jesus had followed this route through Egypt?

And—the biggest question yet—did it matter to any of the true believers?

9. Hills of Sand

D
r. Noshi Abdel-Shahid had concerns about the Holy Family trail, too. He was the third academic I spoke with, and the one whose response surprised me the most. As the director of the Center for Patristic Studies since 1958, Abdel-Shahid was outspoken in his disdain for the Holy Family trail and the "touristic thing" that it represents. Although he has no doubt that the Holy Family was in Egypt, he questions the validity of the Holy Family trail as well as the motives of those claiming there is one.

"The story of the Holy Family in Egypt is a fact," said Abdel-Shahid, his eyes becoming fiery at the first mention of Jesus in Egypt. "But the particulars, I don't know. People hear that places are holy and they go there. They think they are taking spirit from the places he lived or the places that he supposedly drank water. Sometimes these places are true. But many times they aren't true. They are just made up."

I was shocked to hear a man of the Coptic faith make such a statement, especially about one of his Church's most enduring legends. I was even more surprised to hear him place a price tag on these Holy Family sites.

"They do this to make income. It is the explanation everywhere," he said. "But to do this is not the proper guidance. The proper guidance is to help people know their God faithfully and in good conscience and in good faith, and to listen to the commandments of Christ. It is not proper to make money in guiding people to holy sites, only to holiness."

"It sounds as though you don't believe that Jesus really passed through many of these sites," I said.

Abdel-Shahid shrugged, his face a picture of futility.

"There is nothing official in the worship of the Coptic Church about the Holy Family coming to Egypt except the date of them coming to Egypt, which is on June first. The only other thing we have is folk tradition."

"How about the Infancy Gospels?" I asked. "They tell the same stories that are commonly told on the Holy Family trail. And some of them even have place names. Doesn't that confirm belief about the trail?"

"No, it doesn't," said Abdel-Shahid. "You cannot fix all of the facts mentioned in the Infancy Gospels into legality. Since we are not sure when the Infancy Gospels were written, we cannot be sure about all the miracles being mentioned here and there."

Given the nature of his work at the Center for Patristic Studies— which is to interpret and translate the "first fathers" of the Church into Arabic and other languages—it came as no surprise that Abdel-Shahid would take a legalistic approach to the wonders and whereabouts of Jesus as a child. Still, the fact is that much of the Bible itself was built on oral tradition. Wasn't faith in these "folktales" a large portion of the rock that Christianity was built upon? Wasn't faith, as it was said in Hebrews, "the substance of things hoped for, the evidence of things not seen"? I began to think that Abdel-Shahid's dislike of the Holy Family trail went deeper than its money-making proclivities or its inability to prove the exact path of Jesus. For Abdel-Shahid, the Holy Family trail seemed to take away from the spiritual nature of worshiping Jesus. When I asked him about this, he agreed.

"Why would we look for some evidence two thousand years old that says Jesus walked here or performed a miracle there?" he asked. "Why would we search about this? It is very unimportant. We have Jesus Christ in every liturgy. He is with us all of the time."

"Don't you think that these stories help people build up their faith in Jesus?" I asked.

"Perhaps, but I don't think it should be done this way. To make people have true faith is better," he said. "It should not be built on things that Jesus might have touched or wells that he might have drunk from."

"That's your opinion as an educated man," I said. "Maybe the people feel greater faith by walking in the footsteps of Jesus, or at least thinking that they are."

Such a suggestion was exasperating for Abdel-Shahid.

"Look," he said, "I have visited Jerusalem three times because I am very interested in the places where Jesus was born and crucified. When I go to these places I benefit not from putting my hand where Jesus Christ put his hand. Instead I feel more deeply the situation that Jesus was in. Why would I search for something that he touched two thousand years ago?"

"But for most Christians in Egypt, touching a place that may have been touched by Jesus helps them feel the situation of Jesus as a child," I said.

Abdel-Shahid sighed and leaned forward. He was an academic accustomed to fighting over fine points. In this case it was the nature and meaning of geography. Could it inspire? Or was it a false idol, the sort of thing that could lead a person down a path away from righteousness? He believed the latter.

"People need good guidance," he said. "If they are told that they should touch this place because this is the place where Jesus put his foot on the stone, then that is bad guidance. Why? Because Jesus is present everywhere. People pray in his name and he is present in the Eucharist and every liturgy. This is the official face of the Church. It is not one of folk tradition."

Our conversation had reached a dead end. Perhaps there is a "touristic thing" behind the Holy Family trail. And perhaps it does lean a bit heavily upon oral traditions that could not be proven. I could not argue that. But I had seen the inspiration that these sites gave to people. The people who accept the sites of the Holy Family trail have most likely done so all of their lives, with no questions asked. They have left their most heartfelt prayers at these sites and have gone away with more faith, hope, and charity than they arrived with.

Such belief is not a bad thing, in my estimation. It may not be intellectual or up to snuff academically, but it is not a bad thing.

Intellectuals always disagree with the faithful, I thought the next day as I rode through the pockmarked streets of Cairo, victim of yet another punishing ride in one of the city's notorious black-and-white cabs. *That doesn't*

mean they aren't believers. Abdel-Shahid, for instance, is a very devout believer. Just before I left the Center for Patristic Studies, he told me that he visits the tomb of two modern Christians every year, Father Bishoi Kamel and Father Michael Saad Ibrahim.

"I go every year to Alexandria and pray at Father Ibrahim's tomb underneath the cathedral," said Abdel-Shahid. "He makes miracles. People who were his spiritual brothers before his death pray to him and he helps them. These are true Christians making modern miracles. We see them. They are not made up."

He told me something else that I didn't expect to hear from such a devout academic. He said that the vision of the Virgin Mary seen in 1968 at the Church of St. Mary in the Cairo suburb of Zeitoun was a "true apparition" of the Virgin.

"I myself did not see her, you understand. But many people I trust had seen her. And she made miracles for them," he said.

Since then many apparitions have been seen at many different Christian sites in Egypt. From the beginning of the Holy Family trail in Zagazig to the end in Assiut and even beyond, sightings of the Virgin Mary have been claimed by the faithful. Most of these sightings, said Abdel-Shahid, were fraudulent.

"When people have problems in their personal lives it is easy for them to make up stories to make their lives better," said Abdel-Shahid. "They do this for economic reasons and this is bad for the Church."

I found a dichotomy in the fact that he believed in miracles even though he had never personally experienced a miracle. How could he so cavalierly disregard the oral traditions of the Holy Family trail while believing fervently in the modern oral traditions of sacred healings and visionary encounters? Perhaps faith truly is "the substance of things hoped for, the evidence of things not seen." Or as Friedrich Nietzsche so aptly put it, "If a man really has strong faith, he can indulge in the luxury of skepticism." That summed up Abdel-Shahid and many of the other academics I had met and would meet in Egypt. They were walking contradictions: skeptical of the religion they studied, yet faithful to its core beliefs.

Oh, to have the luxury to believe in the resurrection yet deny it at the same time, I thought. That summed up the skeptical nature of some who pursue religious studies.

I put their skepticism behind me and concentrated on the road ahead. Ahead was another site that required faith. I was on my way to

Matariyah and the Tree of the Holy Virgin, one of the most famous sites on the Holy Family trail.

We drove out of the bustling center of Cairo and headed northeast, away from the river Nile and into an area that became increasingly industrial. I noticed fewer of the blue-suited tourist police as we moved away from the city center, and then their absence altogether. The buildings became more faceless and their occupants increasingly blue-collar. Garages lined the road, the snouts of automobiles under repair protruding into the streets from their open bays.

The driver had insisted that he knew right where the Tree of the Holy Virgin was. But now I could tell by the way he looked around nervously that he did not know any such thing. Several times he became lost, and when he did he would turn the wrong way on a one-way street to find his way back to the right path. Signs meant nothing, traffic lights meant nothing, even the stern-faced traffic policemen with their batons meant nothing. When I expressed alarm at an approaching car in which the driver was leaning on his horn, the cabbie rebuked me with a wag of his finger. "For Americans, *beep-beep* is a problem. Not here."

I tried to take the death-defying driving and the *beep-beep* in stride. My life was in the hands of God—or Allah, depending upon which religious camp I fell into at this particular time.

We found our way through the astoundingly dirty streets of this suburb. Around us were stores filled with raw material like wire, pipes, paper, and metal. Some of it was literally bursting out the doors, as though the pressure of an explosion in the back room had blown it halfway out the front door.

We pressed on, down streets piled high with rubbish and dirt. As we did, the cab driver stopped several times for directions.

"A kilometer that way," said a man in a *galabíya.*

"A kilometer or so farther," said two high school boys.

"I can see it from here," said a fat man.

And sure enough, there it was, an oasis in the city, the monument of the Virgin tree.

Surrounded by a modern wall on one side and a cyclone fence on the other, the site of the Virgin Mary tree stands protected from the crush of this crumbling city. This is prime space, and that someone didn't cut the old balsam tree down for firewood a hundred years ago is almost a miracle in itself.

For many years the Egyptian government refused to include this location on the country's heritage list of protected sites. Because of that, locals sold branches, sap, and pieces of bark to pilgrims. Eventually, news reports say, the holy tree became so bare that a stepladder was required to reach the remaining branches.

An enclosure to protect the holy tree and the well next to it was built in 2000 by the National Egyptian Heritage Revival Association, headed by Coptic businessman Mounir Ghabbour. The organization spent more than six hundred thousand Egyptian pounds renovating the site and building a walled compound to protect the tree.

On the day I was there armed guards were plentiful. In fact, the six who stood by the front gate with AK-47s looped over their shoulders outnumbered the pilgrims who were inside touching the tree and admiring the rubbish-filled well across the pathway from it.

I bought a ticket and went inside.

A guard kept waving me to follow him, perhaps to give me a tour. He pulled at me and waved and offered me a cigarette and finally he just gave up. With him gone, I was allowed to walk alone through this famous site.

I entered a tiny museum at the back of the compound and looked at the maps and relics that were on display. Behind glass was a stone tub that looked as though it might be a footbath. The description below it, written in Arabic and English, implied something different. It described the stone tub as "a manger found near Virgin Mary Tree." This artifact was on loan from the Coptic Museum and undoubtedly would inspire awe among the visitors. A manger of any sort will always be linked to the baby Jesus, who is said to have lain in a similar animal feeding trough in Bethlehem, where he was born. As I looked at the tiny tub a couple came up next to me and began admiring the enclosed artifact.

"I wish I could touch," the man said to me in broken English. "That is where the holy baby lie."

I nodded in agreement, which pleased him very much. Then I went outside to a porch with cement tables and benches that overlooked the holy site. I sat down. The air hung like gauze over the city. On all sides buildings crowded against the wall like water against a dam. To one side was an apartment building with the predictable name of Mary's Housing Block. Sandwiching the holy site from the other side was a mosque—Mary's Mosque, to be exact. Its minaret towered over the tree, standing straight like, as one Coptic priest said, "a Muslim guarding his empire." A Catholic church stood on the other side of the housing block, while the entrance was bordered by the filthy main street of Matariyah.

It wasn't always like this, I told myself, closing my eyes for a moment and trying to shut out the sounds and the smells of the teeming city around me. I tried to imagine what this area looked like two thousand years ago. It didn't work. The noise and the odor were so overwhelming that I couldn't remove myself even mentally from these modern-day surroundings.

I picked up my copy of the Infancy Gospels and read what little there was to read about the Holy Family here in Matariyah. First I turned to the First Infancy Gospel of Jesus Christ and read the few lines that pertained to this site. They picked up abruptly after the Holy Family's desert encounter with the thieves who would be crucified with Jesus thirty years later.

> [T]hey went on to a city in which were several idols which, as soon as they came near to it, was turned into hills of sand. Hence they went to that sycamore tree, which is now called Matarea; and in Matarea the Lord Jesus caused a well to spring forth in which St. Mary washed his coat. And a balsam is produced, or grows, in that country from the sweat, which ran down there from the Lord Jesus.

That was all that that gospel had to say about the Holy Family in Matariyah.

I thumbed to the Arabic Gospel of the Infancy and read what little it had to offer about this holy site.

> Hence they turned aside to that balsam, which is now called Matarea, and the Lord Jesus brought forth in Matarea a fountain in which the Lady Mary washed His shirt. And from the sweat of the Lord Jesus, which she sprinkled there, balsam was produced in that region.

I closed my notebook. There were no further Infancy Gospel references to Jesus in Matariyah.

A few city blocks away was an obelisk that marked the central area of the city. An account of Joseph's wedding in the Old Testament book of Genesis has him marrying the daughter of the priest of On.

Joseph likely wed in the area of Heliopolis during its most prosperous period. The city dates back to the third millennium before Jesus, when it replaced Memphis as the greatest of all centers of learning. Egyptians like to claim that they had history's first university in On. There is little doubt that the sons of kings and nobles studied mathematics, sciences, and literature at a revered institute in this city. There was even an observatory, certainly one of history's first, for the study of the heavens. It is believed by some that Moses was raised at Heliopolis, as was Plato, the Greek philosopher from the fourth century B.C.E., who said such things as "Poets utter great and wise things which they do not themselves understand."

The Heliopolis that greeted the Holy Family was truly a shadow of its former self. Much of the statuary had already been destroyed or moved to Alexandria or Rome. Much of the city was occupied by Jews who had left Jerusalem and were now living as expatriates in Egypt. By some estimates there were tens of thousands of Jews in Egypt at the time of the Holy Family's travels there.

The Jews encountered by the Holy Family worshiped at "the house of Onias," a synagogue named after Onias IV. He was the high priest of Jerusalem in about 160 B.C.E., who left Israel for political reasons and was given land in Egypt by King Ptolemy Philometor. He built a synagogue that stood until 72 C.E., when it was destroyed by the Roman government that ruled Egypt.

It is likely—if he was knocking down idols and turning them into "hills of sand," as the Infancy Gospels say he was—that Jesus was not welcomed in Heliopolis. It had already been sacked and damaged a number of times over the past few hundred years. The last thing the people of Heliopolis needed was any of their remaining edifices knocked down.

"Has anyone told you about the spiderwebs?" asked Ra'ed. He had agreed to meet me here after he finished teaching his secondary-school English class. We were going to use this as a starting point to visit the Holy Family sites in and around Cairo. It was shortly after two in the afternoon when he strode into the compound of the Virgin Tree. He looked imperious in the way that teachers are wont to do, sweeping aside one of the armed guards and striding the length of the cobbled walk to get to me at the cement benches. He apologized for being ten minutes late.

"No one has mentioned spiderwebs to me at all," I said.

"Those are among the things that make this site so famous," said Ra'ed. "When the Holy Family came out of the desert they passed through Heliopolis. The baby Jesus was offended by many of the stone idols that he saw, so he destroyed them by turning them into sand."

"That must have impressed the residents of Heliopolis," I said.

"No, it didn't," said Ra'ed, still carrying some of the curtness in his voice that he must have displayed with the children he taught. "There were few residents of Heliopolis at that time but it upset them very much. They didn't want anyone destroying their city, even if he was a holy baby."

"Were they run out of town?" I asked.

"Apparently so, because they ended up here, on the outskirts of town, or at least what was then the outskirts," said Ra'ed. "That is where the spiderweb story begins."

I leaned forward and got my notebook ready. Ra'ed waited while I fished around in my backpack for a pen. It was suddenly like being in class, with the teacher making sure that the student was fully prepared to capture his every word.

"As you remember, the Holy Family was being pursued by the soldiers of Herod. Shortly after the Holy Family was turned away from Heliopolis, the soldiers came through looking for them. Since the people were angry at the baby Jesus, they told the soldiers that the Holy Family was outside of town in a grove of balsam trees. The soldiers left immediately to look for them."

What seemed like an easy catch wasn't, said Ra'ed. The Holy Family saw the soldiers coming across the field and squatted down beneath a balsam tree. Then nature took over.

"There were many spiders in the tree and when they saw the Holy Family in trouble they began to get busy and spun a web around them. Then as the soldiers looked through the grove, the balsam tree itself bowed further down to conceal the Holy Family."

Once again a miracle of nature had saved the Holy Family from certain capture.

"Don't stop writing," insisted Ra'ed. "Get the rest of the story written down. It is because of this miracle that the Coptic Church uses balsam oil in their anointing rituals. That way, when a person is baptized, they will remember the struggles of Jesus as a baby and the miracles that saved him for us."

⁜

We left the Tree of the Holy Virgin of Matariyah and walked toward the metro station to catch a train to our next stop, Zeitoun.

As we wove through the narrow alleyways Ra'ed said that he wanted to make sure I knew something else about the holy tree.

"It is not the original tree," he said.

"I figured as much," I said. "There aren't many two-thousand-year-old trees around."

"Yes, that is true," he replied. "I think the tree that is there now is only about a hundred years old, but they tell us it has been there since 1672. They say it grew from a shoot of the one before it and so on, all the way back to the original tree. That makes sense to me. It is not possible to have a tree like that live for two thousand years, probably not even if it is a holy tree."

I would later find a fascinating story about the tree in the historical writings of Flavius Josephus. According to the first-century historian, Cleopatra wanted to regain Palestine, a province that had been lost to the Romans by the Ptolemies. In hopes of retrieving this province, the beautiful pharaoh visited King Herod with seduction on her mind. Knowing that any sexual dalliance would be answered in war with Mark Antony, Herod rebuffed Cleopatra.

This angered Cleopatra, who managed to turn Antony against Herod anyway. But Herod once again infuriated Cleopatra by presenting Antony with gold treasures and apologies for insulting his girl-friend. The gold was fine, but the powerful Antony wanted something more. He demanded the seacoast of Palestine and all of its cities, which he promptly gave to Cleopatra as a gift. In addition she was given the city of Jericho and all of the plantations around it.

This delighted Cleopatra, who took cuttings of balsam trees found in the area and planted them in the temple gardens of Heliopolis, allegedly at the modern-day site of the Virgin Tree. These trees in Jericho had originally been planted by the Queen of Sheba, claimed the tale, and were thought to be good luck because of their heavenly fragrance.

We caught the metro to the Zeitoun district and then walked the several blocks to Tamambay Street.

We walked in silence through the busy streets. Cairo is the most crowded city in the world, a swirling mass of people, pollution, bazaars, smells, commerce, honking horns, filth, crumbling buildings, calls to prayer, military policemen, traffic policemen, riot policemen, plainclothes policemen, street musicians, donkey-drawn carts, phlegmy coughs, cooking fires, laughter, traffic jams, bright lights, dark alleys, dust, sand, broken glass, and perpetual motion. It looks like the end of the world and the beginning, all at once.

Suddenly we were there, the Virgin Mary Church in Zeitoun. From a distance the stark whiteness of the church made it stand out as though it were glowing. Even though the wind was blowing paper and other garbage down the street and sand was piled in the gutters, everything looked clean because of the color of the church.

We entered the walled compound and were greeted by a deacon named Girgis, a hard-looking man who was dressed entirely in white. Ra'ed greeted him like an old friend and then asked him if he would show me his tattoo.

Girgis nodded happily and began rolling up his right sleeve. There on his arm the Virgin Mary appeared, first her feet and then the rest of her body as he rolled the sleeve to the top of his bicep.

"This is how it is here," said Ra'ed. "Everything has the Virgin Mary on it."

There was a good reason for this. On April 2, 1968, two watchmen guarding a government parking lot across Tamambay Street saw a woman walking on the domed roof of the church just after sundown. At first the watchmen thought it was a young girl contemplating suicide. They ran into the street and began pleading with the young lady, begging her not to jump.

As they shouted, a crowd gathered. Concerned citizens began shouting.

"Wait!"

"Be careful, take care, you may fall!"

Then someone noticed that the curve of the dome was so extreme that no one could possibly walk on it. At that point, their concern turned to awe.

"It's the Virgin Mary," someone cried out.

The priest came out of the church—an affable man named Father Constantin. When he saw the raised faces of the crowd he looked up and gasped.

"It's the Virgin!" he proclaimed.

The priest was ecstatic. The presence of the Virgin at this church was more than just a holy sighting. To him it was the fulfillment of a prophecy by Jesus.

Coptic legend says that Mary was so exhausted from fleeing the soldiers of Herod that she had to stop here for several hours to rest. Although Jesus performed no miracles on this site, as his tired mother rose to continue the journey, Jesus told her: "Be not tired, Mother. Churches will be built in your name all over Egypt, and people will come to them to be healed."

"The Virgin has returned!" declared Father Constantin. "She has come to heal!"

By now hundreds of people had gathered. Before the night was over there would be thousands. Police tried to clear the street but it was impossible. Finally they closed the boulevard to cars and gave it to the people.

All night long and for weeks thereafter, Christians and Muslims stood shoulder to shoulder in front of the church waiting for the Virgin to appear again.

After April 2, newspapers reported that the Virgin began to appear two or three times per week. With each appearance, the interfaith crowd grew. People were streaming to the holy site from all over Cairo. The streets were so crowded that sometimes it took twenty minutes to cross from one side to the other.

At the same time, healings were taking place, and not just of Christians. The first man to see the Virgin Mary, a Muslim named Farouk Muhammad Atwa, had been scheduled for gangrene surgery. The day after seeing Mary, he went to the hospital for his appointment and was declared healed.

People claimed to be healed of such afflictions as infertility, skin diseases, heart problems, depression, "madness." Overnight, the church in Zeitoun became a spiritual medical clinic of sorts for believers of all faiths.

By the end of April, newspaper reports tell of the Virgin Mary hovering over the church for as many as four hours at a time. Some people were literally spending the night on their feet in front of the church, while others were sleeping on the cement floor of the parking garage across the street. The fathers of the Coptic Church declared this a genuine miracle. If it was, it was one that happened at an opportune time for the Christians in Egypt. After the 1967 war with Israel, in which Egypt took a sound drubbing, Islamic fundamentalism was on the rise, and some Muslim clerics were grumbling that it was time to run all Christians out of Egypt and make it an Islamic republic.

But even in these trying political times, the Muslims couldn't ignore such a persistent apparition as this one. Their militant stance against the Christians lessened as a result of the Virgin visions.

It didn't take long for President Gamel Abdel Nasser to recognize the power of the Virgin Mary, too. On May 5, the president picked up the newspaper *al-Ahram* and saw an astounding photograph of a vaporous woman hovering over the domed church in Zeitoun.

The headline written above the photo, in one-inch type, read:

"POPE KYRILLOS DECLARES: THE APPARITION OF THE VIRGIN IS A TRUTH."

Nasser read that the picture had been taken by one of the hundreds of people who now stood outside the church all night waiting for the Virgin Mary to appear. "The photography department at *al-Ahram* has inspected the original film and found no traces of photo-montage," read the caption's last sentence.

Nasser was hooked. He was surprised to learn that the first apparition of the Virgin had taken place over a month earlier. He was even more surprised to find that the first to see the Virgin were two Muslim watchmen at a government parking garage across Tamambay Street.

Nasser wanted to see the Virgin for himself. Within the next week he went to the parking garage several times and stayed there until he witnessed the Virgin Mary with his own eyes. He was dressed incognito so that no one would recognize him. In addition to a phalanx of security police, Nasser brought a member of the Muslim Brotherhood with him to be a witness.

At the church we were introduced to Father Saddik, a priest at Zeitoun who had witnessed the apparition of Mary when he was a young engineering student in 1968. He was also a deacon of the church and had spent a considerable amount of time with the priests during those heady days.

Father Saddik in front of the domed church of Zeitoun, where the Virgin Mary made several appearances in 1968.

"Even though he was disguising himself, all of the Coptic priests knew President Nasser was in that parking garage," said Father Saddik. "He spent at least two nights there in the garage, waiting. It was very strange for the president to be so curious about anything Christian. And the Muslims were dissatisfied that he could believe in a vision of the Virgin. Then he was rewarded. He saw the Virgin Mary!"

The announcement that President Nasser had seen the Virgin Mary riveted the entire country. It was akin to when President Jimmy Carter confessed to having seen a UFO. A committee of high-ranking priests and bishops of the Coptic Church investigated the apparitions and found them to be authentic. Pope Paul VI of Rome sent an envoy, who also confirmed the authenticity of the Virgin visions. There was even grudging recognition by Muslims.

Finally the government's General Information and Complaints Department released this brief statement: "*Official investigations have been carried out with the result that it has been considered an undeniable fact that the Blessed Virgin Mary has been appearing on Zeitoun Church in a clear and bright luminous body seen by all present in front of the church, whether Christians or Muslims.*"

"It was the coming of the Virgin Mary that made this possible," said Father Saddik, pointing across the street to the Church of the Apparition of the Holy Virgin, a massive structure built in 1970 on the site of the parking garage where the Virgin Mary was first seen. This church, enormous inside, boasts the tallest steeple in Cairo, taller even than any of the minarets that mark the Muslim mosques.

"President Nasser donated this land so that we could build a church in honor of the apparition," said Father Saddik. "After he saw the Virgin he became, how do you say, *attracted* to Jesus and the Holy Family. I have heard that he became a student of Jesus and studied much about the years that Jesus was here in Egypt."

The notion that a Muslim president—embroiled in an international war that was full of internal ramifications—would spend any of his free time studying the life of Jesus was hard for me to believe. Perhaps that skepticism showed on my face, because Father Saddik immediately began to address it.

"No, no, no. It is not hard to study Jesus when things like this happen," he said, motioning to the dome of the church where the apparition had taken place. "There is much mystery information about Jesus to know. It is hard not to be intrigued."

Father Saddik then asked Deacon Girgis to show us the photos that were taken of the apparition.

One of the photos was taken at a low angle from behind people who were looking up at the church steeple. The steeple was glowing and next to it was the clear form of a woman of light who seemed to be leaning out slightly.

Another series of photos was taken by Wagih Rizk, a professional photographer from Cairo.

Rizk had heard about the visions and went to the church on April 9, 1968. At 2:45 the next morning, Rizk and hundreds of others saw the Virgin.

"I saw Her in the form of radiating light like clouds," he told a reporter from *Watani*, a Coptic newspaper in Egypt. "The light was very strong, so strong that the eye couldn't bear it, and was seen near the cross over the small eastern dome. The apparition was awesome. Reverence and fear filled me like an electric shock."

Rizk was hooked. He returned the next night and set up his camera on the roof of the parking garage across the street from the church. When the Virgin first appeared again, Rizk was paralyzed by the sight and didn't get the picture.

"Although the camera was ready, I stood in astonishment and couldn't move," he said.

The next night, April 13, he tried again. This time he got a photo and then another. Then he realized something else. He was taking photos with his left hand, the one that had been lame since a car accident one year earlier.

"Five doctors, some of them are among the most famous surgeons

One of Wagih Rizk's photos shows spectators gazing at the apparition of the Virgin Mary on the domed church in Zeitoun.

in Egypt, said [it] was hopeless and will never move again," said Rizk. "[But] the Blessed Virgin had miraculously healed this hand."

Rizk took a number of photos of the apparition and has never sold them or charged a publication fee. The photos that Rizk took are extraordinary and puzzling. In some, forms of light hover over the dome. In others, it appears as though a woman is kneeling in prayer. Despite my Western skepticism I felt a chill run up my spine after seeing the photos. After looking at the evidence of the Zeitoun apparitions, I was convinced that this was a rare occasion when the spiritual universe opens the door and sheds some blessing or *baraka* on our mortal lives.

Even Western science was sufficiently intrigued by the Zeitoun apparition to examine it from a scientific point of view. Noted paranormal researcher Michael Persinger of Laurentian University in Sudbury, Ontario, examined the photographs and the conditions surrounding them and wrote a paper on the Zeitoun phenomena for the journal *Perceptual and Motor Skills* in 1989. He concluded that "the characteristics of these luminous phenomena" were caused by "seismic activity"—earthquakes— that took place four hundred kilometers to the southeast.

He went on to explain that earthquakes can cause "highly kinetic lights" and "coronal type displays" of the variety that appeared over the church during those three years.

What Persinger could not explain was: How could an earthquake four hundred kilometers away produce such light directly over a church?

10. Lost in Babylon

The nun looked at me and slammed the door.

The women behind me laughed.

I knocked again on the heavy wooden door of St. George's Convent and waited. With great effort the nun pulled the door open and shouted something to the women behind me. They laughed uproariously. The nun ducked inside for a moment and then stuck her hand out, handing me a tiny vial of water.

"Congratulations," said a young man who was standing nearby. "You will now become pregnant."

I turned to the women and waved the tiny glass bottle victoriously over my head. They laughed at the absurdity of an American man holding such a votive object. *It is easy to be a funny foreigner in Cairo,* I thought to myself. *Especially if one is willing to look like a fool.*

I was not trying to become pregnant. I had stopped at the convent to ask directions. I was in old Cairo, an area mysteriously referred to as Babylon, and I was lost. When I told the policeman near the Amr ibn el-As mosque that I was looking for the cave of Jesus, he directed me toward a distant tower that was the Coptic Museum. "You will find Jesus there," he said. With the cool wind whipping up a mist of street dust, I walked down Amr ibn el-As Street, ignoring the constant beeping of the underemployed Cairo cab drivers who wanted to drive me the two hundred yards to the heavily guarded entrance of Coptic Cairo.

"I am looking for Jesus," I said to yet another policeman. He did not understand me, so I drew the sign of the cross on my notebook and he nodded vigorously.

He spoke a few words in Arabic, pointing down a long street that had shops filled with tourist goods on one side and the wall of what appeared to be a fort on the other. A roadblock kept the street—Sharia Mar Girgis—blessedly free of automobile traffic. I found out later that the road was blocked virtually all the time to keep Muslim extremists from driving car bombs into the Coptic part of town.

As I walked toward the entrance of Babylon, shop owners strolled slowly out their doors and greeted me like I was an old friend.

"Hello to the U.S.A.," said one owner of a novelty shop. "You must come in and take some Egypt back with you."

"I need to ask you a question," said one young clothing store owner, appealing to any paternal instinct that he thought I might have. "I am about to be married and I need to ask you questions that only a married man can tell me. Come in and have tea."

"Business is not good since September eleventh," said the next store owner. "You can get a very good deal here."

"Come up to my house and have lunch with my wife and I," said the owner of a candle shop. "She is a very good cook and you can eat with us for nothing."

And so it went. Even as I took evasive action by stepping off the sidewalk and heading into the middle of the street, the playful merchants pursued me. I didn't like the constant demands, but I knew it was something they had to do. Since the terrorist attacks on the World Trade Center and the Pentagon, tourism had all but stopped here. After weeks of seeing no Americans at all, I was convinced that I was the only American in Cairo and possibly in all of Egypt. The lack of foreign currency was hard on an economy that is so heavily based on tourism. The night before, a cab driver had told me that the attacks of September 11 had reduced his monthly income by "eighty times."

"All I do now is drive around and look for tourists to give rides to," he said. "But there is nobody so I just drive more and eat my gas. Please tell people to come back. We love Americans."

I left the middle of the street and walked next to the fortress wall. Just as I was about to ask directions again to the cave of Jesus, I saw a stairway with an ornate metal screen of Mary holding baby Jesus. Above the screen was a roughly painted sign with an arrow pointing down a narrow and cobbled alleyway. It read:

THE CRYPT OF THE HOLY FAMILY,
UNDER SAINT SERGIUS CHURCH,
WHERE THE HOLY FAMILY LIVED FOR SOMETIMES

I ducked down the stairs and entered the world of Babylon.

How this area came to have the same name of the famous Biblical city is anyone's guess. And many people have done just that. Guessing about the origin of the name seems to be a favorite pastime for many historians. Although they may disagree on where the name came from, historians almost all agree that it had nothing to do with the famous city of decadence located on the Euphrates River in Iraq and referred to in the Bible.

The Babylon of Cairo is located near the river Nile, directly across from the tip of Rhoda Island. On the southern tip of Rhoda Island was the house of On, called *Per-hapi-n-on* by the ancient Egyptians. Some feel that the name *Babylon* may be a corrupted version of the ancient Egyptian name. Others think it is a twist on the Arabic *Bab ila On*, "gateway to On."

Another theory has it that prisoners from the real Babylon that were captured by Pharaoh Sesostris of the twelfth dynasty may have been imprisoned in this spot. Their homesickness caused them to name their prison Babylon. This theory was given further credence by the classical historian Diodorus Siculus, who added to the legend by writing that these imprisoned Babylonians revolted against the Egyptians and built a fortress to keep their captors out.

Whatever the source of its name, Babylon was an important center of commerce for the ancient Egyptians. In about 600 B.C.E., the Egyptians dug a canal from Babylon to the Red Sea. This became an important shipping lane for trade with India.

The Roman emperor Augustus had defeated Mark Antony and taken Egypt by the time the Holy Family arrived in Babylon. Still, that was early in the Roman history of this area. About seventy years after the death of Jesus, Emperor Trajan cleared the ancient canal that ran through the city and built a fortress to house the Roman garrison.

In the time of the Christian emperor Arcadius (400 C.E.), Copts were encouraged to build churches around the fortress, and build they did. It is estimated that forty-two churches stood in an area of about sixty acres. By the time the Arabs took Babylon in the conquest of 641 C.E., it was a thriving city filled with many cultures.

It is still that way. Completely surrounded by Cairo but not absorbed, the walled city of Babylon is home to about two hundred thousand Muslims, twenty thousand Copts, and about fifty Jews. The Jews say their ancestors helped Jesus when he came through on his escape from Herod. But they say they were here well before then, too. The Jews claim that this is where Moses bade farewell to Egypt and some even claim that this is where he came into Egypt, found in bulrushes right here on the river Nile by the pharaoh's daughter. They claim they have historical documents to prove it and have even built a synagogue on the spot as a memorial.

"I am looking for the cave of Jesus," I said to a woman sitting on a bench outside St. George's Convent.

I don't think she understood anything I said, but she pointed down the alley.

I followed the direction of her finger.

It was the day after our journey to see the Tree of the Holy Virgin in Matariyah and the church in Zeitoun where the apparitions of the Virgin Mary had taken place. My mind was still racing at the photos we had seen there.

Today, rather than wait for Ra'ed to finish class, I decided to strike out on my own and find the Church of St. Sergius. This church was somewhere here in Babylon and was built on top of a crypt that was said to be the cave where the Holy Family hid from the soldiers of Herod. Depending on whom you speak to, the Holy Family stayed here a few days, a few months, a few years, or not at all.

Girgis Daoud, the librarian of the Coptic Orthodox Seminary, says they would not have stayed here at all on their way up the Nile because the soldiers of Herod were staying at the Roman garrison. Others said that they stayed in the cave, which was practically under the feet of the soldiers. The close proximity to the soldiers who were pursuing them is what made the Holy Family's stay in Babylon even more miraculous. Despite being so close to the soldiers, their presence went undetected.

The Infancy Gospels were no help in understanding when, where, and how long the Holy Family stayed in Babylon. There was no mention in any of these gospels about Babylon or any site that might resemble it. The Holy Family's stay in Babylon was an oral tradition with many different conclusions.

Whatever the case, the location of the cave was still unknown to me. Perhaps it was directly under my feet, as it supposedly had been for the soldiers of Herod. I did not know. I just knew that I was still lost.

"Where is the cave of Jesus?" I asked an enormous man with one eye.

"Synagogue that way," he said, pointing down a long alleyway.

Synagogue, I thought. *I'll go there and ask them where Jesus is.*

I walked down the long alley and reached another gate that was being guarded by several soldiers. They stood as I approached and one of them swung the gate open. I stepped through and the gate was clanged shut behind me. I was on the grounds of the Ben Ezra Synagogue.

Named after the twelfth-century rabbi who convinced the Melkite Patriarch Alexander that this site should be returned to the Jews, the Jewish history of this site goes all the way back to Moses.

Jewish oral tradition has it that Moses visited this spot many times when he lived in Egypt. They claim to have found the marks of Moses, ones so distinctive that they could not belong to anyone else. It is in this area, say the local Jews, that Moses made some of his most significant connections with God. In Exodus 9, after the waters of Egypt had turned to blood and the plague of frogs and insects had run its course, God sent thunder and hail and "fire ran along upon the ground." The pharaoh called for Moses and Aaron and admitted that he had sinned in not freeing the Jews from their bondage.

"Entreat the Lord (for it is enough) that there be no *more* mighty thundering and hail," said the pharaoh, "and I will let you go, and ye shall stay no longer."

Moses left the city of the pharaoh and went to the spot of the current synagogue to commune with God. The storm stopped, but the pharaoh went back on his promise of freedom. This cost him dearly, for his army and all of its equipment ended up on the bottom of the Red Sea.

It was also on this spot that Moses prayed for the last time before leaving Egypt for the promised land. Jewish legend has it that Moses returned here after the horrible seventh plague, in which all of the firstborn of Egypt were killed by God. Rather than go around the Red Sea, God told Moses to head straight for it. Hence, this spot in Babylon was the spiritual staging area for the greatest miracle in the Old Testament, the parting of the Red Sea.

It is also here that many insist Moses was found in a forest of bulrushes by the pharaoh's daughter, floating in the reed basket that was made by his mother.

"It is true," said a young man named Abraham, a guide from the synagogue who had been sent for by the soldier who let me in the gate. "I will show you. Then you can believe the fact."

He walked me around the synagogue past a pump that was sucking water from the basement. This is done all over Cairo. Since the Aswan High Dam was built in 1970, the water table along the Nile has risen so much that almost every structure with a basement is threatened by flooding.

"Come," he said, pointing to a modern-looking well with an ornate metal grate covering its opening.

"This is where Moses was found by the pharaoh's daughter?" I asked.

"This is the place," he insisted.

I looked down into the well. The water was at least twenty feet below the rim.

"It was not always like this," insisted Abraham. "He did not float into a well. There was a time when the Nile came all the way up to the ground here and this area was covered with water plants. You must use your imagination but it was here."

If an excavation was conducted on this site, it would reveal a stack of synagogues and churches at least five deep. First was the synagogue named after the prophet Jeremiah, which was built in 605 B.C.E. In 30 B.C.E., the Romans conquered Egypt and destroyed the Jeremiah synagogue.

In 641 C.E., the Arabs conquered Egypt and gave the synagogue property to the Copts, who also claimed Jeremiah as a prophet. They built the Church of St. Michael on the site in the eighth century.

In the twelfth century Rabbi Ben Ezra arrived, possibly from Spain. This wandering Jewish wise man was making a pilgrimage to the sites of Moses and Jeremiah and found himself standing in the Coptic Church of St. Michael.

It was clear to Ben Ezra that this site—now a Christian church— should become a synagogue once again. He appealed to Patriarch Alexander, who agreed to part with the church. There was one catch, however. The Jews would have to pay the annual tax of twenty thousand gold dinars that was demanded by the Arab rulers.

The synagogue was rebuilt and named after Ben Ezra.

Like most synagogues, Ben Ezra contained a *geniza,* a storehouse for religious documents that were damaged or old. These documents were to be stored until they could be buried in a Jewish cemetery. For some reason, however, that never happened at the Ben Ezra Synagogue. They just kept stacking them up in the wooden storeroom.

Some of the documents were of a religious nature. There were Aramaic translations of the Bible, poetry from Spanish-Hebrew poets, and even personal letters between rabbis and philosophers.

Most of the documents are considered "pedestrian," writing that detailed everyday Hebrew life, deeds of sale, even schoolbooks for children. The bulk are from the tenth to the sixteenth century, but some date as far back as the second century B.C.E.

This treasure trove of documents might have been lost or sold on the open market had it not been for the Scottish sisters Agnes Lewis and Margaret Gibson. These classical scholars were traveling in Egypt in the late 1890s when they found an ancient manuscript for sale in Babylon. They purchased it and brought it back to Solomon Schechter, a scholar of Hebrew at Cambridge University. He identified it as a fragment of the Hebrew text of *The Book of Wisdom,* by Ben Sira. The book was authored in 200 C.E. and was known to exist only in its Greek translation.

Schechter was stunned. He went to Cairo to visit the Ben Ezra *geniza* and returned to Cambridge University with stars in his eyes. What he had found was 200,000 fragments of documents, all about ancient Jewish life. He received permission from the synagogue's authorities to empty the *geniza* and took 140,000 fragments, documents, and texts to Cambridge for study.

Many of the fragments and documents that Schechter brought back have been scattered to a variety of academic institutions around the world. The finding of these *geniza* documents has been so consequential that it gave birth to a new field of scholarship, one called genizology.

In addition to providing insight into Jewish customs and rites in the ancient Middle East, genizology has revealed the ways in which Judaism and Islam coexisted. The *geniza* documents show that Jews and Muslims traded freely among one another. They also show that Jews were not only tolerated, they were protected under Islamic law.

"Are there still documents to study here?" I asked Abraham.

"There are still many," he said, taking me inside the synagogue.

The plainness of the building's exterior did not prepare me for its ornate interior. A pair of marble tablets greeted my eyes as I walked in. Words in Hebrew surrounded by gold leaf were carved into the stone. A dozen marble pillars lined the sanctuary and led to the altar. The interior contained an odd mix of Christian and Islamic influences. Vines, sheaves of wheat, and olive branches like those seen in Coptic churches are found here. On some of the carved wood and on two of the chandeliers are the names of four of the caliphs and Sultan Qalawun, all in Arabic. Behind the altar, said Abraham, was a storeroom filled with ancient Torahs. The wooden cases they are stored in are carved with such Hebrew icons as the pomegranate, a popular symbol for longevity.

"There are more documents," said the guide. "We also have some of the *geniza* documents that weren't taken out of the country, and then, of course, there are the graveyard documents."

"What are those?" I asked.

"There are documents found in the Bassatine Jewish cemetery," said Abraham, referring to the world's second oldest Jewish graveyard after the Mount of Olives. "There were two rooms full of documents found in the tombs. Many of them are still there."

"What happened to the rest?" I asked.

"European researchers came and took many of them," said Abraham. "Most of them are in Jerusalem now."

"I am sorry to hear that they were taken," I said.

"Not a problem," said Abraham. "It happened two centuries ago. Now we know better. The government has started a Department of Jewish Antiquities and now they guard these rooms like they are treasure. People can't just come and help themselves anymore. They have to ask now."

The Ben Ezra Synagogue was beautiful and yet sad at the same time. During the time of Jesus there were tens of thousands of Jews in Egypt. Some even estimate that as many as a million Jews lived along the length of the Nile, although such a large population in those days seems highly unlikely to many experts. Even during the Fatimid period (969 to 1171) the Ben Ezra Synagogue and the area around it was the center of the Jewish religion for North Africa and Syria. Signs of Judaism are seen in many places in this country. Despite a tiny Jewish population—less than a hundred and dwindling—there are still eleven synagogues to be found in Cairo, of fourteen in all of Egypt, though many of them are in a state of severe deterioration.

Struggling to survive, the Jews of Egypt seem to be vanishing. Most are aged, and one by one they die off, leaving no one to replace them. There are no rabbis, no kosher butchers, and not enough men to form a *minyan,* or quorum for prayer. The last fifty years of conflict here have caused a modern-day Exodus from Egypt to the Promised Land.

The ancient Egyptian religion had once disappeared in the same way. Once the most powerful institution in Egypt, Egyptian religion dwindled under the force of conquerors like the Romans and then the newly formed Christian Church. Eventually there were fewer and fewer priests who could explain the meaning of the hieroglyphs on the temple walls or provide a coherent interpretation of the religious beliefs that had dominated Egyptian society for nearly four thousand years.

In its own country, Egyptian religion had become a mystery.

Would Egyptian Judaism end up the same way? Would unique rituals and beliefs be lost with the passing of time? I asked Abraham what he thought.

"I think Jews will make a comeback here but I do not know how," he said as we stood on the synagogue steps and watched the armed guards at the entrance gate. "Perhaps the answer is in the Torah that Ezra the scribe left behind."

I shrugged and he smiled.

"Ezra the scribe transcribed a Torah with magical powers," he said. "It is said to be hidden somewhere, perhaps in the documents or perhaps in a secret place in the walls. No one knows. But that magic is strong. It will make us survive."

Perhaps it will, I thought. *After all, the Ben Ezra Synagogue is still here.*

When I told Abraham what I was doing in Egypt, he became excited.

"Jesus was certainly here, too," he said. "Since his family was Jewish they would have relied on the Jewish community that was here."

Still, he was at a loss to recall any Jewish folklore that might relate to Jesus.

"You would be better off talking to the Christians," he said. "They have done a better job of collecting the Jesus stories than we have. Certainly you understand."

So there I was, back in the alleyway that led from the Ben Ezra Synagogue and into the maze of alleyways that make up Babylon. I went past shops and churches and vendors who told me they were Jewish even as they tried to sell small silver Christian crosses. "You can support the last Jews in Egypt by buying this," said a heavy man with a crooked smile. I bought two, part out of sympathy and part for the irony of buying a Christian symbol from a Jewish vendor in a Muslim country.

I pressed on. Past the Convent of St. George, where I had been given the impregnating water. Out the gates of Babylon and back into the street where the vendors had attempted to lure me with their calculated friendliness. Then I turned and headed for the Greek Church of St. George, the only round church in Egypt.

It is round for two reasons, I would discover. The first was religious. The Greek Orthodox who worship here believe that the circle is a symbol of God's infinity. The second reason is practical. The basilica is built atop a round Roman tower, part of the fort that was built here by the Romans to guard the entrance to their newly conquered country. The tower is massive in diameter and three long stories deep. It is in these underground rooms that the Greek Orthodox church conceals treasures of an artistic and spiritual nature that none are supposed to see.

I did not expect to see them, either. But then I met Father David, a Greek Orthodox priest from St. Catherine's Monastery in the Sinai, who was here in Cairo doing temporary duty.

He was standing at the top of the lengthy stairway at the entrance of the Church of St. George. He looked down at me sternly as I labored up the steps. He was a vision of caloric austerity and spiritual abundance. His beard was long and uncombed and his eyes had an intense and spiritual look to them. It was the intense part of the equation that I was concerned about. He did not seem happy to see a stranger. Behind him was a magnificent stone relief of St. George slaying the dragon. The closer I got to him, the more I could sympathize with the dragon as it writhed in agony at the piercing of George's sharp sword.

"Hello," I said.

He nodded.

"Amer-ik-an," I said, announcing my nationality the way the Egyptians pronounce it.

He nodded again.

"Speak English?" I asked, wishing Ra'ed was here to facilitate this conversation.

"No," he said. "Arabic, Greek."

I held up my palms and shrugged. There was no way for us to communicate with one another. Without an interpreter we would be left to sign language. I decided to leave and continue to look for the spot where the Holy Family had hid in a cave. To find it, I tried the only phrase I knew that I thought he might understand: "Coptic Church Jesus."

He laughed at my effort and directed me to a path that passed by the partially excavated Roman fort next door and on to a group of domed buildings. I waved goodbye and headed down the stairs. As I reached the bottom, though, Father David came down after me. He was frustrated by our inability to communicate and he clearly wanted me to follow him. And so I did.

We went back up the stairs and into the church sanctuary, where we paused briefly in front of a magnificent silver-plate relief of St. George slaying the dragon that matched the stone one that graced the front of the church. I thought this was what he wanted me to see but it wasn't. He gestured for me to follow him through the dark sanctuary. Incredible icons watched me cross the room. St. Mark, the apostle of Jesus who spread the Christian word to Egypt, watched my every step, as did St. Anthony, the founder of monastic life. St. Alexandra was there, the wife of the cruel Roman Emperor Diocletian. She had converted to Christianity despite her husband's hatred of the "pagan cult." And then of course there was the magnificent St. George, this time in a color icon. He was not interested in me at all. He was still focused on spearing the dragon that writhed on the ground. The icon of Constantine was ahead of me as I headed for the creaking wooden door that Father David had just opened with a key and disappeared behind. Constantine was the first Christian Roman emperor and the first man of such power to make an effort to assemble a coherent Bible from the hundreds of documents about the life of Jesus that were in circulation in the fourth century. Constantine seemed to be directing me to some secret passageway that I was about to enter.

I followed Father David into the darkness.

The stone steps hugged the wall of the rounded tower, spiraling down into the darkness below. I followed Father David down the steps.

Then, as the light faded away, I slid my feet over the steps from one to the next, making my way deeper into the tower.

Soon I was traveling like a blind man, feeling my way with my feet and relying upon my other senses for any information that was usable. I could hear Father David walking ahead of me. Off to the sides in stone ventilation shafts I could hear the disturbing sound of rats scurrying back into their holes. I was reminded of that scene in *Raiders of the Lost Ark* where Harrison Ford finds himself in the catacombs sharing floor space with hundreds of rats.

And then suddenly there was light. Father David had reached a light switch that offered scant illumination in a room filled with fascinating treasure.

I found out later I was in the first church to be built on the site of the Roman tower. When this church burned in a mysterious fire in 1909, the larger church above us was built. It is identical to this one, only much larger. The Old St. George Church, as this is now called, is packed with icons, pillars, baptisteries, and, yes, even the mortal remains of the patriarchs of the Greek Orthodox Church in Egypt. Father David took me into one room where these remains were neatly stored in boxes approximately three feet long. Large bones were saved, he said, and sealed in these stone boxes that were now stacked on shelves with glass doors.

He was reverent as he led me through the brick room filled with these body boxes, all engraved with the names of their occupants and arranged by the dates of their service to the church. Overseeing this solemn space was the stone statue of a praying angel, perched atop a pillar, his wings pressed against the corner of the room.

Father David was patient as I examined the boxes and admired the truly incredible gold-leaf icons. In addition to the iconic paintings of saints, there were stunning renderings of biblical scenes such as Adam and Eve being chased from the Garden of Eden. In the back of the room was a painting of a very calm Jesus, his right hand held up as though he was trying to capture the viewer's attention. In his left hand he displayed an open Bible. It was as though he was handing its grace to everyone who looked at this painting.

The gold-leaf sky around the head of Jesus was mesmerizing. As it drew me into the painting, I wondered what the world of art would be like without the stories of the Bible to give much of it a theme. Then my thoughts were disturbed by a polite cough from Father David.

He motioned for me to follow him down another flight of stone steps.

Once again a light was clicked on and we were standing in a stone room with a well. We were at almost the deepest part of the tower now, and the room we had entered had the appearance and scent of the dungeon in a castle.

Father David had a frustrated look on his face as he tried to explain the significance of where we were. First he spoke to me in Greek. Then he pointed to an icon of St. George and the dragon and began to make a flailing motion with his hands, as though he was beating someone. Suddenly I realized what he was trying to communicate. This was the room where St. George had been tortured for his faith. This was the room where George started his incredible march to sainthood.

After Jesus and Lazarus, the legend of St. George is probably the most famous resurrection story in Christianity, though its veracity is widely doubted. According to a study conducted by the Catholic Church, the only thing that can be confirmed is that George actually existed and "suffered . . . in Palestine, probably before the time of Constantine."

Popular belief has it that George was born in 280 C.E. to the governor of Palestine. At a very early age, probably about eighteen, George became an officer in the army of Diocletian.

Apparently George participated in some of Diocletian's persecutions of Christians and became repelled by these atrocities. As legend has it, he complained to the emperor in person. The murderous decrees of Diocletian were too harsh, he insisted. Then he further infuriated the emperor by admitting that he himself had become a Christian and believed in the divinity of Jesus.

Diocletian was reportedly beside himself that an officer in his army was a member of the cult that he was attempting to eliminate. He ordered that George be imprisoned and tortured until he recanted his faith. This imprisonment and torture took place right in this room, Father David told me later through an interpreter. Here the future saint was physically beaten by the same Roman soldiers that he had once commanded. When he failed to renounce his faith, George was taken to Palestine, where he was killed by soldiers and cut into pieces. Yet despite deep burials and even destruction of his body by fire, George was resurrected three times by God.

There were massive conversions to Christianity as result of George's resurrections, say his biographers, and new resolve among Christians to keep the faith. Even Diocletian's wife, Alexandra, converted to the new faith, only to be martyred by her husband.

Finally George was beheaded. Although milk instead of blood flowed from his severed head, George finally died and stayed dead.

The legend of St. George was embellished many times over the years. The tale of St. George and the dragon did not come to be until the fourteenth century, when crusaders from Europe heard the stories of St. George from the Byzantine Christians who had joined them in the sack of the Middle East. Troubadours in England eventually heard the story and developed it into the tale we know today. A horrifying dragon was ravaging the marsh town of Selena, Libya. The dragon "breathed pestilence" whenever it approached town. To appease the beast, the townsfolk gave it two sheep per day. That worked for a while, but soon the reptile was approaching town again, searching for a more varied diet.

The townspeople decided to offer human sacrifice to satisfy the dragon's hunger. Daily they would draw lots to determine the loser, and daily someone went off to become the monster's meal.

One day the king's daughter drew the short straw and was led to the marsh dressed like a bride. As she waited to be devoured, St. George rode by and asked her what was wrong. When she told him, he made the sign of the cross and attacked the surly beast with his lance.

The rest is, well, the stuff of icons. St. George killed the dragon and chopped its head off. Then, despite being offered half the kingdom, he rode off into the sunset, leaving nothing but legend behind.

Although many in the Middle East believe in the historical validity of the story, most Western scholars read the story as allegory. The dragon was meant to be Satan and the virginal young maiden the Christian Church. And St. George? He was the force of light, fighting the forces of darkness and keeping them from devouring the faithful.

By the time Father David and I left the tower and went outside, a translator had arrived. Ahmed Shaker El-Sobky was a teacher of English at a local high school. But he also spoke Greek, which was the Father's native language. Finally we could communicate.

"The story of St. George reminds me of the story of Jesus," I said to Father David.

Father David in the catacombs of the Church of Saint George in Babylon where St. George was tortured for his faith.

"It reminds you of him because of the resurrections?" he asked. "Yes, it does have that element. What it says is that God holds the power of life over death at all times. If he wants to make a point to people, he can make us come to life whenever he wants. He can heal us, he can make us happy or sad or rich or poor. That is the nature of God."

I told Father David why I had come to Egypt and what I was doing in Babylon. When he heard that I was here to see the cave of the Holy Family, he took my hand and led me down the stairs and around the bishop's house to the Greek cemetery on the other side.

Without the elevated crypts that are required because of Cairo's high water table, the graveyard would have looked like a sculpture garden. Headstones and grave markers had been made with great care, and each one reflected a unique view of death. Hosts of angels adorned many graves, each in a different pose. Some were vigilant as if standing guard, while others were in repose as if preparing for the long slumber themselves. Some tombstones were engraved with more macabre visions such as the skull and crossbones, while others displayed the noble busts of the dead who were contained in the crypt.

Father David passed these quickly and headed for a lone statue of Jesus. Beyond was the Church of St. Sergius. It was here, underneath this eleventh-century Coptic church, that the crypt of the Holy Family can be found.

What was surely once a cave was now the heavily renovated basement of the small church above. The walls had all been smoothed and plastered. Stairs from the church sanctuary led to the Holy Family's hiding place. Dominating the room was a classic stone well. The few visitors who were there used a plastic bucket with a rope tied to its handle to dip water. This was holy water because, Father David told me, this was the well that Jesus ordered to spring up so they wouldn't have to leave the cave for water and risk being captured. Today's visitors dipped water from the well and drank it, dabbed it on their heads, or carried it away in bottles. One couple drenched their surprised infant son with a small cup of it. A Muslim scooped water into his palms and then splashed it across his face like a Bedouin at a desert oasis.

"It is refreshing to wash with the water of such a wise man," he said. "To do so is not at odds with my religion at all."

If there was any question that this room was a shrine to the Holy Family, all one had to do was look at the art that filled it. Every one of the fifty or so icons was a stunning representation of the Holy Family. Some showed the familiar image of the Holy Family crossing the desert on a donkey. Others were less common, like Mary breast-feeding the baby Jesus or the angel appearing to Joseph with the news that King Herod was dead and they could now return to Israel.

Three steep steps took us down into a tiny room. There was a portrait of Mary and Joseph with the lively little Jesus standing on his mother's lap between them. The space was so small that I experienced mild claustrophobia as the three of us crowded into the room.

"This was the actual cave that the Holy Family lived in," said Father David. He fell silent for a moment and so did I, trying to soak up as much of the original grace as I could in this heavily plastered room. I discovered later that this was the site at which the Greek Orthodox Church believes the Holy Family stayed. The site revered by the Copts is nearby.

"How long did the Holy Family stay in this spot?" I asked Father David.

"They stayed here for three years and then they went back to Palestine," he said. "This was a good hiding place for them."

I was surprised by his answer. The Coptic Church has gone to great pains over the years to outline a Holy Family route. In their version of the events, the Holy Family stayed only a few days in this cave before pressing on to the south.

Father David disagreed with the Coptic version. He was insistent that the Holy Family only came as far as Babylon and its vicinity, including Memphis, the ancient capital of Egypt. Located about twenty miles south of current Cairo, Memphis was considered the juncture between Upper and Lower Egypt and was therefore almost always considered the center of Egyptian government as well as of religious, medical, and intellectual matters.

"Jesus visited the temple of the pharaoh in Memphis just to know what it was that was taught by the priests," said Father David. "But that is all I am allowed to tell you. I am a priest and I cannot talk about such things."

That Father David had brought up the possibility of Jesus learning from pharaonic priests surprised me. Such thinking aligned the priest—and perhaps the Greek Orthodox Church—with the teachings of the Infancy Gospels. In those books there is no account of the Holy Family in Babylon. But there is mention in both the Infancy Gospels and the Arabic Gospel of the Holy Family coming to Memphis and seeing the pharaoh. In both books it mentions that the Holy Family remained three more years in Egypt after seeing the pharaoh, although in fact Egypt did not have a pharaoh at that time.

In the First Gospel the final verse about the Holy Family's stay in Egypt reads: "Thence they proceeded to Memphis, and saw Pharaoh, and abode three years in Egypt. And the Lord Jesus did very many miracles in Egypt, which are neither to be found in the Gospel of the Infancy nor in the Gospel of Perfection."

The Arabic Gospel reads essentially the same way.

Does that mean that the Holy Family went no further? Or does it mean that there was no attempt by anyone outside the Coptic Church to detail their remaining time in Egypt? And if they did stay in Memphis, did Jesus learn the healing tricks of the Egyptian physicians and priests, perhaps the same tricks he used to perform the miracles written about in the Holy Bible? Some scholars and historians think so. They see Jesus as a magician who learned his magic from history's greatest medical magicians, the Egyptians.

I had once read the words of an ancient historian who claimed that Jesus had tattoos on his body, ones that recorded the magical healing formulas that he received from his Egyptian teachers. I had never given these claims much credence. But now, sitting with a learned man of a Christian church in the cave of the Holy Family in Babylon, the subject was irresistible.

"Did Jesus study with the priests of ancient Egypt?" I asked.

"This is a difficult question," said Father David. "It is forbidden for me to answer. I have my opinion but I cannot tell you my opinion and you know why. You cannot hear this kind of information from a priest. I can say nothing."

I continued to bore in.

"But much of what you say seems to agree with the Infancy Gospels," I said. "Yet many Christians think the Infancy Gospels should not be read because they say untruthful things about Jesus. Do you agree?"

"This is another difficult question to ask of a priest," said Father David. "The Greeks only believe in the words of the Holy Bible. But in my opinion there is not one key to spirituality but many keys. The Bible is one of those keys. I believe in the Bible, of course. But I believe that you can learn from other stories about Jesus, too. Not as much as from the Bible, but you can learn from them because they are historical."

"So do you think that much of Christianity came from the ancient Egyptian religion?" I asked, trying to steer him back to my original question.

"There is some tradition in the Christian religion that you find in the old pharaonic religions," said Father David, treading lightly on this holy topic.

"Like what?" I asked.

"Like the ceremony where incense is burned in the temple. That is the same as it was in pharaonic religion," said Father David. "The symbol of the cross, too. The symbol used for the giving of life in pharaonic times, the ankh, is very much like the cross for Christians. Copts believe that this symbol is the source of the cross that is the symbol of Christianity."

I wanted to ask Father David more questions but he was clearly finished talking about this uncomfortable subject. He wanted us to take the metro downtown, where he knew of an American-style coffeehouse where we could have cake and cappuccino.

As we started for the stairs that led from the tiny grotto, Father David turned and pointed to the iconic portrait of the Holy Family.

"We all want to know the truth about him. But the truth is in love," he said. "Love is a big word, a real word because it encloses all of nature. It is a word that has many keys, just like knowing Jesus has many keys. But if it is at the center of our soul, we will know the truth."

Part II

11. Just Passing Through

"We must be careful right now, Paul. We are in a very dangerous situation."

"Dangerous situation? We are sitting at a stoplight, Kees."

"Precisely, my American friend. Red lights are decoration here. These drivers coming up behind us are as likely to drive over us as stop. It is dangerous to stop at red lights here. People look to policemen for traffic directions, not to lights. They might run us right over if a policeman waves them on against the light."

The light changed and Kees put his foot to the floor, as did all of the drivers around us. A thick orange cloud spewed into the air from the exhaust pipes, adding to the pollution that wraps Cairo in a stifling haze.

Kees did not seem to notice. Perhaps he had lived here too long to be bothered by the smog. More than likely he had just given up and accepted it. *Insha'allah,* as the locals say, "God willing." What has gone wrong will maybe someday go right, by either human or divine intervention. Until then, it is out of our hands. . . .

We were speeding up the Cornice el-Nil, the busy highway through Cairo that hugs the Nile River. The thoroughfare could at times be a Mad Hatter ride of cabs, cops, and private cars. Its saving grace was its wide promenade and tall trees, a touch of class that makes nighttime

Drs. Cornelis "Kees" Hulsman

Cairo seem the Paris of the Middle East. In a city that is officially the most crowded in the world, a drive down the Cornice offers a fresh river breeze and a mile or two of driving relaxation—or at least it did for me.

"This road is madness," said Kees, throwing daggers with his eyes at the cab that was swerving way too close to us. "They should turn this whole road into a sidewalk and give it to the pedestrians. That would teach these drivers a lesson."

As Kees continued his hyperkinetic complaining about his adopted country I went into a cocoon of thought, pretending to read the notes in my notebook.

As we turned west on the Sharia al-Ahram and headed toward the Great Pyramids, I thought of the first time I had heard of Drs. Cornelis "Kees" Hulsman. It was from Shems Friedlander, a noted Sufi writer and filmmaker and the head of the Graphic Arts Department at American University in Cairo.

I had known Friedlander for fifteen years, since we first worked together at a magazine in New York City. Shems was a convert to Islam and became an expert in the life of Jalaluddin Rumi, the thirteenth-century Islamic poet. The first line of Shems' book about Rumi, entitled *Rumi: The Hidden Treasure*, reads: "The spiritual traveler can make a great journey while not moving in space."

Shems decided to make a great journey while moving *in* space. He left the magazine in New York and moved to Cairo, where he took his position at American University. When I first decided to follow the Holy Family trail, I contacted Shems. I was hoping that through his connections at the university he might be able to recommend a guide with knowledge of the sites as well as of the Christian community in Egypt.

The name that came back from Shems was Drs. Cornelis Hulsman, a Dutch sociologist who was an affiliate assistant professor of journalism at the university.

Hulsman's interest in the Middle East began with his friendship with Daan van der Meulen, a Dutch diplomat and explorer who ventured widely throughout the Arab Peninsula during the 1930s. Hulsman was fascinated by the stories of van der Meulen and decided to explore the Middle East himself. In 1976 he began in Israel, making it as far east as the gates of the holy city of Medina in Saudi Arabia, where he was not allowed to enter because he was not a Muslim.

Kees (as his friends call him) then went to Egypt, where he developed an interest in that country's pharaonic times. He visited all the temples and monuments of the country and then turned his focus to modern Egypt. He became so fascinated with Egyptian society that he received permission in 1982 from Leiden University to do doctoral research in his newly adopted country.

This was also the year that Kees discovered the Coptic Orthodox Church. While researching milk production in the town of Damietta, he met a charismatic priest who regaled him with stories of the Copts. The stories intrigued Kees, as did the notion that Christianity could exist so well alongside Islam.

In 1988 he married an engineering student named Sawsan who happened to be a Copt. Since 1994 Kees has been an accredited Dutch news correspondent, writing primarily for Dutch newspapers. He also founded The Religious News Service from the Arab World (now Arab-West Report), which reports on the content of the Arab-speaking press.

The real appeal to having Kees as a guide, Shems had said, would be the research he had done on the Holy Family trail. For the past year, Kees had been one of the researchers and writers on a picture book of

Holy Family Coptic sites that was being produced by the National
Egyptian Heritage Revival Association and American University. Since
Kees was familiar with most of the sites I planned to visit, Shems felt
he would be the perfect guide for this voyage.

"I want to be a bridge, creating an understanding in the West
about Christianity in the East, and in the East about Christianity in the
West," Kees later stated as his personal goal.

Unfortunately, Kees was not available for my first trip to Egypt. He
met me at my hotel when I first arrived and told me that a full slate of
teaching would prevent him from accompanying me. Still, he graciously
arranged for me to meet Ra'ed and at the end of my first trip was available to answer any questions I had about Egypt, Copts, or the route of
the Holy Family.

By the time of my second voyage, for reasons that were never made
clear to him, Kees' contract with American University had not been renewed. I knew poor teaching abilities were not the reason he was let go.
I had attended two of his classes when I was in Cairo and was impressed with his teaching methods and enthusiasm. The students loved
him and even felt comfortable enough to poke fun at his Dutch accent.
Kees was an authoritative teacher who had the rapt attention of his students. This is no small feat in Egypt, where the students have a bad
habit of talking to one another right through a teacher's lecture.

In e-mails to me from Egypt, Kees had speculated on possible reasons that his contract was not renewed. One possibility was The Religious News Service. He was not afraid to question many religious
leaders in print. He frequently called into question claims of persecution, especially those by members of the Coptic faith. It was not beneath him to travel to the site of an alleged persecution only to find
that the incident had not taken place as stated. Now that Kees was
again a foreign correspondent, he would have plenty of free time to
visit the remaining sites of the Holy Family trail with me. He personally
knew all the priests and bishops at each of these sites and he would
arrange for us to stay at the churches in each location. This would make
travel much easier and safer.

"There are no hotels to speak of below Cairo anyway," said Kees a
day or two before we hit the road. "We are going into what some people term Fundy Land."

"Fundy Land?" I asked. "What is that?"

"That, my American friend, is the area where all of the Egyptian religious fundamentalists came from," said Kees, a faint lilt of humor in his voice. "All of the Egyptians who are with Osama bin Laden in Afghanistan came from the area we are going into now. Well, maybe not all of them, but most. You get the picture. They ran the area between Mallawi and Assiut like the Mafia ran New York. It can be dangerous, especially for an American. While we are in Fundy Land would you like me to introduce you as a friend from Holland?"

We crossed the bridge over the Nile island of Rhoda and headed west toward the Giza Plateau and the Great Pyramids. It was morning, and the sun from behind us made the world's greatest man-made wonders stand out in bright relief.

"Look at those," declared Kees, a tinge of disgust in his voice.

"I am," I said. "They are absolutely magnificent. I don't think anything like that could be built these days."

"Not those," he said, flicking his wrist to dismiss the pyramids. *"Those."* He pointed toward a row of brick apartments that were lined up in an agricultural field. Although they could have had a view of one of the world's wonders, there appeared to be no attempt to take advantage of it. The windows were small and the front doors faced a damp field that surely spawned millions of mosquitoes.

"That is the problem with Egypt," he said. "It is overpopulated and they let people build illegal houses like those. That's just old cheap stuff that will shake down in an earthquake."

Earthquakes are a serious concern in Egypt. A fault line runs approximately the length of the Nile and has led to many devastating earthquakes in the past. Among the most deadly was the one in Dahshour in October 1992. Estimated at 5.9 on the Richter scale, the quake damaged more than a thousand schools and killed over seven thousand people. It also laid waste to our first stop, the Monastery of Abu Sefein at Tamua.

The monastery at Tamua had not been on my list of Holy Family sites. According to the Coptic priests at the Holy Virgin Church of Maadi, the Holy Family did not go there. They claim that the Holy Family fled the soldiers of Herod by boarding a boat on the banks of the Nile in Maadi and sailing south to Deir al-Garnous. That means they would have passed Tamua and not touched the shore again for more than a hundred miles. The priests at Maadi insist that Joseph paid for this boat voyage with the gifts of gold, frankincense, and myrrh that the wise men had given to Jesus at birth.

There are at least two reasons why the priests believe that the Holy Family left from Maadi. For one, the church occupies a spot that was thought to be a Jewish synagogue during the time of the Holy Family's flight to Egypt. Then there is the miracle of the floating Bible. On March 12, 1976, a young Coptic deacon named Sama'an Megalli walked down the steps leading to the Nile and found a Holy Bible floating in the river. Megalli picked up the Bible and found it open to Isaiah 19, the chapter that prophesies the arrival of Jesus by saying, "Behold, the Lord rideth upon a swift cloud," and ends with perhaps the line in the Bible most often quoted by Copts, "Blessed be Egypt my people."

However, the priests at Tamua agree with everything their brothers at Maadi say about the Holy Family except the boat trip. They claim that the Holy Family did not take a boat past the site of their beloved monastery. Rather, the Holy Family *walked* there using a secret tunnel that passed *underneath* the Nile.

Proof of this, said Father Salib, the head priest at the monastery, was revealed in a dream to Pope Kyrillos VI in the late 1960s.

"The pope lived here sometimes," said Father Salib. "One night he had a dream in which he saw the true route of the Holy Family. In the dream he saw them walking underneath the Nile and coming here instead of boating down the river."

We were sitting in the church office only a few feet from the Nile. Surrounding the front door were people young and old lined up to speak to the priest. They were anxious to come in but the priest ignored them, concentrating instead on our conversation. Explaining the route of the Holy Family was important business for the priest and he wanted to make certain that it was done properly. We, as influential foreigners, needed to be properly informed of his church's place in Holy Family history.

"You may wonder why you never find written reference to Tamua as being part of the Holy Family trail," said Father Salib.

"Yes, I wonder that," said Kees.

"It is this," said Father Salib. "There are places where the Holy Family passed through and there are places where they stopped. The places where they stopped are recorded in writing. The places where they passed through are kept alive only by oral tradition. Tamua has been talked about from father to son for two thousand years. Many people doubted this was one of the Holy Family locations even then. Finally Pope Kyrillos had his dream and that confirmed it. Now no one can doubt that the Holy Family passed through here."

Kees shrugged. I could see that *he* had his doubts.

"This sounds an awful lot like Moses crossing the Red Sea," said Kees. He translated his own words into Arabic so the priest could understand him and then translated the words of the priest to me.

"He says that there is a link between Jesus crossing the Nile through this tunnel and Moses parting the Red Sea," said Kees. "He also says that Joseph the son of Jacob was living in this very spot many centuries before Jesus passed through."

"Then there is a connection between the stories of the Old Testament and those of the New Testament?" I asked Father Salib.

"Yes, there is," said the priest. "But no one knew that until St. Mark came to Egypt. Everyone here was pagan then, but he came and told them the stories of the Old Testament and the New. It was then that they understood the word of God and the prophecies that connect the old days and the new."

St. Mark was the apostle who literally followed Jesus to the grave. He was also Egypt's first Christian, arriving in Alexandria possibly as early as 42, according to Coptic historian Otto Meinardus, and maybe as late as 50–62. It was through him that the Egyptians first heard the prophecies of the Old Testament as well as the "good news" about the life, death, and resurrection of Jesus Christ. Angry pagans dragged Mark to his death through the streets of Alexandria on May 8, 68. Before his horrific ending, though, Mark linked many of the Bible stories to events in Egypt.

The Holy Family's crossing of the Nile in a secret tunnel was apparently one of those stories, said Father Salib.

"It was no surprise to people that Jesus would come to a place that had significance in the Old Testament," said Father Salib. "When they heard the sermons of St. Mark they understood that he was like those who had come in the Old Testament."

"Were there miracles performed here by Jesus?" asked Kees.

The priest shrugged. "You have to remember that the Holy Family just passed through here to Upper Egypt," said Father Salib. "There may have been miracles but we don't know about them yet."

The room we were in was a clutter of books, papers, an ancient rotary telephone, desks and chairs. It seemed as though everything was vying for space. But alone on the wall was a picture of Pope Kyrillos VI, the holy man whose dream gave substance to the notion that the Holy Family crossed beneath the Nile in a tunnel. Bearded and munificent-looking, he looked down at us with kind and knowing eyes. The people outside were pacing and ready to speak to their priest, and the priest was clearly ready to get on with his day. But Pope Kyrillos looked down with a beatific look, a serenity that made me feel relaxed and welcomed, despite the imposition we had caused.

"I must deliver Mass," said Father Salib, rising from his chair. "Are there more questions?"

"Only one," said Kees. "We would like to see the tunnel."

Father Salib shrugged.

"There was a tunnel underneath the Nile from the church at Maadi to here, that is for sure," he said. "But we do not know where it is today. They have not been able to find the entrance."

Father Salib gave us a quick tour of the church and then invited us to stay for Mass. We stayed for a short period of time before Kees tapped me on the shoulder and motioned toward the door. "We need to leave now," said Kees. "We have already spent more time here than Jesus did when he came out of the tunnel."

It wasn't until we drove out of the walled churchyard and were back on the road to Upper Egypt that Kees made his true feelings known.

"Did you hear what the priest said?" Kees said, navigating the pock-marked agricultural road that runs along the eastern side of the Nile. "He said, 'Jesus may have performed miracles here but we don't know about them yet.' Do you know what that means?"

"I'm not sure," I said. "What does it mean?"

"It means that the tradition of the Holy Family is still changing," said Kees. "It means that this is a living tradition that can change when a pope or a bishop—even a priest—has a dream or vision. In a few years there will probably be stories about the miracles that Jesus performed here. Where there are questions, answers usually emerge.

"Let me show you how important people are to keeping the route of the Holy Family alive," said Kees. We were maybe fifty miles south of Tamua. He slowed down and began looking for a road that would take us to the other side of the canals that ran next to the highway. A green strip of crops less than a mile wide ran next to the road. Beyond the green was raw desert. Pyramids dotted the landscape. Most of them had been built poorly or with angles that were too steep and had crumbled under their own weight. Other than these man-made mountains, there was an expanse of desert all the way to Libya.

Kees turned down a road that took us across the canals and then onto a dirt road through green fields of cotton and groves of date palms. Soon we came to a very primitive village with houses fashioned from mud bricks. The streets were narrow, barely wide enough for two cars to pass. The citizens walked slowly in front of the car and stared back at us, curious about these two foreigners who were driving through their town.

"This is the town of Saudiya," said Kees, tapping his horn to convince the driver of an ox-drawn cart to give us more room. "In medieval times there was a monastery here that was built in honor of the Holy Family passing through. This is even mentioned in the Coptic Encyclopedia. Now this town is completely Muslim; there are no Christians here. Even though Christians in a neighboring village acknowledge that this is the site of the monastery, nobody can locate it, let alone determine what the Holy Family did while they were here."

To make his point, Kees rolled down his window and asked some of the citizens where the site of the old monastery might be. Young and old pondered the question, yet no one could answer.

"I'll show you where I think it is," said Kees. He had been out here a few years earlier and thought he had found the most likely spot. He steered down a rutted road past a large Muslim cemetery that was shaded by a giant tree. We were deeper into the desert now and before long the sand in the road overwhelmed our wheels and we were stuck.

"Not a problem," he said, climbing out of his car and pointing to a spot on top of a small hill. "That is probably where the monastery was."

Kees looked up at the hill and then turned 360 degrees, taking in the harsh desert that surrounded us. Next to us was a cone-shaped mountain covered with a scraggly sort of rock. It turned out to be a pyramid and like most of the ninety in Egypt it had crumbled beneath its own weight. This ancient funerary symbol represented our closest reminder of civilization. The village of Saudiya was several miles behind us. We were stuck in the sands of the eastern desert.

I became fixated on our situation.

"Kees, we are stuck in the desert," I said. "We don't even have a shovel to dig our way out."

"A shovel would probably be worthless anyway," said Kees. "The sand would just pour right back into the hole."

Realizing that the monastery was not on top of the hill he had originally pointed at, Kees continued to scour the landscape for some sign of
the long extinct structure. He didn't seem to care about being stuck in the
sand. Instead he was stuck in a different type of sand, the sands of time.

"This proves my point," Kees said, giving up on the monastery.
"The story of Jesus in Egypt is a living tradition, one that requires a
strong living faith. If there is no one around to keep it alive, it disappears like old ruins or flattens out like that powerful pyramid. It has
nothing to do with history. That is a Western mistake. It has everything
to do with faith."

We leaned against the car and looked out at the white desert. I forgot for a moment about being stuck and concentrated on the raw
beauty of our surroundings. I realized now what I would be struck by
many times in the days and weeks ahead: that the edge of the desert
allowed for a vista that placed little between you and God. For this reason, it was the perfect place for a monastery.

"Here comes help," said Kees, pointing to a tall man in a traditional *galabiya*. He was walking toward us from beyond the pyramid and
didn't seem to be at all surprised to see two foreigners stuck in the desert.

His name was Ragab Mohammed Hassan. He offered to help us
push the car from the sand, which he and I did as Kees piloted from the
driver's seat. Once the car was back on solid ground, he asked for a ride
to town.

"I have a garden and a beautiful house," he said from the backseat
as Kees translated. "I would like to invite you to see my garden and
have tea."

"What should we do?" I asked Kees.

"If he knows any stories of Jesus in this area, then we should stop
and join him for tea," said Kees. "Otherwise it will take too much time.
We will drink tea half the afternoon and then get stuck out on the road
at night. We really should stay on schedule."

Kees asked Ragab if he had ever heard any stories of Jesus being in
the area. He had not, he said. The only Jesus stories he knew were the
ones he had read in the Quran.

"I have told him that we have an appointment in Upper Egypt and
must leave immediately," said Kees. "I have not lied to him. The priest
at Deir al-Maimun is waiting."

⟰

But there was no priest waiting when we arrived at Deir al-Maimun. Instead a nervous deacon greeted us and said that the priest had given up on us and gone home.

"He expected you more than an hour ago," said the deacon to Kees.

"He is Egyptian, not Dutch," replied Kees in good humor. "He should expect us to be late. Go find him and tell him that we are on Egyptian time."

With some time to kill, Kees suggested we take a walk around the town.

"There is more to see here than meets the eye," he insisted.

Although it was only about five in the afternoon, there was no one outside. The rows of mud brick houses that lined the narrow streets gave me a claustrophobic feel as we walked between them. Many of the doors were painted colorfully, but other than that the walls were the color of the mud bricks they were made from. We walked down one street and then another through this maze of sameness that makes up so many Egyptian villages. In short order there was nothing to orient me. I was lost.

Luckily Kees was not. He turned down one street and then another and soon the Nile was dead ahead.

"In the days of Jesus this village was not here," said Kees, stopping at the banks of the Nile and taking in the sunset as it lit the palm and poinciana trees that lined the bank. "But there must have been something about this area that appealed to Jesus as the Holy Family passed by in its boat. The Copts believe that Jesus blessed the site of Deir al-Maimun. Maybe they stopped here or maybe he just blessed it from the boat, but Jesus declared that someday greatness would come to this site."

"And did it?" I asked.

"It certainly did," said Kees, turning his back on the sun and walking toward an iron fence that encircled a small stone basin. "This is the workshop of St. Anthony, the first official hermit and the father of monasticism."

We would hear more about St. Anthony later from the priest of the church. Now, however, Kees was cut short by the opening of the door to a house that was next to the fenced-in basin. An older woman came out, dressed in a long housedress and wearing a scarf around her gray hair. When she saw us her eyes lit up with pleasure. It was like we were beloved relatives making a surprise visit.

"God has brought you to my home," she shouted, holding her arms out to us as though she expected us to leap into them. "You must come in right now and eat dinner. It is ready."

Kees explained that we had a meeting with the priest, otherwise we would gladly join her for dinner. "We just wanted to stop here before the sun went down, to see the basin of St. Anthony," he said.

The woman knew everything about St. Anthony, she said. Why, it was here that he had come every day to wash his feet and to talk to the people who came to seek his wisdom.

"You must have known him personally," quipped Kees.

The woman laughed. "No, I am not *that* old," she said. "But the stories that are still here are that old."

Kees thanked her for the offer of dinner and agreed to return later for a cup of tea. Then I followed him through the village maze back to the church of St. Anthony, where we met Father Girgis.

Father Girgis was a bear of a man, with a round face, round glasses and a black beard that accentuated the size of his smile. He had been here twenty years, he said. When he arrived this village was very near collapse from lack of care. He had initiated a restoration project among the villagers that restored much of the luster to this town, most of which was originally an ancient monastery.

"When I arrived there was no electricity, no running water, not even candles in this church," said Father Girgis. "Now it is different."

He turned on the lights of the church and proudly began showing us around. As he talked to Kees about the improvements he had made I focused on the floor. It was solid stone and grooved as though a massive hair comb had been pulled through it. I had seen this kind of floor somewhere else, but I wasn't sure where.

"It's the floor from a pharaonic temple," said Kees, translating the priest's words. "He says this church is built on top of the site of a pharaonic temple."

The priest waved us to a stone pillar that extended from the floor to the roof. He stood proudly next to it and posed while I took a picture.

"This is amazing," said Kees, listening as the priest spoke. "This pillar is from the original pharaonic temple. Rather than destroy everything and start over, the Coptic monks who built this incorporated portions of the original temple into the design."

"Why would they do that?" I asked.

"Because of that," said Kees, pointing to a deep hole in the floor of the church. "That is the cave of St. Anthony."

The priest raised an iron grate and I peered inside. The "cave" was the approximate size of a human grave, about six and a half feet long and four feet wide. A short fence surrounded it. I opened the gate and climbed down a ladder to get inside. I was in a box of stone—a pharaonic grave, according to the priest, that had been turned into living quarters for a saint and was now a revered religious relic that would remind the entire congregation why it was they were in church.

"Did St. Anthony actually live here?" I asked the priest.

"Yes," he said, a warm smile gracing his face. "He slept here every night for at least twenty years. You are experiencing for a few minutes what he experienced for twenty years."

I sat on the floor of the tiny tomb and looked up. I tried to imagine what it was like for St. Anthony, alone in this dry cave in the third century. There would be no fence surrounding this hole, and no church roof—or any roof—over his head. There was only the magnificent sky of Egypt to gaze at and the lonely eastern desert to surround him.

"This is what St. Anthony wanted," said the priest. "He wanted to connect with God. To do that he had to live here, sleep here, and pray here. He was a hermit. He wanted to be far away from the people and the world and this is where he initially found the place to be solitary."

I looked at Kees and he nodded.

"What he is saying is probably historically correct," he said. "There are many stories that I doubt, but not this one. Historians have researched what he is saying."

The priest continued speaking.

"St. Anthony was a rich man. His father owned many *feddan* across the river," said Father Girgis. "St. Anthony inherited all of his father's land. Then he read the scriptures and they spoke to him. He decided that he wanted to give all of his riches to the poor and follow in the footsteps of Jesus."

"What spoke to him so loudly in the Bible that he gave up all of his possessions?" I asked.

"It was Jesus talking to wealthy people, those verses in Luke," said the priest. "When St. Anthony read those, he realized that he wanted to follow Jesus."

I closed my eyes for a moment and tried to imagine St. Anthony reading those verses in the eighteenth chapter of Luke.

And a certain ruler asked him, saying, "Good Master, what shall I do to inherit eternal life?" And Jesus said unto him, "Why callest thou me good? None is good, save one, that is, God."

Thou knowest the commandments, Do not commit adultery, Do not kill, Do not steal, Do not bear false witness, Honour thy father and thy mother.

And he said, "All these have I kept from my youth up."

Now when Jesus heard these things, he said unto him, "Yet lackest thou one thing: sell all that thou hast, and distribute unto the poor, and thou shalt have treasure in heaven: and come follow me."

And when he heard this, he was very sorrowful: for he was very rich.

And when Jesus saw that he was very sorrowful, he said, "How hardly shall they that have riches enter into the kingdom of God!

"For it is easier for a camel to go through a needle's eye, than for a rich man to enter into the kingdom of God."

I opened my eyes and looked up at the priest and Kees. "Couldn't he have sold part of his wealth and lived in a house instead?" I asked.

"No," said Kees. "Not St. Anthony. It was all or nothing for him. He lived in the extreme, which is what being a hermit is about. It was the only way that he could truly connect with God."

"He heard that Jesus had blessed this spot and decided that this was where he would come to be a hermit," said Father Girgis. "This was the holiest and loneliest spot he could find. He slept here all night and prayed all day, and when he needed money he made baskets in a stone tub down by the river and sold them to people who passed by. I will take you down there later so you can see where he worked."

"Doing things like making baskets is repetitive work," said Kees. "Even today many monks do it because it lets them pray during labor."

St. Anthony came to this spot in the year 275 C.E., when he was twenty-five years old, said the priest. Here he lived for twenty years, until he was forty-five years old. By then living in Deir al-Maimun had become a burden for history's first hermit. People in nearby villages had heard that there was a wise man living in a tomb at the site of this former pharaonic temple and they went to him for advice. Gradually, St. Anthony's life of solitude turned into one of frequent interruption, as a constant stream of people came to seek his counsel. Finally he left his stone tomb and moved deeper into the eastern desert, where his followers organized a monastery, Deir Mar Antonios. Here, according to the *Catholic Encyclopedia*, he spent the second half of his life. He died probably in 355 C.E., at the age of 105. At his request, his gravesite was kept secret by two disciples who buried him so his body would not become an object of reverence.

"Many people come here and scribble prayers on pieces of paper and leave their wishes in the grave," said Kees, pointing past me at the sandy floor. I looked down and saw many pieces of paper. "On these papers are prayers for healing or for good grades in school exams or to get a job or find a partner in life. This is a place where people ask for help with daily life problems, not major world problems."

"Is anyone ever helped?" I asked the priest.

The pleasant Father Girgis looked at me as though I had made a joke. A big grin crossed his face.

"There have been many miracles here," he said. "I will tell you one. Recently a woman who had problems in her back came to the cave and prayed. She was very sick before she prayed, but the day after the prayers, she was well."

I am not sure that it would please St. Anthony to know that people were still seeking his intervention in prayer. All of his life he told his followers that they did not need his help in communicating with God. "If you believe in Christ whom I serve, go, and according as you believe, pray to God and it shall come to pass," he told them. But sufferers do not always listen. The biographies of St. Anthony tell of people sleeping outside his door, beseeching him to pray for them. "Seek and it shall be given unto you," he told them. They still sought his saintly prayers. Now, nearly seventeen hundred years later, they are seeking them still.

"Do you ever sleep in the tomb?" I asked the priest.

"Sometimes, yes," said Father Girgis.

"Why?" I asked.

"It gives me wisdom," he said, beaming. "When I sleep down there I get special wisdom on how to deal with the problems of the people in the church. The revelations I receive are never big ones like the Vision of Theophilus. They are always community-related. They are small revelations, but important to the people of my congregation."

I climbed out of the tomb. It was late now and Kees was anxious to get back on the road. We were going to Cairo for the night and he was nervous about the road trip ahead. He had good reason. The desert road was also known as "the highway of death." Not only do many people drive with their headlights off because they think it conserves fuel, but dust storms sometimes kick up out of nowhere, causing deadly pileups.

He made his concerns clear, but the priest still wanted more of our time. "Follow me," he said, walking out of the church and down a street that took us back into the village maze. Both Kees and I knew that we were going back to St. Anthony's stone trough, the place we had visited when we first came into town. Kees tried to explain that we had seen this religious relic already but the priest kept walking, winding down one dark hollow after another until we saw ahead of us a single porch light illuminating the fence that surrounded the stone bath.

What Father Girgis saw on the fence froze him in his tracks. Draped over the railing in a most indecorous fashion was the old woman's laundry. It was soaking wet and dripping water into the sacred trough of St. Anthony.

It was a blasphemy to hang one's laundry on such a holy relic. Father Girgis' warm demeanor turned cold, and the grin on his face that had been present all evening turned to a frightening grimace.

In a rage he tore the wet clothes from the iron fence and stomped them into the dirt. Then he kicked them down the street until they were well out of the circle of light that illuminated the sacred trough.

"I must come by tomorrow and forgive these people for what they did," said the priest, taking a deep breath to compose himself. "What they did is wrong. You do not hang your laundry on sacred relics. But they are very ordinary people. They need to be educated."

12. Visions or Dreams?

It was late at night when we left Deir al-Maimun and got on the desert road back to Cairo. Kees had made a point of calling this highway the "road of death," but it wasn't until we began our perilous journey home that I realized how correct that description was.

A light wind blew off the desert, suspending a cloud of sand that gave the road ahead an orange haze. Every few miles a double or triple row of speed bumps rose out of the pavement, causing drivers to slam on their brakes to avoid the jarring that could break an axle.

As Kees navigated this nerve-wracking route, he regaled me with stories of dust storms and deadly accidents, the worst involving a bus filled with students that collided head-on with a truck in the middle of the night.

One conversation evolved into another and soon we were talking about the happy priest at Deir al-Maimun and his angry response to the parishioners who were drying their laundry on the fence around St. Anthony's stone basin.

"Don't you think he overreacted to their mistake?" I asked.

"Maybe by your standards in the West, where everything can be questioned," said Kees. "But here you don't question authority, especially religious authority. In some places in the Middle East it could be a death sentence for a Muslim to question the Quran. Christians can be

very strict, too. You show respect to everything in the Church. You simply do not question higher authority."

That presented a problem, I said to Kees, because I wanted to
question authority.

Although the locations visited by the Holy Family have been compiled by combining oral traditions, Infancy Gospels, and homilies by
important bishops, the most puzzling source of information about Jesus in Egypt came from the visions of important church leaders. For the
most part the visions deal with the sites in Upper Egypt. Pope Theophilus, the late-fourth-century Church leader, was the first to have a vision related to the Holy Family. He had an extended conversation with
the Virgin Mary during a dream at a house in Deir al-Muharraq thought
to have been occupied at one time by the Holy Family. It was during
this visionary dream that the Holy Mother provided some of the place
names that they had visited, including Tell Basta in the Delta and Deir
al-Muharraq, the southernmost stop for the Holy Family before returning to Israel. Other visions by holy men have added to the Holy
Family trail. Bishop Cyriacus of al-Bahnassa wrote about a vision that
was experienced by a "Father Antonius." In that vision, the Virgin Mary
identifies an area in al-Bahnassa as being "an altar of glory" placed
there by the Virgin as the Holy Family passed through on their way
south. To test the authenticity of the vision, Bishop Cyriacus spent the
night praying with the priest who had it. By night's end he, too, had had
the same vision.

And then there was the story of Shenute. The fifth-century monk
reported that he encountered Jesus while walking in the mountains of
Upper Egypt. Jesus and Shenute came upon the unburied corpse of a
man who had lived in the first century. Jesus resurrected this man, who
recounted tales of the Holy Family in Hermopolis, the current-day village of Ashmunayn.

These and other visions were puzzling to me. Why, I asked Kees,
were these visions so readily accepted as gospel? What authority made
them so?

"In short, Kees, when is a vision a vision and when is it a dream?" I
asked.

"That's a heavy question to ask of any religion, not just the ones
around here," said Kees. "All religions have plenty of visions in their
backbone. When you question the truth of a vision, you can be questioning the truth of a religion. That can be dangerous. People don't like

to have their beliefs questioned." We rode in silence for several minutes as I pondered the meaning of what Kees had said.

"However, it is a *good* question. When is a vision a vision and when is it a dream?" repeated Kees. "Yes, we must ask that question, if just to see the answers that come back."

The first church official we questioned was Bishop Marcos of Shubra el-Kheima. He was the moderator of the committee to establish the official route of the Holy Family. Founded in 1999 by Pope Shenouda III, the committee's goal was to establish once and for all an official version of the route of the Holy Family in Egypt. Surprisingly, there was no official Church version in existence. Other than a nineteenth-century map that was deemed inaccurate by the committee, there was no sanctioned way for a modern-day pilgrim to find all of the sites.

Although there were no real maps, plenty of historical documents gave strong hints as to where the Holy Family was thought to have traveled. The committee of eight bishops spent considerable time reading the historical documents, including those recounting a variety of visions. Then once a week they came together to talk about the sites that definitely hosted Jesus and the sites that *might* have.

By the end of 1999 they had compiled an official map. Their work was completed just in time for the new millennium.

We visited Bishop Marcos in his bishopric in northeast Cairo. He was a witty man with a mastery of the English language and a quick laugh. Over tea I told him that I was interested in knowing how a committee of modern bishops was able to chart the course of the Holy Family through Egypt, a trip that took place two thousand years ago.

"I am sorry to say that there is no way to know exactly where they went the entire trip," he said, emitting a chuckle. "After all, there was no one following them and there were no spy satellites from the United States to map their exact course. We do know from the documents we studied that the Holy Family was in certain spots. But what about the areas in between? Those we arrived at by logical thinking."

"What do you mean by logical thinking?" asked Kees.

"Many of the places now named as sites were not there when Jesus came through," said the bishop. "For example, Zeitoun did not exist at that time. But the exact points of Farama [near El-Arish] and Tell

Basta were known and so were Babylon, Maadi, and Deir al-Muharraq. But how did they get from Farama to Tell Basta? And what route did they take to Babylon and then to Deir al-Muharraq? There was nothing there in those days, so we had to use our imagination."

"Imaginations?" asked Kees.

"Yes, that and logical thinking," said the bishop. "For example, from the vision of Pope Theophilus we know that they went from Farama to Tell Basta. And we know there was only one way to get there, so that route was no problem. But after that we had to use our imaginations. We had to figure that this foreign family with a different language was left to help themselves because they could not ask for help. So they would have to travel near to the banks of the Nile. Doing that would make it easier for them to get water and food and also to find their way."

"So plotting out the trail of the Holy Family is not an exact science," I said.

"Some of it is exact, because we have place names and we know where those places were," said Bishop Marcos. "We know from the documents where, say, point A and point D are. We just had to use logical thinking to tell where points B and C were."

The sites not found in the ancient documentation were often decided by the oral traditions that exist in an area. If people have always told stories of Jesus in a given area, then chances are the Holy Family was there, said the bishop. Also there was the matter of place names. Sometimes places were named after the Holy Family yet no one in a region knew why. On the edge of the western desert in the north of Wady el-Natrun, for example, there is a well with the curious name of the Maria Well.

"No one knows where that name came from, but it has always been called that," said Bishop Marcos. "Where did they get this name? Local people did not name it. So we can imagine that the Maria Well means that the Holy Family came to this place, used the well to drink from, and continued down the Nile. In that case, we are using logic, not oral tradition."

"Was there ever a time that you doubted one of those sites?" I asked.

"No, because it was easy to see how they had to travel," said the bishop. "There is not any problem between these points. Maybe they went one kilometer to one side or the other, but we knew they were close."

I mentioned that in a study of how the itinerary of the Holy Family was assembled, New Testament scholar Stephen Davis found that the sources fell into four categories: homilies attributed to prominent Egyptian bishops (visions are included in this category), historical-geographic works on the church in Egypt, liturgical documents such as lists of saint's days, and Infancy Gospels.

Bishop Marcos concurred with all of these but added one of his own: modern-day visions.

"As a group, we would pray for guidance," said Bishop Marcos. "If I would pray alone for guidance and I imagined something, that doesn't mean that the Holy Spirit put it inside me. But if we all pray about a site and all have the same dream or vision, then we know we have the right site. For example, if we all prayed about something—you in the United States, Kees in Holland, and me in Egypt—and we all have the same dream or vision, then this means it is right by the Holy Spirit."

Kees nodded. "That's one way to tell if a vision is a vision," he said.

I saw the logic of this. This form of vision quest seemed to be as scientific as possible, especially in an environment of strict orthodoxy where science was often seen as the enemy of religion. But what about visions that are experienced by only one person? How is it possible to know if Pope Theophilus' richly detailed encounter with the Virgin Mary is truly a vision or a dream?

When I asked this question of Bishop Marcos his bright smile wilted and his forehead wrinkled in a spasm of deep thought.

"We don't know when a vision is truly a vision and when it is a dream," the bishop finally said. "But we do know that trustworthy visions and dreams can come to one person. Joseph in the New Testament, for example, had a visionary dream that told him to come to Egypt for safety. Later he had a visionary dream to leave Egypt. And Pope Theophilus was also alone when he spoke to St. Mary in his vision. So we believe it is possible, even today, that one person can have a vision. But that vision or dream should refer to the Bible or books or information that we know is true. That way we accept that the vision is true because we have built on faith. It is on faith that we go."

The next day we boarded a bus and headed for Ishneen al-Nassara and Deir al-Garnous, two rival Holy Family sites 120 miles south of Cairo. Boarding a bus was an act of faith in this country, declared Kees *after* the door was shut and we started moving.

"There are many accidents on the roads of Egypt," said Kees. "Before you board any kind of public transportation, you have to have faith that God wants you to make it to your destination."

Kees was joking, of course, but only partially. It was not uncommon to look out the front window of the bus and see a heavily laden pickup truck or a passenger minibus heading straight for us. More than once the other passengers leaned forward like moviegoers at an adventure film to see if the oncoming driver was going to plow into us or get back on his side of the line. *Insha'allah,* "God willing," was muttered frequently during these brushes with death, as were other words that I could not understand but took to be some form of deliverance prayer.

The two people on the bus who didn't seem fazed by these near misses were the bus driver and Kees. The bus driver seemed to take a long view of the road. He gazed at the distant highway from his elevated perch at the helm, ignoring the smaller cars that raced toward him from up close. Kees took a long view of a different sort. He laughed at the oncoming cars as though protected by an invisible shield. It seemed to me that for him this was like a fun-house ride.

Watching Kees, the words of Bishop Marcos came back to me. *It is on faith that we go.*

"What did you think of Bishop Marcos' point of view on faith?" I asked Kees.

"You mean that you have to have faith to believe in these sites? I agree with him," said Kees. "One thing he didn't talk about was all of the miracles that take place at many of these sites. Virtually every Holy Family location has had miracle healings associated with it. To many of the faithful, that is proof enough that the spot is blessed by Jesus."

There are other phenomena that add grist to faith, said Kees. There were the apparitions of light that have illuminated sites in the past or do so even today. These are thought to be proof of special approval by Jesus, a visible manifestation of his blessing. Sometimes these light apparitions are said to take human form, as the one in Zeitoun was said to take the form of the Virgin Mary. Others consist of light radiating from a source inside the church or site, while still others are lights that shower down from the heavens.

"This heavenly light is a very special thing," said Kees. "It means that a site is certainly blessed and that the people who see it are blessed. Many people who see it are changed forever. And of course the site is changed forever, too, because if it is a logical continuation of the trail, it becomes part of the Holy Family story."

Such was the case with Deir al-Garnous. It was here that the Holy Family stopped on its way to Ashmunayn, Kees informed me, and added that the site had been discovered by both light and a vision.

Bishop Cyriacus, who perhaps lived in the eleventh century, was responsible for recording these visionary encounters. He claimed that a manuscript written by Joseph the Carpenter had once been found in the area. Joseph declared that the Holy Family had stopped in the area of Deir al-Garnous. They rested here for four days, refreshing themselves with cool water from a local well before continuing southward.

Although the manuscript of Joseph the Carpenter was now lost, a contemporary of Bishop Cyriacus named Father Antonius later confirmed its content in a vision. During this revelation he saw a "miraculous light" on a hill and went to that spot to read the gospel of St. John. As he read, the Virgin Mary and Jesus appeared to him. "This is the altar of glory I placed here until the end of generations," said Jesus. "Even if the place is desolate it will be remembered forever."

Father Antonius reported his vision to Bishop Cyriacus, who spent the night praying with the priest. By the end of the night, the Holy Virgin had appeared to Bishop Cyriacus, too, delivering the same message to him. A church was soon built in honor of the Holy Virgin.

In the seventeenth century another church was built in Deir al-Garnous with the help of the Virgin Mary. She appeared to the workmen, telling them where to find building stones.

The old church stood until the 1920s, when yet another miracle occurred. The Virgin Mary appeared to Father Yuhanna al-Shuwayli and told him to build a new church. The priest was initially angered at the request. He had no money and no bricks with which to build. But the Virgin Mary took him to a tree that had renewed itself with its own shoots many times throughout the centuries. The priest realized that renewal was necessary and so a larger and better church needed to be built. By telling others about this vision, al-Shuwayli was able to obtain funding and building material to create the structure that is there now.

"The church was built on the spot where Father Antonius first saw the miraculous light," said Kees. "In one corner of the church is a well that is believed to have originated with Jesus."

"And what about the town of Ishneen al-Nassara?" I asked.

"They only passed through," said Kees. "But there is a twist. As they were walking through, Jesus was thirsty, so they stopped to drink at a well. But the water was too deep for them to reach. This time, though, Jesus held his finger over the well and water rose to the top so they could drink.

"That miracle took place on August twenty-second at four P.M., or so the oral tradition says. Now, every year on that date and time, the water in the well rises to the rim."

Kees wore a puckish grin as he told the last part of that story.

"Is it really true that the water rises every August twenty-second?" I asked.

"We will be staying at Ishneen al-Nassara for a couple of days, so you can investigate all of these questions for yourself," said Kees. "First we will stop at Deir al-Garnous, just as the Holy Family did."

⟊

The donkey was frightened. He brayed as our driver eased the car past him, pressing him against a mud wall on the narrow street leading to the Church of the Holy Virgin. The people laughed. They had obviously seen this kind of competition before, the one for road space between the hoofed transportation of the old days, which this street was designed for, and modern mechanical transport.

I felt for the donkey, literally. I had my hand out the window and was trying to push him away from the car. He wouldn't change his path. He kept pace as best he could with us, vying for road space even though he was scraping the wall. It was as though the transportation of yesteryear did not want to give way to that of modern times.

Finally we reached the end of the road and stopped.

In front of us was a metal gate decorated with a cross. Flanking the gate were two guard posts, each one manned with armed guards. Despite the fact that Deir al-Garnous is a city of twelve thousand Christians and no Muslims, a Christian church in Fundy Land still needs to be protected.

Across the church courtyard and out the gate came a tall priest wearing sunglasses and a broad smile. He made straight for Kees, who welcomed his friend loudly.

"Father Shenuda," he shouted. "It is good to see you again. I wish you much *baraka.*"

The two men embraced and then Kees told his friend why I had come.

"Oh, that is wonderful," said the priest. "This church is now called the Church of the Holy Virgin, but the first church to be built here was called the House of Jesus. That is because the Holy Family came through here, without a doubt, and that is why the churches that have been here have been named first after Jesus and then after his mother."

"There is even a well here where the Holy Family stopped to drink," said Kees.

"Just like Ishneen al-Nassara," I said to the priest.

Kees translated my comment and Father Shenuda's smile clouded over.

"Do not compare us to Ishneen," said the priest. "This is the real place, not Ishneen. It is doubtful that the Holy Family stopped at Ishneen."

Kees smiled as he translated.

"It looks as though there is some rivalry between the two sites," he said. "He does not want to be mentioned in the same breath with Ishneen."

Nonetheless, that is exactly what Kees did. When he found out that Father Shenuda's church had a celebration of the coming of the Holy Family on June 2, he mentioned that a similar festival took place in Ishneen.

"Nothing takes place in Ishneen," said the increasingly agitated priest. "It is only here. Here the church is named after the Holy Virgin. There it is named after St. George. Holy Family sites are always named after the Holy Virgin. That is one reason that Ishneen is not a true Holy Family site."

As we walked toward the church, Father Shenuda counted the Holy Family sites, skipping several we had already gone to and, of course, leaving Ishneen out of the picture entirely. Ishneen, he said, was a recent addition to the Holy Family trail. It was clear that he didn't believe it belonged.

Father Shenuda took us inside the church and showed us the holy well that had been created by Jesus to quench the thirst of the Holy Family. The well was positioned in one corner of the church and was about the size of a large washbasin. When a deacon lifted the lid to draw water with a bucket, I could see the brick-lined shaft and the water about twelve feet below the rim.

"So does your water level rise on June first to honor the arrival of the Holy Family? It does that at Ishneen," said Kees.

The question clearly annoyed Father Shenuda.

"Ours rises on June first," said the priest. "This is the day we cele-brate the arrival of the Holy Family at Deir el-Garnous."

"That makes no sense," Kees said to me, not translating his com-ment to the priest. "At Ishneen they say the Holy Family came through on August twenty-second. Here they say it was June first. That is how these things go. There is a lot of jealousy and envy about the Holy Family trail."

We found out later that the rivalry over this site had become so in-tense that Bishop Agathon of Maghagha had ordered each church to respect the other's claim to the Holy Family by not staging rival reli-gious festivals.

Father Shenuda did not want to talk about that right now. Instead he was focused on the miracles of the well.

"People come here with all kinds of diseases," said the priest. "Chris-tian or non-Christian, it doesn't matter—they are healed when they drink from this water."

"What kind of illnesses do they have?" asked Kees.

"Oh, all kinds," said the priest. "Some have leg problems, someone has had kidney problems, internal problems, eye problems. It doesn't matter. They come here and drink and they are healed."

"Why is this healing water?" I asked.

"Because the Holy Family rested here for four days and drank wa-ter from this well," said Father Shenuda. "Just the presence of Jesus graced it with healing properties."

"What is the most miraculous thing you have seen?" asked Kees.

The priest paused to think a moment.

"One day two men were up there painting, fifteen meters high," he said, pointing up at the towering ceiling of the church. "The platform they were on broke and both of them fell. One of them, the Muslim, was badly hurt. But the Christian had only scratches and he walked away. He was not hurt in the fall because he had just drunk from the well."

"That is quite a miracle," said Kees. "Would it be possible to talk to the Christian who was not hurt?"

"No, I don't think so," he said. "He has moved away to Maghagha and we don't know where he is."

"I see," said Kees, skepticism showing on his face.

By now the deacon had pulled up a metal bucketful of water and was pouring two cups of the miracle water for Kees and me. He walked

Father Shenuda displays an ancient Arabic Bible in the Christian town of Deir al-Garnous.

through the sanctuary, approaching carefully to avoid spilling any. The priest held his hands out to the deacon and took the two plastic cups from his hands. The cups were quite old and looked as though they had been used thousands of times. I tried to look happy at being given the opportunity to drink from the well at the same time as I recalled the number one rule of healthy travel: Don't drink the water. I think that even goes for water that is blessed.

"You must drink it," said Kees, holding his cup at the ready. "It is a gift and it is holy water, so nothing bad would dare swim in it. Come now, you must drink the *baraka* of the well."

When he could see that the cup was not moving toward my mouth, Kees continued his relentless questioning of Father Shenuda.

"People are healed by this water, so it is healthy, correct?" he asked.

"They drink the water, but they are only healed when they believe they are healed," said the priest. "So it is drinking from the water plus faith."

"So there you have it, Paul," said Kees. "If you drink this water and you do not have faith that it is clean, then it will make you sick. But if you drink from the water and have faith, then it will not make you sick."

"But I don't need this water," I said to Kees. "I have no afflictions."

"Are you sure?" asked Kees.

"One can never be sure," I said.

"Then drink this miracle water with faith and you will be sure," he said.

And so I did.

Our next stop was the agricultural village of Ishneen al-Nassara. Although Father Shenuda did not believe the Holy Family visited this area, the Pope's committee did. So that is where we went next.

Here we met Father Yu'annis, the human dynamo who runs the Church of St. George.

Father Yu'annis is a powerfully built man, with a winning smile and a strong handshake. He is a twenty-seventh-generation priest who is bringing up his son, Michael, to be number twenty-eight. In addition to the son, Father Yu'annis and his wife have four beautiful daughters who are the most modern dressers in the village. He has a cell phone that never stops ringing, its "Yellow Rose of Texas" chime going off at all hours. And he has a personality that is demanding yet pleasant at the same time, making it almost impossible to say no to any of his requests, as I would find out soon.

When I got to know him better, I told him that if he lived in America, he would be running a major company. He thought about that for a moment and said, "Take me to America."

I assumed he was kidding, just like I assumed he was kidding when he pulled me from the car in Ishneen and declared me an honorary member of the congregation. The strength of his welcome was so strong and its sweep so broad that I felt as though I had been pulled into a fast river. It wasn't a frightening feeling, though, just an overwhelming one. Kees said it was like "being swept up in grace," which I thought was a good explanation of the feeling.

Father Yu'annis had a deacon escort us into the church compound's guest quarters, five floors of Spartan rooms that serve as a place to stay for travelers of all kind. While there we would encounter soldiers, people returning to Ishneen for funerals, and clergymen from other places.

Guest houses like these represent a safe place for Copts to stay in a land that has been plagued by religious intolerance.

We left our gear in the room and quickly went up to the roof to see Ishneen al-Nassara in the late afternoon light. From our rooftop perch we were in the middle of town. Below us was the twelve-domed church of St. George, a stunning house of worship that is mentioned by Arab historians as far back as the twelfth century. There is a dome for each of the apostles (Judas not included) and a larger dome representing the presence of Jesus.

From our aerial view, the church sat like a jewel surrounded by a setting of brightly painted houses and deep green agricultural fields.

The vista was beautiful, but it was not one we could enjoy for long. Father Yu'annis was standing in the courtyard below us, waving us down. He wanted to take a walk around town before dinner and let his foreign guests meet members of his congregation.

"What is that?" I asked Kees, pointing to a domed circle of pillars with a lighted cross on top.

"That is why you have come," declared Kees, pointing to the strange edifice. "This is the well of the Holy Family that has put this church on the map of the Holy Family trail."

"It looks so new and conspicuous," I said to Father Yu'annis. I told him that I had expected a classic well, like the one I had seen at Mostorod or Tell Basta. This well had been entirely encased in marble and surrounded by the pillars and dome to give it a contemporary look. Over the top of the well was a gate that was locked with a padlock. This was to keep people from getting the miraculous water when they weren't supposed to, said Father Yu'annis.

Father Yu'annis hailed a deacon who was walking by and told him to get the key that would unlock the metal cover. As we waited, Father Yu'annis said proudly that this was the well that the Holy Family drank from as they passed through Ishneen.

"They were running from the soldiers of Herod, who had been sent to kill them," said Father Yu'annis, his face beaming as he told the story. "They stopped here to take a rest when someone told them that there was a well for drinking water nearby. This was that well.

"When they got here the well water was too low for them to reach it by hand. But that was not a problem for Jesus. He ordered the level of the water to rise and it did, all the way to the top. Then they could drink and continue their journey."

Father Yu'annis' version of the journey was different from the official

Coptic one. The Holy Family passed through Ishneen twice, said the priest. The official version has them going through only once. The first time they passed through they did so quickly, with no miracles, said Father Yu'annis. After four days in Deir al-Garnous, they returned again. It was the second time that resulted in the water-raising miracle.

The deacon returned with the key. Father Yu'annis wrestled with the lock for a few moments and then it clicked open. He raised the metal lid to reveal the ancient circular well that I had expected to see to begin with. The old well had simply been encased in the marble. This sort of thing is done frequently in Egypt. Ancient wall paintings are painted over, old churches remodeled, even most holy altars plastered over, all for the sake of modernization. At least this well had only been encased and would still be there if future generations wanted to restore it to its former glory, I thought.

"Because Jesus caused this water to rise, it is now healing water," said Father Yu'annis, filling two cups from the bucket that the deacon had pulled up.

"Oh look, Paul, it's time for more holy water," said Kees.

This time there was little argument. I drank from the cup, as did Kees, putting full faith in the hope that a miracle would keep us from becoming sick.

That evening Kees and I were the guests of honor at the service in the Church of St. George. Father Yu'annis gave a rousing sermon to the more than five hundred parishioners who jammed the pews. The subject of his sermon that night was the connection between the Old and New Testaments. The Copts, like all Christians, believe that there are many references in the Old Testament to the coming of Jesus Christ. Because of that, said Father Yu'annis, the Old and New Testaments are a single unit.

"The Old Testament is the question and the New Testament is the answer," said the priest. "The Bible is like a big palace that is built by many people but designed by only one, and that is God."

As Father Yu'annis spoke in commanding and forceful Arabic, I looked behind me. The women were on the right side of the room, heads covered with scarves. On the left were the men. It was a sight I had come to call the "Egyptian split," the physical segregation of men from women in public places. In some of the churches there were high balconies that were blocked from the sanctuary by wooden screens

Father Yu'annis, the human dynamo of Ishneen al-Nassara, delivers the liturgy in the incense-filled Church of St. George.

with holes in them. These aren't used now, but in the old days, women were required to sit in these balconies to keep from distracting the men. Today women could at least join the men on the same floor.

Father Yu'annis stopped speaking and I turned back around. He was smiling at me and holding his hand out, an indication that Kees and I should come to the podium. Reluctantly we rose and found our way to the side of the charismatic priest.

All eyes were on me as the affable priest put his arm around my shoulders and spoke in rousing Arabic to the congregation.

"He says you are here from America to write a book about the well of Jesus that is here at the church," said Kees. "And he says that you are visiting all of the other sites along the Holy Family trail as well."

I smiled and nodded as he spoke, nervously expecting Father Yu'annis to hand me the microphone to say a few words.

"He says that America has become very interested in the time Jesus spent in Egypt and that you will carry the message of the Holy Family trail back to your country. . . . And then he says—"

The congregation began to applaud as Father Yu'annis clapped

me on the shoulder and began to laugh, his face lit up with mischievous joy.

"What did he say?" I asked.

"He says that you will deliver the sermon in the church Sunday
night," said Kees, laughing out loud. "You must prepare, Saint Paul of
Arizona, because you are now going to become a preacher."

13. Words That Stay with Us

The next afternoon we went to al-Bahnassa and saw what happens when the faithful are not present to keep a site alive.

In ancient times, al-Bahnassa was known as Oxyrhynchus, after a sharp-nosed fish that was once worshiped at this spot. Christian legend has it that the Holy Family stopped to drink water but found the well dry. Pained by his thirst, Jesus began to cry. When his tears hit the ground, the well responded by gushing water for the Holy Child to drink.

The Muslims have attributed at least two stories about the Holy Family to this site. One was recorded by Muhammad al-Baqir, an eighth-century imam of the Shiite branch of Islam. He wrote of Jesus being taken to school in al-Bahnassa when he was nine years old.

> The teacher said to Jesus, "Say the alphabet." Jesus lifted up His head and said, "Dost thou know what these words mean?" The teacher wished to strike Him, but Jesus said, "Do not strike me, but if thou dost not know, ask me and I shall explain to thee." "Speak," said the teacher. "Come down from thy desk," answered Jesus. The teacher came down and Jesus took his place and began to say, "The Alif stand for the good deeds of God, the Da for the glory of God, the Gim for the splendor of God, the Dal for the religion of God, the Ha for

the abyss of Hell, the Wa indicates the misery of those living in Hell, the Ha means the remission of sins of those who ask for forgiveness, the Ka is the word of God which will never change, the Sad is the measure for a measure, and the Ta stands for the serpents of Hell." "Well," said the teacher to the Holy Virgin, "take thy Son and watch over Him, for God hath given to Him wisdom and He doth not need a teacher."

Another eighth-century scholar, Wahib ibn Munabbih, recorded a story that has the baby Jesus using his powers of observation to solve a crime. The Holy Family is staying at a poorhouse in al-Bahnassa that is funded by a *diqhan*, or wealthy man. Mary becomes very upset when a large portion of the kindly *diqhan*'s personal fortune is stolen by thieves. Feeling his mother's pain, the baby Jesus says to her, "Mother, dost thou wish me to show where the *diqhan*'s money is?"

The *diqhan* joined Mary and Jesus as they approached a lame man who was being carried by a blind man. "Arise," said Jesus to the lame man. "This I cannot do," he said. "How then was it possible for you to steal?" asked Jesus.

The *diqhan* beat the blind man until he revealed the stolen fortune. Both men had misused the few talents they had. The blind man used his strength and the lame man his eyes to steal from others.

Documents of early Christianity, including papyri fragments of the Gospel of Thomas, were also found here by Oxford archaeologists who dug through the rubbish pile of al-Bahnassa between 1897 and 1907. Called the Oxyrhynchus Papyri, this material is still being reconstructed and translated.

✠

With material like this found there, I expected al-Bahnassa to be a richly preserved site. But it wasn't. Where there were said to be 365 churches as early as the fourth century in this town, inhabited by ten thousand monks and twenty thousand virgins, there was practically nothing now. The Muslim conquest, followed by the rapid decline of the Egyptian Christian population, led to the disappearance by destruction or neglect of all the ancient Christian churches in this place. All that remains is the ruins of a sixth- or seventh-century monastery and that was found only when Muslims were digging a grave and happened to poke into the buried roof.

"It is right over there," Kees told the driver of the car we had hired in Ishneen al-Nassara. He parked the car on a side street and we began walking up the rutted road toward an enormous pile of dirt that looked like it belonged in a gravel pit. With us was a deacon from the Coptic church of Sandafa, a neighboring village.

At the top of this dirt mound we could look down into a pit where workmen had dug deep to clear dirt from around a massive stone building. Although much of the structure was still buried, what I could see appeared to be the basement of a much larger building. There was a labyrinth of rooms with vaulted ceilings. If this basement was any indication, the structure that once stood above it must have been magnificent.

"Ah, the lost glory of the Holy Family trail," said Kees. "Christians have tried to protect it but it hasn't happened. Holy sites only flourish in a flourishing Christian community."

Unpacking my camera, I kneeled down to take a picture that would have included the ruins in the foreground and the Muslim cemetery in the background. But before I could get my gear turned on, a man came out of a tiny stone house, waving his arms and shouting, "No pictures, please! No pictures, please!"

The man stood in front of us and put his hands on his hips.

"You must buy a ticket before you look," he said. "And then you can still not take pictures."

"Why?" demanded Kees.

"Because this area is not ready to be photographed," said the man, who eventually introduced himself to us as Ahmed Abdel Gawg, the site archaeologist. "It is what I have been told to do."

We paid the few Egyptian pounds that were required of us and walked around the rim of the site. In between constant reminders to not take photos, Gawg told us that this area had once been a *patrium*, a residence for monks. He pointed out tiny rooms or cells that the monks had lived in and took us to what he described as an industrial area.

"Here they made things like baskets for sale to the public so they could support the church," said Gawg.

"What was here?" I asked, pointing to the area aboveground where nothing now stood.

"That was a church," said Gawg. "And when it went away this whole area became a graveyard. It started over there and eventually they were burying bodies over here. That is why this site was found. Someone dug a grave and found this church."

" 'Muslim Gravedigger Finds Christian Site,' " quipped Kees. "Now there's a headline for you."

Gawg said that clay tablets from the Christian era had been found but "no proof" that there were once 365 churches here—one for each day of the year—as Christians have claimed.

"Oh, certainly you believe that there were three hundred sixty-five churches here," declared Kees playfully. "All of the books say it is so."

"There is no proof," insisted the archaeologist.

"Of course there is," said the deacon, stepping into the argument. "It is written in Church documents that there is a church for each day here in al-Bahnassa."

"And I suppose that next you are going to tell us that the Holy Family did not pass through al-Bahnassa," said Kees.

"I cannot tell you that they did," said the archaeologist seriously, failing to catch the playfulness in Kees' voice. "We have no proof, no certainty, that the Holy Family came through here."

The deacon was stunned by this declaration.

"Certainly you accept that the Holy Family came through al-Bahnassa," he demanded. "It has always been told that they did."

"Perhaps, but we have no certainty that the Holy Family was here," maintained the archaeologist.

"What would convince you?" asked Kees.

"It would take evidence. Archaeological, perhaps. Or historical documents. You find stories of Jesus being here that are written after the Islamic conquest of Egypt, but not before. We would need evidence from before."

"Have you not found any?" asked Kees, a mischievous smile on his face.

"We have found clay tablets from the Christian era, but no stories of Jesus being here," said the archaeologist. "I am sorry."

The deacon and the archaeologist continued to argue as Kees and I walked away.

"This kind of thing happens even here," said Kees. "Science and religion argue about the past. Get out your camera. While they are arguing you can sneak some photos."

Kees told the deacon we were leaving and we all started back for the car.

"I am sorry to have interrupted your conversation," Kees said to

the deacon, who appeared to be still riled by his argument with the archaeologist. "We could have stayed here a while longer, but we need to
get Paul back to Ishneen so he can prepare for his sermon tomorrow.
His time to speak will come very quickly, as all good things do."

Kees knew I was nervous about my pastoral debut. I had never delivered a sermon before and on only a few occasions had spoken before
more than five hundred people. I readily admitted that I was frightened, but Kees did his best to put my mind at ease.

"Don't worry about it," he said. "You are an American, so they
don't expect much. And if anything wrong comes out of your mouth,
you can blame it on the interpreter."

That slight comfort was all I was going to get from Kees. We rode
back to the church compound at Ishneen, where Father Yu'annis was
anxiously awaiting our arrival. He had an active evening planned, he
said, and he wanted to make sure we were well fed.

"Tell him I want to take dinner in my room," I begged Kees. "I
need to work on my sermon."

"Nonsense, Paul," said Kees. "He wants to have a meal with you.
And besides, this will be your chance to talk about the Holy Family's
visit to Ishneen."

In the priest's dining room, trays were set up and the lights were
turned off to discourage flies from coming into the room. Father Yu'annis'
daughters brought in heaping plates of vegetarian fare, including falafel, brown beans, and a tasty flatbread. Father Yu'annis assured me that
we would be dining on meat if it weren't for the fact that we were
here in the middle of the seven weeks of fasting leading up to Coptic
Easter.

"We can eat no meat or dairy during this period," said Father
Yu'annis. "It is out of respect for Jesus that we do this."

"It is out of respect for Jesus that you do everything," said Kees.
"But you show special respect to Jesus on August twenty-second, isn't
that right?"

"That is true," said Father Yu'annis, his eyes bright with excite-
ment. "August twenty-second is the anniversary of the day that the
Holy Family came through Ishneen."

"What did they do when they passed through here?" I asked.

"Jesus caused a miracle," said Father Yu'annis. "They got to this
well and planned to drink from it. But the water was very deep and
they could not reach it. So Jesus passed his hand over the top of the
well and the water rose to a level from which they could drink it."

"How is it that you know this is the day they came through?" asked Kees.

"Because it is on that day that the water rises every year," said the priest. "Every year on August twenty-second the water rises at four in the afternoon. It does not do this for the other wells in this area, only the one here at Ishneen. That is why it is a miracle and why we celebrate the passing of the Holy Family through here."

Kees clearly was skeptical about this legend, because he next presented a tricky question to Father Yu'annis.

"A few years ago Egypt went on Daylight Savings Time. That means what was four o'clock before that time is now five o'clock. Does the well still rise at four like it used to?" asked Kees.

Father Yu'annis said nothing for a while as he ate. Then he slowly nodded.

"The rising of the well is a miracle," he said.

"So at four o'clock on August twenty-second it rises?" reiterated Kees.

"Yes, it does," said the priest. "Two years ago they came from Egyptian television to film this miracle and at exactly four o'clock it rose. It was on TV."

I could tell that Kees still had his doubts. So did I. The likelihood of this happening seemed slim to me, but Father Yu'annis insisted that it was true.

"People come from all over the country to see this," he said. "And they come to drink the miraculous water. It is miraculous because if they believe, then they are healed of their sickness or their problems are solved."

"So they have to believe for the healing to take place?" asked Kees.

"It helps," said Father Yu'annis.

To both Kees and me this seemed an example of faith healing. When we mentioned this to Father Yu'annis, he merely shrugged.

"There is nothing wrong with being healed by faith," he said.

We ate in silence for a while and then Kees bore in again, obsessed with the notion that the well could rise like clockwork at 4 P.M. every August 22.

"You come from a line of twenty-seven priests," declared Kees. "Did any of them ever say that the well did not rise at exactly four o'clock on that date?"

"I don't think so, but I did not know all of them," said the priest.

"How about your father?" asked the persistent Dutchman. "Did he ever not see it rise at four in the afternoon on August twenty-second?"

"No," said Father Yu'annis, smiling broadly at the interrogation. "Not one time did the water not rise at four in the afternoon."

We spent another evening in church and then at least an hour afterward talking with the townspeople about life outside of Egypt. They were all curious, especially about the United States. It seemed as though everyone had a cousin or uncle in America or knew someone who had emigrated there, and everyone wanted to hear about the way we live.

Most curious were the young people, especially those who had recently graduated from college and were now trying to find jobs in a country that had none. All of them crowded around me, asking if it was true that jobs are easy to find in America. Most were living with their parents, as they had in the years before they went to college. Now that they were educated, they wanted to know how they could leave Egypt to find a better life.

These conversations conveyed a certain amount of desperation and were painful to participate in. I was happy when Father Yu'annis waded into the crowd and led me to his house.

"When everyone leaves, we will take my car and go visit my brother and father," he said.

Soon Father Yu'annis brought his car out of the garage, a 1980s Mercedes 200 sedan. It was late at night and I was openly nervous about the drive to the next town. Over the past decade there has been considerable violence against Christians in this part of Egypt. Several have even been killed for religious reasons. Even though political unrest has lessened considerably since President Mubarak's declaration of war against violent Islamic fundamentalism, I was nervous about riding through darkened villages at night with a Coptic priest.

"Aren't you concerned about driving so late?" I asked Father Yu'annis before we got into the car.

"Not at all," he said, reaching beneath his heavy garment and pulling out a semiautomatic pistol. "I can handle almost anything myself with this."

"Now there's a realist," said Kees, climbing into the car.

I was still nervous, but for Father Yu'annis this time.

"If you get caught with that, you'll go to jail," I said.

"No problem," he insisted. Reaching into a pocket, he pulled out a concealed-weapon permit. "The chief of police takes good care of me. Let's go."

Night driving through a village such as Ishneen is a study in automobile durability. Deep ruts crossed the dirt roads, their bottoms disappearing in shadows. The priest drove slowly around them but had to be careful of the massive stones and blocks that dotted the roadside. Although his father's house was only a few miles away, it would take us nearly an hour to get there.

But it was worth the trip. Number twenty-six, as I called him—because he was a twenty-sixth-generation priest—was a commanding presence even at the age of eighty. He was slim and tall and wore a long beard that went to his upper chest and was gray with age. His eyes were clear and took it all in. As we came up the stairs he checked us out like a man accustomed to reading a person's story in his walk or mannerisms. He had acquired this talent in a lifetime of priesthood.

Number twenty-six lived in a prosperous three-story townhouse. On the first floor lived one of his other sons, a deacon in the local church, which was the parish of another son, Father Mikhael, who also joined us. Number twenty-six lived on the second floor. On the third floor—the roof, actually—was an entire barnyard of animals, including goats, chickens, rabbits, and turkeys grand enough for a major Thanksgiving dinner.

Kees and I were invited into the living room, where we sat quietly with the priests and watched television. On the screen the men and women of the World Wrestling Federation duked it out on a stage somewhere in the American South. Frankly, I was embarrassed to be watching this display of my own culture. I drank a nonalcoholic beer called Birell and watched silently as the three priests devoted rapt attention to the worst American TV has to offer. *What you are watching does not represent my country,* I wanted to say to them. In retrospect I really don't think they cared. The specter of giants fighting is entertainment in any country and apparently to any group, including Coptic clergymen.

Before long Number twenty-six tired of wrestling and flipped the channels to an interview in progress between an Egyptian TV newswoman and Pope Shenouda III, the reigning patriarch of the Coptic Orthodox Church.

We tuned in just as the brilliant seventy-nine-year-old pope was addressing the importance of Egypt to Christians worldwide.

"Even Pope John Paul of the Catholic Church says that Egypt is an important Christian center," said Pope Shenouda. Quoting his Catholic counterpart, he said, " 'I believe Egypt is a holy land for a number of reasons. Number one of these reasons is that the Holy Family visited Egypt.' "

This proclamation led to a rousing response from the three clergymen, the type of response I would have expected from them during the wrestling match.

"That is why you are here," said Father Yu'annis. "You are here because the Holy Family's voyage is important even to Christians outside of Egypt."

I agreed and the three priests began talking to one another rapidly. Suddenly I realized that Number twenty-six was addressing me.

"He is asking you if you are prepared to speak at church tomorrow," said Kees, interpreting.

I sighed heavily and shook my head. The three priests laughed.

"He is making a suggestion," said Kees, listening and interpreting. "He says that you should speak about love. He says that there is not enough love in the world right now and that everyone needs to remember the words of St. Paul the apostle."

I immediately took note of his recommendation in my notebook. This was professional advice and I didn't want to forget it.

"Yes," said Father Yu'annis, aka Number twenty-seven. "Tell people how we are all the same. Tell them how love is important in small communities like ours and how it is important in the world."

"And tell them how there are many different types of love," said his brother.

I wrote down all of this advice so I would remember it. The three holy men had given me a place to start. Now all I had to do was build a framework around it.

⁜

The next afternoon I began working in earnest on my sermon. By now I was horrified at the thought of standing before five hundred people while expressing my thoughts on anything religious. Although my father had been an ordained Baptist minister, there was nothing in my past to make me think that his talents had been passed on to me. Although the sins of the father are said to be visited on the son, I had never heard it implied that the same could be said for talents.

Still, there was nowhere to hide, so I prepared. As the sun dropped and the shadow of the steeple grew longer, I faced the fact that I was making my pastoral debut today, like it or not.

And then something happened. Shortly before sundown the church bell rang three times and people began streaming into the church. Thinking it was my time to speak, I left my room and crossed the courtyard just in time to fall in line behind a group of wailing men carrying a coffin on their shoulders.

"What has happened?" Kees asked Father Yu'annis.

"Mr. Marcos has died," said the priest, his face a picture of sadness. "He was a deacon and was sick for some time. We must bury him now."

The tradition in the Middle East is to bury the deceased before sundown on the day of death. For Father Yu'annis that meant a race with the late afternoon sun. Expertly he purified the sanctuary with a thick cloud of incense and then delivered an impassioned sermon. The family wailed over the loss of its patriarch, genuine in its grief.

At the end of the sermon the entire congregation stood and streamed out. Outside we followed the coffin, which was borne to the graveyard on the shoulders of the deceased's sons. Around us swirled a river of women dressed in black. They were wailing like the men, some of them waving to the coffin, which was held above the crowd.

As the procession reached the graveyard, the women turned away and went into the house of the deceased to comfort the widow. Burying a man is men's business in Egypt. There were no women to watch as his coffin was slid into the aboveground tomb and its door closed and locked forever.

It was dark now as we walked slowly and somberly back to town.

Amidst the weeping men, Kees and I said little. I had never seen a faster funeral, nor had I seen one so intensely emotional. For the next three days the male members of the Marcos family would sit in a room at the church and receive condolences while the women did the same at the family home.

"Are you ready?" said Father Yu'annis, putting his arm around me as we walked back to the church.

"I thought the funeral would take the place of the evening sermon," I said hopefully.

"You are not getting off that easily," said Kees. "You are tonight's main attraction."

With a talented young interpreter named Mena Girgis Hanna at my side, I delivered a one-hour sermon on love and understanding, just as my priestly advisers had recommended.

Not much of what I said to the congregation is relevant to this book. But in looking back at my notes I realize that I delivered one pearl of wisdom that summed up the reason I had come so far to examine

The author delivers his unexpected debut sermon, helped by local translator Mena Girgis Hanna.

a voyage that was an intriguing web of myth, magic, and reality. It had to do with the power of both words and stories.

"Many billions of words are written and spoken every day," I said at the start of my sermon to the farm families of Ishneen. "We talk, talk, talk, and the words go out into the air and evaporate, disappear like a chicken's squawk or a dog's bark.

"The same is true of writing. Billions of words are written each day. We write letters, books, stories of our lives, and these writings disappear, never to be read again.

"But some words—written or spoken—touch us so deeply that they stay with mankind forever. They become the stories we live by, the gospels that rule our lives."

I was talking about the Bible, and most specifically the words that St. Paul the apostle wrote about love in 1 Corinthians 13, which reads:

Love is patient; love is kind and envies no one.
Love is never boastful, nor conceited, nor rude; never selfish,
    not quick to take offense.
Love keeps no score of wrongs, does not gloat over another's
    sins, but delights in the truth.
There is nothing love cannot face; there is no limit to its faith,
    its hope, and its endurance.
In a word, there are three things that last forever: faith, hope,
    and love, but the greatest of them all is love.

Looking back, I could easily have been referring to the words and stories that Egyptians live by in their beliefs about Jesus in Egypt.

"How is it that these stories have continued to survive in Egypt?" I asked Father Yu'annis later that night, when my debut sermon was long over.

"They have survived because they are true, and because people need all of the stories they can have about the Savior," said the priest. "Can you imagine what a wonderful thing it is for Christians in this village to know that the Holy Family came here and drank from their water? It makes them much closer to God."

"Do you believe that all of the stories about the Holy Family in Egypt are historically true?" Kees asked Father Yu'annis.

"Stories do change over time," said the priest. "But the message has remained the same in all of the stories. The people need these stories for their faith. If they are the written word, that is fine, but if they are the spoken word, that is just as good. These stories are very, very old and have been told many times. But the people need these stories for their faith, so the hearts of the stories do not change. They keep our beliefs alive."

⚜

One of Coptic Christianity's most important stories about Jesus was not ancient at all. It had been first put on paper by an international authority on Coptic Christianity in the early 1960s. It was made famous when it was delivered as part of a sermon before a congregation of Christians in the United States. From there it made its way around the world to become an important morality tale for the Christians of Egypt.

The story in question involves a meeting between St. Bishoi, a late-fourth-century ascetic, and Jesus Christ. Known by some as simply "St. Bishoi carries Jesus," the story is not known to have existed in Egyptian Christian lore until the noted historian (and theologian) Otto Meinardus recorded it. Now it has become one of the most often told parables in Coptic Christianity. It even exists as icons in many churches.

The new story is a variation of an old one. In the original story, St. Bishoi washes the feet of a sickly-looking person (in some versions he is a monk) who passes by his cave. The man turns out to be Jesus, who praises Bishoi for this act of kindness that none of the other monks in the area would extend to him. Otto Meinardus expanded this ancient story:

> Jesus then told Bishoi that he would return the next day to a nearby mountaintop. With a blessing, the monk who was really Jesus ascended into heaven.
>
> A short time later, several monks passed by Bishoi's cave. He told them what had happened but none of them believed what he said.
>
> "Drink this water," he commanded them. "It is water used to wash the feet of Jesus."
>
> They all refused, and when they did the water disappeared.
>
> Bishoi told them that Jesus would appear on the nearby mountaintop the next day.
>
> Word spread, and the next day all of the monks were hurrying up the path of the mountain so they could spend time with the Lord. As Bishoi hurried up the mountain he saw an elderly and frail man sitting by the path. The old man implored each passing monk to help him make the climb to see Jesus. He received no response, since each of the monks was thinking only of his own grace and not that of anyone else.
>
> As Bishoi passed the elderly man asked him for help. Without hesitation, Bishoi hoisted the elderly man onto his back and continued to climb. Soon Bishoi fell far behind his fellow

monks and the man on his back seemed to increase in weight so much that Bishoi could not move. He gently put the man down on the ground and turned to speak to him. He found himself gazing into the face of Jesus Christ.

Bishoi was blessed that day. While his fellow monks waited on the mountaintop for Jesus, Bishoi had a long and satisfying conversation with Him down below.

As the sun began to fade and the monks started to trickle down the path, Jesus arose and asked Bishoi to remind the other monks to remember the needy. "When they help the needy, they help me," he told Bishoi before once again ascending to heaven.

The other monks wept when they discovered that they had missed the opportunity to help their Savior. But they had learned an important lesson about submission the hard way.

I had heard this story from at least two priests and one bishop, including Bishop Marcos of Shubra el-Kheima, who confirmed that the story was not known to monks in Egypt until they read it in Meinardus' book on monks and monasteries.

Personally, I have found this to be one of the more inspirational of the saint stories. I had a difficult time believing that such a respected scholar as Otto Meinardus had created the story and then accidentally let it slip into the tradition of Coptic tales about saints. But it was true. I was able to telephone him at his home in Ellerau, near Hamburg, Germany, where he confirmed that he had preached the story on October 21, 1962, at Washington National Cathedral in Washington, D.C., and "from there it went on."

"That's how oral tradition is," said Meinardus. "Once a story leaves someone's mouth, it spreads like wildfire."

It's not as though Meinardus made up a story that wasn't true. It was that he created a story to make a *truth* even *truer*. The fact that his story is now a proud part of the Coptic culture is a sign of just how true it is.

14. Stairway to Heaven

In the morning, government security police met us at the front gate of the church. There were two pickup trucks full of them, officers in the cab with the drivers, ordinary soldiers in the back. The soldiers waited patiently as we said our goodbyes to Father Yu'annis and his family. They slung their Egyptian-made AK-47 rifles over their shoulders and smoked cigarettes and talked. The officers were a little more edgy. They rested their hands on the tops of their holstered 9-mm pistols and paced in front of the car, chatting to one another and looking at their watches as though they had a train to catch.

Father Yu'annis told them to wait a few minutes and took us into the church for one last visit. He wanted to make sure that we saw the relics contained in the glass cases—fragments of the holy bones of St. George, Father Mikhael El-Behery, and the children massacred by Herod in his fruitless attempt to murder the child Jesus. These revered body parts are divided among several churches, so it is common to see relics of the same saints or martyrs in several churches.

"Half a century ago, the foundation and walls of this church began to crack," said Father Yu'annis, opening a relic case and bringing out the bolster that held the bones of St. George. "There were plans to tear down the church and build a new one because they did not want it to crumble. But a parishioner had a dream of St. George. He came to the parishioner and said, 'I do not want to leave my home.' After that it was decided that the church should simply be restored."

"That was a decisive vision," said Kees.

"Yes, such visions are good because no one has to make decisions," said Father Yu'annis. "They are made for you."

We talked for a few minutes more but it was obvious that the security police wanted us to get going to our next destination. They were already surprised by the fact that we had arrived here from Cairo undetected by the undercover police. When the guard at the church in Ishneen reported that we were staying there, the police telephoned Father Yu'annis a number of times asking how we had arrived without their knowledge.

Father Yu'annis convinced them that we were safe in his village, where there were a number of armed guards protecting the church at all times. But now that we were about to leave the protection of the village, police would be around us like a cocoon. It was not pleasant, but there was nothing we could do about it.

We said our goodbyes to Father Yu'annis and his family and got into our hired car, an Italian/Turkish Shalin that was driven by a Copt from Maghagha. Father Yu'annis walked behind the car for a short distance as we made our way slowly through the narrow dirt streets of Ishneen. The police honked their horns at virtually everything, including dogs, donkeys, old women in doorways, and chickens. I looked behind us to see Father Yu'annis waving and smiling as he talked on his cell phone. Then he disappeared in a cloud of dust.

"We are stuck with the police but it's better than it used to be," said Kees, relaxing into the well-used car seat. "Just a few years ago they came to pick you up in armored personnel carriers when visiting Mallawi."

I jokingly said that the area we were going into should be named "the gateway to Fundy Land," but Kees said that the signs would be ripped down. Religious fundamentalism in this part of the country has been devastating to everyone concerned. No one wants to remember the days of fighting that took place between government forces and extremist groups such as Islamic Jihad and Gama'at al-Islamiya.

"Further south beyond Minya they took whatever they wanted and most of the time they took it from the Copts," said Kees. "They ran parts of Upper Egypt like the Mafia until President Mubarak got tired of them."

When he got tired of them, reprisals were swift, massive, and deadly. Security forces from other parts of Egypt occupied places like Samalout,

Minya, Mallawi, and Assiut, towns where we would be staying in the days to come. Armed soldiers were assigned to these areas from other parts of the country. They traveled in armored personnel carriers and fought pitched battles with armed fundamentalists. More than fifteen hundred people were killed between 1992 and 1997. Then things became even worse. A group from Egyptian Islamic Jihad murdered fifty-eight tourists—most of them Swiss—in Luxor and returned to their base of operations in Fundy Land.

Over the next four years, security forces arrested hundreds of people, while judges used emergency detention laws to jail hundreds of people for indefinite periods of time. Battles were fought in the countryside, cities, even mosques, and because of them the political climate has changed rapidly for the better.

Now it is relatively safe to drive past the cotton fields we were now passing and not have to worry about being shot at, or walk down a city street and not be physically attacked for being a Christian or a foreigner. But just being "relatively safe" isn't good enough for a modern Egypt that is trying to prevent religious extremists from taking over. So the government now regulates mosques, at least to the best of its ability. And it still controls much of Upper Egypt with a force that is observant and responsive. Many people think that all of the terrorists in Upper Egypt have been killed, jailed, or exiled to places outside of the country. But the government is taking no chances, according to Kees.

"That's why we have to have the police with us all day," he said.

Security forces may be a value to the safety of a region, but the police can be a hazard on the highway. They speed, pass illegally, and sometimes run other cars off the road. At one point they were driving too recklessly for our driver to keep up. When that happened they stopped and one of the officers came back to our car and lectured him.

"Whatever traffic violation I make, you do the same," he scolded. "Don't worry. You will not be ticketed. You are with us."

We were with them until we saw the cliffside church known as Gabal al-Tair, or "mountain of the birds." The setting was so perfect that I only remember looking across the green fields of sugarcane and up the steep white cliff at the church and village that seemed to be carved right out of the rock.

It was afternoon, and the city on the hill was bathed in sun, its limestone surface both reflecting and absorbing light so that it glowed with a radiance that seemed to emanate from within. I could see why. After the monastery of al-Muharraq, where the Holy Family was actually thought to have lived for six months, this church was considered the most important spot on the Holy Family trail. In looks alone it was spectacular. But I was wrong to think that the beauty of the spot had anything to do with its religious importance. This was the spot, said Kees, where Jesus left his handprint in stone.

"When the Holy Family came to Gabal al-Tair they arrived by boat," said Kees. "As they pulled close to shore, a large rock dislodged from the cliff and threatened to fall on them. Everyone on the boat was quite frightened, except Jesus. He stood and put his hand against the huge rock and caused it to rejoin with the rocks of the cliff so it would not fall down. When he did this, his handprint was left in the stone."

"So this represents archaeological proof of Jesus actually having been to Egypt," I said, half seriously.

"I suppose it could, if you believe the oral tradition it came from," said Kees. "Of course there is no way of examining the stone, because it is no longer here."

"Why not?" I asked.

"Because like all good Egyptian artifacts, this too has been stolen, and by whom we don't know."

Some accounts link the disappearance of the handprint stone to Almeric, the twelfth-century king of Jerusalem who took many Holy Family relics. Another account has the sacred stone still buried in the silt beneath the Nile. The most likely story, according to a local priest, is that the British took the stone sometime during the first half of the twentieth century, when they occupied Egypt. Some relic hunters have reported that this holy stone is in the British Museum. But Kees had a person in England query the noted museum, which denied having the stone in its collection.

"Whoever has it, they came, saw, conquered, and stole," said Kees. "It has always been like that here, so why should it be any different with the handprint of Jesus?"

We stopped at the base of the stairway that would take us to the church, 166 steps carved up the mountain by Egyptian masons. But before we started the climb, Kees had an archaeological mission of his own. He was going to see if he could buy Shagaret al-Abid, the worshiping tree of Gabal al-Tair.

A wealthy Cairo businessman, Mounir Ghabbour, had asked Kees to purchase the remainder of the tree so it could be protected, perhaps housed in a museum with other religious relics.

"There it is," he said, leaving the car and striding to the trunk of an acacia tree that had obviously been felled some time ago. "That is Shagaret al-Abid."

As the police milled around their trucks, puzzling as to why we had stopped here, Kees told me the story of the tree. After Jesus prevented the rock from falling on his boat, oral tradition has it that the Holy Family put ashore only to find themselves walking into the midst of a pharaonic temple. Recognizing the divinity of Jesus, the stone idols fell to the ground and broke as the Holy Family passed through. Upset by the destruction of the temple that their presence had caused, the Holy Family ran up the mountain. As Jesus touched the mountain it opened, revealing a pathway to a cave. There, oral tradition says, the Holy Family found refuge for three days.

When they came back down the mountain to resume their journey up the Nile, legend says that the acacia tree bowed to Jesus as he passed.

The story of Shagaret al-Abid was considered oral tradition until about twenty years ago, when Bishop Samuel (at that time a monk) visited Gabal al-Tair and identified this particular acacia tree as the one that had bowed to Jesus. This created a new site for Christian tourists, who came to see the noted tree, whose branches did indeed bow to the ground. Bishop Samuel then asked Bishop Marcos' Holy Family Map Committee to list the tree as an official Holy Family site. The committee added the tree to its list and it became part of a photo book put out by the Ministry of Tourism to promote Holy Family pilgrimage to Egypt.

This was not good news for the squatter who lived on the site. With official attention being drawn to the tree, he now risked the loss of his house and the land he had been illegally farming.

Then everything changed for the squatter's advantage. Sometime in the middle of the night the tree was chopped down and its roots completely dug up so that nothing could ever grow back.

The destruction of Shagaret al-Abid became an international scandal. Some people claimed that it represented a major religious theft. Others declared that it was a further example of the antagonism that still existed between Christians and Muslims. But Kees said it was neither.

"The problem was a simple one," said Kees. "That guy right there didn't want to lose any land to a tourist attraction, so he cut down the tree."

"That guy," the one Kees was referring to, was standing about twenty feet from us, selling oranges from his grove at a roadside stand. Kees waved to the man, whom he had shared tea with, and went over to him and began speaking in Arabic.

I went to the butchered acacia to see the damage. It had a long trunk, maybe twenty feet in length, that was doubled over like a man bowing low. Both of its ends had been burned and there was no sign of a stump.

"I got it," said Kees, beaming with a sense of conquest. "I bought the tree from him for a hundred Egyptian pounds. It was a good deal for him. He doesn't make that much in a month."

The squatter seemed very happy to get rid of the dead tree. It had been bad luck for him but now his luck had changed. He smiled and waved at us. When business got slow he came over to us and gave us two oranges, free of charge.

"He is very happy with this deal," I said to Kees.

"He should be," said Kees. "It is better to get something for these remains than nothing at all."

Kees pulled out his cell phone and placed a call to the businessman. Ghabbour was as delighted as Kees, who felt as though he had worked a good deal and accomplished a good deed, both at the same time. For the mere price of a hundred Egyptian pounds, he had purchased an important Holy Family relic, which would now be preserved in a museum, where it would be appreciated by the faithful. If it stayed here much longer, the bowing tree would become firewood or termite fodder.

However, when Kees returned to the site with a pickup truck a few months later, the man told him he could not surrender the fallen relic without a permit from the Egyptian Antiquities Organization. The tree lies there still.

✛

With the tree expedition behind us, we got on with the business at hand, climbing the 166 stairs to Gabal al-Tair. With green fields of plenty and the Nile below us, blue sky and church steeple above, this was indeed a stairway to heaven.

"At the top you will see a sign on the church that says this was built in the fourth century by Queen Helena, the mother of Constantine," said Kees. "Some archaeologists believe it was built in the sixth century, but no one knows for sure, since many churches have been built on top of older churches and have left no trace. They also say there is no evidence that Queen Helena ever came to Egypt, but many churches are attributed to her anyway."

The church itself is somewhat of an optical illusion. The block walls and steeple make it appear as though it is built aboveground, but once you are inside it is clear that the church is hewn from the mountain. Twelve pillars that have been carved from rock support the roof, benches of stone line the walls, and a thin red carpet covers the stone floor. At the rear of the church is a small crypt that is no larger than a good-sized broom closet. Occupying most of the space inside is an icon of Jesus and Mary with a shelf in front for votive candles.

It is in this pocket cave, said Father Matta, that the Holy Family stayed in Gabal al-Tair. He took us on a quick tour of the church and then settled down on one of the stone steps leading to the altar. It was a quiet day in the Church of the Holy Virgin and Father Matta was relaxed. This was the off-season in Gabal al-Tair. In June, thousands of pilgrims visit the church to celebrate the arrival of the Holy Family in Egypt. At the end of August, nearly as many pilgrims visit the church to celebrate the Feast of the Assumption of the Holy Virgin, who is thought to have ascended to heaven from here on the twenty-second of that month. These months can be chaos, said Father Matta. But now there was just the normal load of people coming to ask for the ordinary miracles that prayer could grant them.

"People come here from all over Egypt to pray," said Father Matta. "They might have specific problems with their father or mother or in their marriage. Or they might even be looking for a marriage partner. Anything personal that people need help with will bring them here.

"People come here with problems and I pray with them. Then they come back later, maybe months later, and their problems have been solved," said Father Matta. "In some places Jesus works instantly, like a flash of light. Here the problems are solved over time, but they are miracles just the same."

Father Matta was a pleasant man with a giggle that came at odd times, as though he was privy to secret jokes that were being whispered in his ear. The jokes stopped when Kees mentioned the bowing tree.

That tree had caused him considerable pain, Father Matta said. And the final resolution had been no way to treat a religious relic. The Christians had hoped for some kind of legal solution to the tree incident. Punishment for the guilty party would not have been asking too much, although the government did demolish a building that was erected on the site of the tree by squatters. Nor, for that matter, would enshrinement of the remains of the destroyed tree be out of the question. But none of that would happen now, said Father Matta. A loophole had been found by the competition.

"The Muslims declared that this tree was not bowing to Jesus, as Christian tradition says, but to Muhammad the Worshiper, a noted local follower of Islam. The local government says that since it is a Muslim site, Christians have no claim or anything to worry about."

A light came into Kees' eyes that seemed less than angelic.

"What if I can get the tree for you?" asked Kees.

"This could bring trouble because it is something we want to forget," said Father Matta. It would be better, the priest implied, to let bygones be bygones and forget about possession of the tree itself. Perhaps just the stories themselves would be sufficient to sustain the image of nature bowing to the child Jesus.

"Perhaps it is best that this tree goes to Cairo," said Kees as we left the church. "It is too controversial to bring the remains to the church at Gabal al-Tair."

⳨

We left Gabal al-Tair with a question that Father Matta could not answer. Who was it that identified the handprint on the rock as being that of the young Jesus? We knew that the story had been handed down orally from generation to generation. But a relic, especially one so important as the handprint of Jesus, has to be approved by the Church. Who had done that? And how was it done?

We asked these questions of Father Matta but he did not feel it was his place to answer them. Some questions are too important for priests to answer, he said. When those questions come up, he refers the questioner to a bishop for resolution.

"Maybe you should ask Bishop Paphnutius," said Father Matta. "He will certainly know the answers."

And so we did.

We got back into the hired Shalin and caravaned to Samalout accompanied by the police. Samalout is a town of about two hundred thousand that relies heavily upon agriculture and its stone quarries. It used to host a considerable number of tourists, but that was in the days before this area became known as Fundy Land. Now it looks tired and tough, its streets pockmarked from lack of repair and its buildings in need of a face-lift, which makes the bishopric of Samalout stand out even more.

Near the center of town is the area known as "the home of the five-star bishop." A medical doctor and a gourmet, Bishop Paphnutius has combined his three loves into a stunning compound that contains the most modern hospital in the Samalout region, a church, and a five-star restaurant on the ground floor of a European-style hotel and residence. There is even a grocery store around the corner that could easily occupy a spot on Madison Avenue.

We spent the night in one of guest rooms and met with Bishop Paphnutius in the morning in his office. A very elegant man, the bishop has a mission that he describes as "serving the public by building hospitals and schools and making life better for the people." In the future, he said, he plans to build a miniature version of the Holy Family trail next to the church on Gabal al-Tair. It will be inside a large building and will consist primarily of panoramas, like those found in a natural history museum. He wants to do this so people can visit all of the sites covered by the Holy Family, from the dream of Joseph that ordered him to flee King Herod and go to Egypt to the dream in Deir al-Muharraq that allowed the Family to return home again. This museum, he said, would allow people to follow in the steps of the Holy Family without ever leaving the building.

"Our Lord Jesus could have crushed King Herod and finished him, but he did not for two reasons," declared the bishop. "He escaped from him the human way to show us all how to escape from evil. The other reason he came was to bless Egypt by fulfilling the Old Testament prophecy from Isaiah, chapter nineteen, verse twenty-five, which says, 'Blessed be Egypt my people.' We suppose that this prophecy and the Holy Family trail are two of the most important reasons there is still Christianity in Egypt. We have suffered much in Egypt. But if you enter a church on Sunday you will find it full of people praying and paying good spiritual attention."

The Holy Family trail gives the faithful more faith, said the bishop.

"In every place that he went through in Egypt, we feel in our hearts the blessing of the Lord. If his foot touched there and his hand touched that—the faithful love these places because they feel blessed."

"I am glad you mentioned these special sites because we have a question about one of them," said Kees. "We would like to talk to you about the handprint of Jesus at Gabal al-Tair."

"Yes, that is one of our most holy objects," said the bishop. "Unfortunately it is missing."

"So we hear," said Kees. "But that is not what we want to talk about. We want to ask you how it is known that this was truly the handprint of Jesus."

"I see," said Bishop Paphnutius. "As you know, the story must have originated with people who saw Jesus prevent the rock from falling. Then when they were able to see his handprint on the rock, they told the story of what they saw."

"Yes, but isn't there more to it than that?" asked Kees.

Bishop Paphnutius explained that in the year 383 C.E., Pope Theophilus visited the monastery at Gabal al-Tair. In those days the monastery was known in some accounts as Deir el-Bakara, or "monastery of the pulley," because visitors were hoisted to the top of the mountain by means of a pulley. He had heard about the handprint of Jesus and had been asked to determine its authenticity.

Most likely he was hoisted to the top of the cliff by nervous monks (no one wants to be responsible for dropping a pope from a mountain) and was presented with the stone for his examination. At this moment, said Bishop Paphnutius, something miraculous took place.

"The holy stone was placed in his hands and he said that he could see a light coming from it," said the bishop. "That was confirmation enough for everyone in those days and remains confirmation enough for everyone now."

Pope Theophilus may have been returning from what is now Deir al-Muharraq, where he had his visionary encounter with the Virgin Mary. The bishop did not know for sure. All that matters, he said, is that the pope saw a holy light coming from the rock with the handprint of Jesus.

"This was a vision that happened to a pope of the church, not an ordinary man," said Bishop Paphnutius. "I suppose that would be good enough assurance that this was a true vision."

And what of visions that happen to ordinary men? I asked the bishop. How is it possible to tell that their visions are truly genuine?

"Of course our Holy Bible speaks of visions, but I don't agree that we have to accept every vision as being from God," said the bishop. "We have to be very cautious and very strong to deal with every vision. For a vision to be a vision, there should be some signs."

As an example, Bishop Paphnutius cited miraculous healings that had taken place at some of the Holy Family sites, especially ones after seeing the visions of light like those over the church of St. Mark in Assiut. When flashes of heavenly light have been reported emanating from above the church, people have reported healings that have been confirmed by medical doctors. These must be true visions, said the bishop, because they are accompanied by true healings.

"These miracles happen in many of the holy places, and many of them are accompanied by visions," said the bishop. "Many of these miracles are certified by X rays and lab exams. There may be cancer before the vision, but now there is no cancer. I have seen it."

"You have seen this in your own hospital?" Kees asked. "Tell us one that you have seen here."

The five-star bishop shrugged.

"I have not seen it here," he said. "But you can find these stories in many holy places with the priests in various parts of the country. Places like Assiut have many of them."

Still, Bishop Paphnutius continued, you may have a vision but not experience a miracle. Only if you have personal faith for a miracle will one happen. In other words, he said, "Miracles, like healings, only happen depending upon your faith in God."

I was surprised to hear such a proclamation from a medical doctor, especially one who took such pride in having advanced X-ray equipment, an eye surgery clinic that specialized in detached-retina surgery, and a CT scanner that provided a three-dimensional digital image of the insides of a patient in a few minutes. Wasn't he espousing a belief in faith healing by saying such a thing?

"No, not at all," he said when I asked him bluntly. "If you think receiving the miracle of healing is all psychological, then you are canceling the power of religion completely."

God can heal, he said. But first you have to be open to the idea and have faith that a miracle can take place. In short, to be given healing grace is not enough. One must accept it, too.

I was intrigued by what the bishop said but not particularly surprised. As a thoroughly modern medical doctor, Bishop Paphnutius knows the effectiveness and limitations of medical technology. In the

Western world, where medicine and religion never mix, the notion that divine intervention could actually be a force in healing is almost considered blasphemy in many medical circles. There are some scientific studies in the West examining miraculous healings or the power of prayer but these are rarely taken seriously. Western doctors tend to ignore the possibility of miracles, which is usually okay with the patients, who want pills, not prayers, anyway.

It is different for doctors in the Middle East. They are steeped in a culture that is different from that of the West. They study Western medicine, many at Western schools, but they are willing to recognize where the miracle of Western medicine ends and where divine intervention begins.

"Here they do not question medical miracles like you do in the West," said Kees as we packed our belongings and prepared to continue our voyage. "They accept miracles as things that are awe-inspiring, not things to be picked apart and questioned. In this culture, you do not question the work of God."

Ashmunayn was more than the work of God. To some early Egyptians it was the womb of God. An ancient Egyptian creation myth has it that the eight gods that comprise water, air, darkness, and boundlessness mated here to create the "great explosion," or what we would call the Big Bang. What came of it, say writings on the walls here, were the "primeval waters" from which all of civilization has crawled.

There were no primeval waters visible anymore as we drove into this ancient city. The city, formerly a port, was now high and dry. Perhaps that was the reason it was abandoned, said Kees.

The ancient city is flanked on one side by the new (but I would never say modern) city of Ashmunayn. The ancient city is a crazy salad of civilizations that once occupied this ground during antiquity. Two dozen or more Corinthian columns stand like proud sentries over a mishmash of ruins. Ancient Egyptian temples that were dedicated to Thoth, the god of science and writing, have been toppled over time. A giant Roman bath stands neglected near where the road to the Nile would have been. Crumbled but still visible are the remains of the Ashmunayn basilica. Built in 431 C.E., this once famous church is now a memory. Goats were grazing among some of the ruins. Other than that, there appeared to be no caretakers.

Ashmunayn, considered the "womb of God" in pharaonic times, is now a ghost town of Corinthian columns and Roman ruins. It was here, according to a variety of stories, that Jesus caused idols to topple and trees to bow.

"Use your imagination and you can see what a magnificent place this was when the Holy Family came here," said Kees, standing next to the baths. "This was a trading center, so it was a very active city. The boats would unload at the river and the passengers and sailors would go into town to enjoy themselves after their long river journey. They must have passed right by here."

Although most of the city had been pulverized over time, enough remained to help create a mental picture of this once beautiful town. I could imagine the Holy Family leaving the boat that they had sailed on from Gabal al-Tair. Mary was probably frazzled by this time and anxious for some rest. She had wept in Gabal al-Tair when the mere presence of her divine son had caused a pharaonic temple to collapse. Here, she might have thought, she could get some peace and quiet and enjoy the luxuries of a large town.

But there was to be no rest and relaxation for Mary in Ashmunayn. A number of stories from a variety of sources create an image of Jesus moving like a tornado through this merchant center.

No sooner did the Holy Family enter the city than three statues of Thoth fell to the ground and shattered "into small pieces as if broken with a hammer." Word of the destruction spread throughout the town and soon the inhabitants gathered to see what kind of divine destroyer had been able to topple their idols.

They watched as a tree used by Satan worshipers shuddered as Jesus passed, shaking the evil spirits from its branches. Then the tree bowed to worship the Holy Child. The tree, wrote Sozomen, a fifth-century historian, became a healing plant, one that would cure the illness of believers who touched its bark. "On the expulsion of the demons, the tree was permitted to remain as a monument of what had occurred," he wrote. "[It was] endued with the property of healing those who believed."

Jesus was detained for questioning, but no magistrate in his right mind would attempt to restrain someone who exhibited such powers. He was released into his parents' custody and told to leave the city before further damage could take place.

Bishop Demetrius of Mallawi had expressed interest in restoring parts of Ashmunayn to their former glory, especially the basilica. He would also create a Holy Family monument, one that told the story of Jesus in Ashmunayn. Such restoration was highly unlikely, said Kees. To rebuild the basilica the bishop would need a permit, which would more than likely not be issued. Anyway, the new town of Ashmunayn had a Christian population of only five hundred or less, hardly enough to get the kind of support needed to create such a monument.

"This is just another example of how the faithful are needed to keep a local tradition alive," said Kees.

We walked through this ancient ghost town a while longer but there was little to see. A forest of stone columns marked the site of the destroyed basilica but other than that the place looked like a boxful of puzzle pieces that had been shaken hard and dumped onto the ground.

"There is another Holy Family site farther up the road, but I am told it is almost impossible to find," said Kees. "It is a holy well in the town of Dairout Um Nakhla, which is now practically a hundred percent Muslim. They respect Jesus as a prophet, but they have taken over some sites in areas that are now almost entirely Muslim."

In Dairout Um Nakhla they had never heard of the well of the Holy Family.

We started with the police in that town, asking them for the address of the well of Jesus. No one in the mud brick post knew, so they directed us to the post office next door. The postman was dozing at the counter when we walked into his cement hut. Kees apologized for waking him and then asked again for the well of Jesus. The postman didn't know, but he pointed toward the ceiling.

"Ask the guard," he said.

We stepped outside the building and shouted up to the cramped gun emplacement that had been built from brick on the corner of the post office.

"Where is the well of Jesus?" shouted Kees.

The head of a soldier poked out of the gun port. He didn't know, he said, but maybe we should go that way and ask someone else.

We walked down the dirt road that ran next to the canal and turned into the city. The narrow streets and high buildings made me feel as though we were walking through a deep canyon.

"Do you know where the well of Jesus is?" Kees asked a passerby.

"Not the well of Jesus," he said. "But I know where the well of the Companion of the Prophet is."

The man gave us directions and soon we wound our way through a maze of streets to a small mosque. The house of worship was very old and parts of it were crumbling. A row of outdoor toilets with shower curtains to block the view made this the least appealing building entrance I had seen in Egypt. Across a narrow walkway from the toilets was an open-air area for worship. At the end of the row of toilets, in a stall of its own, was the well of the Companion of the Prophet.

Our arrival was announced and the imam came racing out of the mosque. He was a tough-looking fellow, shaped like a fireplug, who looked as though he was about to start a holy war with the wayward Westerners.

It didn't take long to realize that our initial impression was wrong.

His name was Muhammad Meggie and he was delighted to meet us, he said. His young assistant arrived with a tray of sodas, and in short order we found ourselves surrounded by members of the congregation as we talked to the imam about his mosque.

"This building is very old," he said. "It marks the spot where Shaikh Omar, one of the Companions of the Prophet, lived after the Arab conquest of Egypt in the seventh century."

Kees told the imam that some Copts believe a church is buried underneath the foundation of this mosque.

"They think it marks one of the sites where the Holy Family stopped for water," he said. Pointing to the well, he went on, "And that, they believe, is the well of Jesus."

The imam was quick to disagree.

"That is the holy well of Shaikh Omar," he said. "It has always been so. The well is used to wash before the holy prayer. And yes, it is *baraka* [blessed] water. It is that way because it is a well that was made by a Companion of the Prophet."

One of the members of the congregation began working the handle of the well's pump and soon water was spilling out of the spigot. Before I could say "no thank you" a cup of the holy water was handed to me as the congregation watched expectantly. I thought about the row of toilets next to the well and then about the emergency supply of antibiotics I was carrying in my backpack.

"Bottoms up," said Kees.

I took a deep breath and drank from the cup.

As it turned out, I did not need the antibiotics at this or any other well. As Kees put it, "Holy water is clean water in any religion. Usually."

Later that night we had a chance to speak to Bishop Demetrius at his bishopric in Mallawi. He expressed dismay at the insensitivity of the Muslims for building a mosque over such a holy site as the well of Jesus in Dairout Um Nakhla. He had written at one point to a government agency to complain about the desecration of the site and said that they were threatening to tear the mosque down.

The chance of tearing down a mosque seemed highly unlikely in a country where 95 percent of the inhabitants were Muslim, I said to the bishop. He agreed but insisted that the matter was still very sensitive.

"The larger question to me is this," said Kees. "If a mosque is built on a Holy Family site, do you take the blessing away?"

"Oh no," said the bishop. "The blessing stays forever. When our God blesses a place it stays forever."

"What if a person drinks from the well of Jesus in Dairout and no longer feels as though the water is blessed?" I asked.

"That is their problem," said Bishop Demetrius.

"I will tell you a story about blessings that has to do with a well," the bishop continued. "A non-Christian once drank from one of the

holy wells that Jesus created. He told the priest that the water was dirty.
The priest prayed over the well and had faithful Christians drink from
it. They found the water to be very good. But when the non-Christian
drank from it again, he believed that it was still dirty. To me that shows
the meaning of blessings. If a person believes an area is blessed, then he
will take the blessing. If he doesn't, he will receive no blessing."

The one-eyed ferryboat captain gave us the evil eye before starting the
engine. He had been ordered by the police to hold his boat until we arrived and he wasn't happy about the delay. This was the last boat of the
evening and now he would have to wait on the other side until the police were sure that we were safely in the hands of Father Yousab, the priest
at the Church of Abu Hinnis. Then he would have to bring the police
back to the western side of the Nile in the dark. This would be no easy
task, I assumed, for a man with limited vision.

He started the engine and edged the boat out into the current. The
glassy water rippled and bumped against the smoke that drifted across
the surface of the Nile from the burning cane fields. Everything shim-
mered as we moved: the water, the smoky air, even the sound as it
reached our ears from the puttering engine.

We had spent the day visiting a couple of the more questionable
Holy Family sites. The Church of Apa Hor, at the foot of a large Christian cemetery, was rumored to be an area that the Holy Family had
passed through. Possibly true, possibly not, said the region's bishop.
There were no manuscripts from the early Church fathers to lend credence to this being a true site.

The same was true of the impressive pharaonic tombs of Beni Hassan. Built in the eleventh and twelfth dynasties, these colorfully painted
tombs are an Egyptophile's dream. Paintings depicting the heavenly life
of the pharaohs share wall space with Coptic crosses and other writings
that have made historians such as Otto Meinardus think that this may
well have been once used as a classroom for Coptic children. Bishop
Demetrius of Mallawi thinks that this area may also have been visited
by the Holy Family. But there is little documentation to support this
thesis, so we kept our visit short.

Now we were crossing the Nile and heading for one of the more
impressive sites on the Holy Family trail, the legendary cave church of

the Virgin Mary. There are several Holy Family sites in Abu Hinnis, including another holy well and a hill where the Virgin Mary supposedly rested. These sites were significant, but they paled in comparison to the cave church.

I had read about the cave in a variety of sources, including the *Coptic Encyclopedia* and the Coptic histories of Otto Meinardus. It was one of dozens of caves and quarries that were built in the mountains east of Abu Hinnis by the ancient Egyptians. They used the caves for the burial of high-ranking citizens.

Eventually, Christian hermits moved to these mountains and created monastic communities called *lauras*. They lived in solitude during the week, but on Sunday they came together in the cave church for worship. It was there that the more artistic among the hermits were said to have painted scenes of the Holy Family coming into Egypt. These paintings were made in the sixth or seventh century, according to the *Coptic Encyclopedia*, and include the first paintings of the slaughter of the innocents, the flight into Egypt, and the angel Gabriel appearing to Joseph.

Our dilemma was that no one we had talked to seemed to know where the cave of the Virgin Mary was. The mountains where it is located are peppered with pharaonic tombs and enormous rock quarries from ancient times. We would be looking through dozens of caves and trying to find the one with the artistic prize inside.

When we expressed our concerns about finding the cave to Father Yousab, he said it would be no problem. The pleasant young cleric said that he knew the exact location of the cave. What were lost now, he said with a very worried look on his face, were the keys to the guest house where he intended to house us for the night.

"If we do not find the keys, then you will have to sleep in the church," said the priest.

He did not look happy about that prospect, so of course we were not happy, either. *It is always best to trust the locals,* I thought. *If he is not happy about our accommodations, then we should not be happy, either.*

That proved to be the right instinct. As it turned out, the keys could not be found, so after dinner we were driven to the Church of St. John the Short, where we were taken to one of the youth halls by a deacon.

"Security will not be a problem," he assured us before he left. "The church is surrounded by a wall and manned by guards. And of course we will lock the church doors."

We would have been better off sleeping in one of the guardhouses. There was no water in our youth hall, no operating toilet, the twenty-one beds were jammed tightly together like something out of the nursery rhyme about the old woman who lived in a shoe. And since the windows on the veranda didn't close, there was a stream of mosquitoes to keep us company all night long.

In the morning we went in search of something to drink and ended up in the stairwell of a home where the lady of the house sold sodas. We purchased two bottles of Sprite but gave up on those quickly when we noticed the heavy smell of goat urine each time we took a sip. Had these sodas been stored in the room where the goats lived? We didn't ask. We left the house and went in search of Father Yousab.

By the time we found him, Father Yousab was ready to take us to the cave church. We boarded the church's Russian-made van and drove the dirt roads out of the village to the base of the mountains of Ansenna. Both Kees and I offered mild complaint about our lodgings. But as soon as we drew closer to the mountains, I forgot about the bad beds and the swarm of mosquitoes. From the base of the mountain I could see the pharaonic catacombs. As far as I was concerned, one bad night in a church youth hall was worth the view we had now. If Father Yousab really knew the way, we would soon be looking at one of the world's great art treasures.

Two armed guards from the church joined us and we began our climb up the flinty white mountains.

"Why do we need armed guards?" I asked Kees.

"Because there are villages on the other side of these mountains that have many fundys," said Kees, jokingly. "It is best for Christians to be protected."

We followed the narrow paths up into the mountains, past tombs with hieroglyphs carved into the walls and past deep shafts dug for mummies. I stopped to look at the first five or six of these burial chambers, even dropping stones down into the deep ones to count the number of seconds it took for them to hit bottom. *If I stop at all of them,* I told myself, *I'll never get to the church.*

Near the top of a craggy mountain Father Yousab stopped at a fork in the trail. He conferred with his guards, who pointed in opposite directions. Father Yousab kissed his cross and followed his own instinct.

After another brief consultation with the guards, Father Yousab waved us to a hole about the size and shape of a large window that was cut into the mountain. It was a side entrance to a massive quarry that went deep into the mountain. We all climbed in through the hole and waited for Father Yousab to make his entrance before following him. Then he led us to a stone wall that on closer inspection was an iconostasis. Above this sacred wall were the paintings I had read about. They were badly damaged, with many of their features pounded off by tools wielded by the various conquerors of Egypt who wanted to destroy the icons. But despite the damage, features could still be readily seen.

In a cave church in Abu Hinnis, Father Yousab smiles serenely among the sixth-century paintings of the Holy Family's flight into Egypt. Painted by hermits, these represent the world's first renderings of this mysterious Bible story.

On the left side of the iconostasis was the beginning of the story, the Holy Family fleeing to Egypt. Next came a graphic rendering of soldiers holding children by the throat and killing them as King Herod watched from his throne. Then there was a painting that was possibly of mothers crying. Finally there was a rendering of Joseph being told by the angel Gabriel that King Herod had died. Even given their condition, the talent of the painter was evident and the intent of the painting obvious.

I remembered the verse from Matthew 2:20, in which an angel of the Lord appeared saying, "Arise, and take the young child and his mother, and go into the land of Israel: for they are dead which sought the young child's life."

The priest gazed in appreciation at the wall paintings. He had been here many times and still the paintings made him feel "much love for our Savior." He added, "I come up here alone sometimes. It is a good place to pray and think and spend time with God."

I could understand what Father Yousab was saying. From the front entrance of the church was a westerly view of the Nile River valley and all of its green lushness. To either side of us and under our feet were mountains as barren as mountains could be. Lining these mountains were tombs and quarries from pharaonic Egypt in its prime, while behind us was one of the most ancient of Christian churches, its walls adorned with the oldest existing images of the Holy Family coming into Egypt. It was a spiritual view indeed, one that provided a vista of the extremes of nature as well as civilization, a sort of alpha to omega in one breathtaking panorama.

Both historians and clerics link this cave to the Holy Family. This link is a tenuous one, however, relying entirely upon oral tradition. And the tradition it relies upon is not very well developed. Some people believed that the Holy Family rested in this cave before continuing south. No miracles or interesting events are claimed beyond that.

I asked the priest if he thought the Holy Family had stayed at this cave.

"Maybe they did," he said. "Some think they did and I have to say that I sometimes feel their presence."

We continued to walk through the mountains as the sun lengthened our shadows. We examined tombs and the mysteriously beautiful writing of the Egyptians that decorated them. Father Yousab knew the turf well and pointed out crosses and other signs of early Christianity that were carved amid the hieroglyphs.

As the day darkened we wound down the steep little paths that people have followed for centuries. I paused for a moment to look back up the mountain and imagine just what it was like for those hundreds of hermits who lived, worked, struggled, and prayed alone in their caves yet together as a community.

"He wants to know what you are looking at," said Kees, nodding to one of our armed guards who was holding his shotgun at the ready.

"Ask him if he ever sees ghosts in these mountains," I told Kees.

"No, never," said the guard seriously. "Only terrified people see ghosts. Not courageous ones."

15. The Holiest Spot in Egypt

The year was 385 C.E., and the twenty-third pope of Alexandria had been invited to visit Qusqam in Upper Egypt by its bishops and the more than three hundred monks who lived there. The voyage from Alexandria to Qusqam, near what is now Assiut, would be an arduous one. The pope and his party of clerics, guards, and servants would have to travel more than 250 miles to reach the stark desert outpost in the middle of the country. On the way they would pass through dangerous deserts where lions were known to pick off unsuspecting travelers, and through areas known to be crime-ridden and lawless.

Still, Pope Theophilus set out on this voyage eagerly. In all of Egypt, there was no more holy spot than the grim desert of Qusqam. It was here, in a desolate and sun-drenched house, that the Holy Family was said to have resided for six months and five days. And it was here, according to Coptic legend, that an angel of the Lord broke the good news of Herod's death to Joseph in a dream.

The presence of the Holy Family in this place had been prophesied by Isaiah, the greatest of the Old Testament "writing prophets," more than seven hundred years before the birth of Jesus. In the nineteenth chapter, nineteenth verse of the book that bears his name, Isaiah declares that there will be "an altar to the Lord in the midst of the land of Egypt." The Copts believe that this altar was a stone from a pharaonic quarry that was inside a house in Qusqam. Jesus slept on this stone. Moreover, because the Holy Family worshiped in this house, Copts feel it is the world's first true Christian church.

Pope Theophilus considered it "the will of God" that he visit the "dwelling place of God, of His angels and of His holy Virgin mother." On the way to Qusqam, the pope certainly passed through many of the same spots that the Holy Family was said to have visited. He surely saw the tumbled ruins of Tell Basta. He certainly visited Ashmunayn and saw the healing tree and heard its legend. And it is known that he saw the handprint of Jesus at Gabal al-Tair, because he consecrated the relic after seeing the imprinted stone glow with heavenly light as he held it.

By the time Pope Theophilus reached Qusqam on January 13, 385 C.E., he was steeped in the folklore of the Holy Family and well versed in the knowledge of the sites.

According to scholars, Theophilus went to Qusqam for two reasons. One was to attend the festival of the mother of God, which was to take place three days after his arrival, on January 16. Another reason was to repair the church, which had apparently fallen into disrepair. On a recent trip to Alexandria, Emperor Theodosius of Rome had given the pope the authority to loot the ancient temples of Egypt as a source of funds to erect new churches and restore old ones.

Now, seeing the tiny residence of the Holy Family, Pope Theophilus had the grand idea of razing the house and building a large new church. This idea apparently met with some objections from the ten bishops who were with the pope.

With both the fate of the house and his just-completed voyage on his mind, Pope Theophilus retired to the upstairs of the Holy Family's home to sleep. Before doing so, he prayed. His vision was translated by Alphonse Mingana, a professor of Oriental languages in England in the 1920s and 1930s:

> I stretched my hands, prayed and implored my God and my Saviour Jesus Christ and said: . . . O my Lord and my God, have mercy upon me, and do not let me return empty handed, me who have fixed my mind on you from my childhood to my old age. I beseech you to reveal to me your coming into the world and to this mountain which you visited together with your Holy Virgin mother, and to this desolate house in which you established your habitation. I pray you to help me to build a big church, and we will glorify, exalt and honour your holy

name. You are the one whom are due power and glory with your Father and your Holy Spirit, now at all times and for ever. Amen.

At the prayer's end, Theophilus declared that a light shone on him that was "so dazzling that I believed that the sun itself was shining on me." Out of the light a throne became visible. Sitting on that throne was the "Queen of all women," the Virgin Mary. Around her, the pope saw the angels Gabriel and Michael and a host of lesser angels. The sight was so stunning to Pope Theophilus that he claimed to have fallen on his face and "become like a dead mar [horse]."

According to the written account of the vision, Mary calmed Theophilus and praised him, calling him "the athlete who fights for the Christians."

"I have revealed myself to you by the will of my beloved Son," said Mary.

She then launched into the story of their flight to Egypt, an account that was impressed so deeply in Pope Theophilus' mind that he was able to recount it verbatim the next day to the assembled bishops and priests. His story so strongly affected everyone who heard it that they too were apparently able to recount the vision verbatim, and so on for hundreds of years. Most scholars believe it was not until the eleventh century that the Vision of Theophilus was committed to paper. It is this written account that became the framework for the Holy Family trail as it now exists.

As part of the vision, the Holy Virgin told Pope Theophilus that she did not want the house torn down. It had always been her favorite house, she said. She wanted it left just the way it was.

But that did not happen. Somehow over the centuries everything except the altar stone has been torn down. Now there is a beautiful new church surrounding the altar stone. The altar itself is believed to be the original stone from the time of Jesus, but that may not be true, either. Sometimes even the holiest of spots change when no one is watching. Or perhaps they were never the way people thought they were to begin with.

It was midafternoon when we arrived at the monastery of the Holy Virgin at Deir al-Muharraq. From across the agricultural fields the monastery resembles a medieval castle, complete with turrets and a wall that is topped by spaced blocks that protect archers while they aim at the enemy below. When I mentioned this resemblance to Kees, he corrected me.

"Those are the kind of walls found around old Jerusalem," said Kees. "The Copts built the same kind of walls around this monastery to link the two places. After Jerusalem, this is the holiest site for Coptic Christians."

With the flourish of dust and noise that only a caravan of vehicles can deliver, we pulled up in front of the main gate and piled out. An older monk with a large and bushy beard approached Kees and told him that we would not be able to enter the monastery on this day.

"He says that because it is the fasting period, there is no one here who will be able to show us around," said Kees.

The monk drifted away and Kees asked a deacon to find a monk that he knew. Soon a slim young monk came trotting down the walk from inside the fortress. He had a broad face that carried a wide smile as he made directly for Kees. The two hugged like long-lost brothers and then Kees told him what we wanted to do. Father Stephanous, who was the historian for the monastery, nodded thoughtfully and shrugged.

"No problem," said Kees. "He will be glad to show us the church of the Holy Virgin."

Leaving our guards behind, we went through the main gate and then through a second gate that brought us into the monastery's main yard. Inside the walls of this Coptic castle was the most bizarre collection of buildings I had ever seen. Off to one side was an enormous colonial-style building that Father Stephanous called the monastery palace. It consisted of four three-story sections that were placed in such a way that the inner space was in the shape of a cross. It had a total of sixteen bedrooms as well as a large conference room and library. Built as a bishop's residence in 1910, the palace is now used as a guest house for the pope as well as important visitors.

"Sorry," said Kees, reading my mind. "You do not qualify."

Dead ahead were three intriguing buildings. On the left was the massive, two-steepled Church of St. George. It had the twelve domes of the classic Coptic churches and managed to dwarf even the palace to our left. Two buildings to its right was the monastery keep. Built of block, this protective tower was erected in the fifth century and could be used by the monks to wait out attacks by barbarian tribes. To get inside, one had to cross a drawbridge. When the drawbridge was retracted, the monks survived on water from a well in the basement, and dried lupine, which could be moistened and eaten.

"Luckily, no one ever had to use it," said Father Stephanous. "This is the only monastery in Egypt that was not attacked by Berbers."

The building in the middle was where we were headed. It was set like a jewel between the two larger structures, its slanted walls making it look as though it had squeezed itself into this space instead of the other way around. Humble in appearance, the church had an air of authority, an unmistakable dignity.

"This is the Holy Family's first house and the first Christian church in the world," said Father Stephanous.

We went inside.

There was nothing left of the original house, but then how could there be? The house was said by oral tradition to have been built by Joseph out of mud and palm leaves.

"The altar is in the same place that the Holy Family had it," said Father Stephanous. "The house was built around the altar."

The area he pointed to was about fifteen feet square and encompassed the holiest portion of the sanctuary. Although the house is no longer there, its form has been kept the same as it was in the first century, or so says an archaeological history of the monastery that is published by the Copts.

There are no written accounts of this being the house of the Holy Family before Pope Theophilus' fourth-century vision, which was not written down for many centuries. As a result, no one knows for sure what the house looked like, said Father Stephanous.

It was several minutes before the daily liturgy, so we had time to get close to the altar. It was covered with a white communion cloth and other accouterments of the daily worship. Because this is the holiest spot in Egypt, Father Stephanous said, the liturgy must be carried out every day on this altar until the end of time.

"This is such a holy spot that anyone who comes here to ask a favor of God will be given that favor," said Father Stephanous. "This is true as long as it is asked in faith."

"Go ahead," said Kees. "Ask God for a best-seller."

I thought about doing that for a second, but then I thought of something that I wanted even more. I wanted some kind of sign from God, a sign that would answer the questions I had about the Holy Family trail.

I stood silent for a moment while I formed the question in my

In the holiest of Coptic sites, Father Stephanous stands next to the altar in the monastery at Deir al-Muharraq. The altar is believed by some to be stone from a pharaonic quarry that Jesus slept on during the Holy Family's six-month stay in this desert region.

head: *Is there truth in the Holy Family trail or is it all just folklore?* Then I let it go.

"What did you ask for?" asked Kees.

"Something I really want," I said, and left it at that.

Outside the church I mentioned to Father Stephanous that we had heard rumors about the recent renovation of the church. Someone in Cairo had told us that some of the plaster from the altar had been chipped away and what was discovered underneath was not a stone at all, but bricks. That meant one of two things: Either the altar stone had been encased in bricks and covered with plaster hundreds of years ago, or there was just a pile of brick with no stone in the middle.

Father Stephanous confirmed the recent discovery. He said it had become a battle between two different camps of monks, those who want to take the altar apart to prove things scientifically and those who are happy with the notion of faith and want to believe that the altar stone of Jesus is inside those bricks.

I suggested the names of some American archaeologists who could carefully disassemble the bricks underneath to see if there was indeed an altar stone. Father Stephanous simply laughed at the recommendation.

"I think we will keep this matter inside the monastery," he said. "The important thing here has always been the knowledge that our Lord Jesus Christ has been here on the altar."

The monk seemed saddened about the altar issue, as though the discovery that there was no stone underneath the bricks would be like discovering that Jesus had never been here.

But his was not the only voice on the issue. Later in the day we had a chance to enter the keep, the magnificent fortress that stood next to the Church of the Holy Virgin. It was an ancient structure, a thick-walled stronghold designed to repel the most savage opponents. We reached the keep by climbing a high stairway and then crossing a drawbridge. The walls of the keep were as thick as a car is wide, and the rooms were small. We went all the way downstairs to the basement floors and up again to the top, where a liturgy was being carried out in a small chapel by several monks.

At the end of the service a tall, dignified monk named Father Philoxenos came to talk to us. He knew Kees from other times he had been to the monastery and seemed happy to see him.

When talk turned to the questions that had been raised about the altar stone, the monk felt less anguished than Father Stephanous about the validity of the stone. Leave it alone, he declared, because faith is more than bricks or stone.

"Forget about the age of the altar," he said strongly. "The altar is in the center of Egypt as Isaiah says it is supposed to be. And we are sure that the Holy Family has been here. Whatever an archaeologist might find doesn't matter."

That night we had been invited to stay at the bishopric of Bishop Thomas in the town of al-Qussia. This was great news, said Kees. Bishop Thomas was another of the "five-star bishops." And the guest house in the bishop's church compound was among the finest of its kind in Egypt.

"Royalty could stay in this house and be happy," said Kees. "It is many, many times better than the youth hostel in Abu Hinnis."

Another reason that Kees was happy to be staying in al-Qussia was that it would give us a chance to visit one of the most controversial sites of the Holy Family trail, the town that Jesus cursed.

Just the mention of a town being cursed by Jesus makes some Copts cringe. Yet in the vision of Theophilus, Mary tells the pope that things got bad as soon as the Holy Family entered the town. Idols fell down and the pagan priests became fearful.

"Go out of town lest the children should come out and kill you," said the priests to the Holy Family. Taking their cue, the townspeople of al-Qussia chased the Holy Family to the city limits and told them to be on their way. "That was when," said Mary to the pope, "my beloved Son turned and cursed the town: 'Let its people be in an estate lower than all other people, and let them be more lowly and subdued than all the inhabitants of the land of Egypt. Let its earth be cursed so that nothing shall grow in it except [alfalfa] and rush-nut, and let its soil lie uncultivated and remain as it was before I cursed it.' "

Yet most Copts deny that Jesus cursed this town. Or, in some instances, they deny that the present-day town of al-Qussia is the same one that Jesus was chased out of two thousand years ago.

Father Boutros does not agree with either of these assessments. He is a priest at St. Michael's Church, which is located near the land in question, and he thinks that Jesus did indeed curse al-Qussia. Luckily, he says, al-Qussia was much smaller in those days.

"The area that was cursed is easy to find," said Father Boutros. "I will take you to it."

We got into our hired car and made our way through the tight and dirty streets of al-Qussia. Kees had met Father Boutros before and knew that he was a playful man. As the car jolted its way through the town, Kees bantered with the priest about getting a "cursed" parish.

"You are in a cursed church on cursed land," joked Kees. "What did you do to get this parish? Doesn't the bishop like you?"

"Of course he does," laughed the priest. "It is not as you think. You will see."

In a moment we did see. Turning a corner, we came to a large open area. It was about the size of two or three city blocks and it was depressed in the middle. Nothing at all was built in this area. Instead this prime real estate was clearly a garbage dump.

"*This* is the cursed town of al-Qussia," said Father Boutros. "This was the size of the town when the Holy Family came through."

I found the explanation that Father Boutros gave to be very convincing. Hidden in the middle of that garbage dump was a pharaonic temple, complete with idols and pillars. These were the idols that Jesus had caused to tumble when he came through town, said Father Boutros.

"As you can see, the curse is not on the people," said Father Boutros. "The curse is that this area can never be built on."

As we drove from the area, Kees shook his head and smiled. "I'll bet we are the first visitors asking for directions to the cursed land of al-Qussia," he said.

In the morning, a cloud of incense filled the bishop's house, its sweet smell reaching my room all the way on the fourth floor. I came out of the room and looked over the railing. There was a flurry of activity in the reception area below. I could see the bishop and monks in their black garb swirling around three men in suits. In a moment they all funneled into the bishop's meeting room, a long and narrow space lined with Louis XVI chairs. The door clicked shut behind them.

"That incense means that the bishop is back from his trip," said Kees, coming out of his room. "Today he is meeting the British ambassador to Egypt and his successor."

When we had arrived the night before, the bishop was not home. His assistant, a serious young man named Bazam, had seen to it that our rooms were ready and our meals prepared. He put us both on the fourth floor of this guest mansion, which must have at least twenty-five guest rooms.

The guest house was located inside a walled and guarded compound. Inside was a church, some church buildings, and the bishop's own residence. It occured to me that the church might be embarrassed to make such a show of wealth in a town in Upper Egypt that didn't seem particularly wealthy. It was quite the opposite, said Kees.

"The people here love a rich church," said Kees. "It allows them to show off their religion."

When we arrived downstairs, Bazam was in the kitchen, riding herd on the cook to make certain that our breakfast of beans, rice, and potatoes was done quickly.

We had a busy day planned. First we had to stop at the press center in Assiut, where we would meet our press escort for the day. After that we were going to Dronka, a hillside pilgrimage site that has been proclaimed in modern times as the last stop on the Holy Family trail. This site is controversial. According to ancient documents, Deir al-Muharraq is the spot from which the Holy Family returned to Israel. Dronka is more than thirty miles farther south. Many Copts believe that the Holy

Family came farther south to this pharaonic stone quarry before boarding a boat. Even though the vision of Theophilus clearly indicates that
the boat was "manifested by Jesus," the Copts in support of Dronka
say that it was the nearest river port to Deir al-Muharraq and most certainly the Holy Family would have left from a port. Bishop Mikhail of
Assiut supports these claims. He also declared that a first-century
monastery had been built on this site in Dronka honoring the Holy
Family's stay. The presence of this ancient monastery has never been
proven. Nonetheless, Dronka is now considered the final site on the
Holy Family trail.

Also, its status as a Holy Family site has been confirmed, say believers, by the appearance of mysterious lights over the last twenty years,
and even of the Virgin Mary herself.

Our final stop would be an interview with Bishop Mikhail himself.
This would be a rare treat. Known as one of the most mysterious fig-
ures in modern religion, Bishop Mikhail rarely grants press interviews.
Through an emissary we had asked if he would talk with us about two
of his favorite subjects, the Holy Family trail and visionary encounters.
Surprisingly, he agreed.

We ate hurriedly and then loaded our gear into the car. That was
when our problems began. The driver was there, but our security escort
was nowhere to be seen.

We waited for an hour and then waited more. Kees was pacing the
courtyard. We said our farewells to the British diplomats as they left
their meeting with the bishop. Then the bishop himself came out, a
smile of understanding on his face.

"I don't wait for them any longer," he said, passing by us on the way
to his own car for a trip to Cairo. "If security is not on time, I just
leave."

Kees took his lead from the bishop. With a great flurry of anger, he
approached the church security guard and asked him to open the gate
so we could leave. The man refused. The security police with their
trucks had not yet arrived from town, he explained nervously.

"Open the gate," demanded Kees. "I am taking responsibility for
our safety, not you."

A shouting match ensued between Kees and the security guard as a
dozen or so Copts gathered to watch the argument. They were delighted
to see a European in a pitched verbal battle with a member of the police. It was something only a foreigner could get away with. An ordinary
Egyptian would be severely disciplined for this kind of transgression.

Finally the security man folded. He ordered the heavy metal gate to be opened and our voyage to the south began.

We were intercepted by security by the time we reached the main highway. Today we had only four guards instead of the eight we'd had the day before. The lieutenant in charge stopped our car and began to chastise the driver for leaving the compound without him. When the driver and Kees explained what had happened, the lieutenant gave us a wave of resignation and returned to his truck. We were on the road again.

"Even as a foreigner, you can only yell at the lower guys," said a calmer Kees. "You don't want to try this with a lieutenant on up. It wouldn't work."

By the time we were on the outskirts of Assiut, two trucks escorted us, containing a total of eight security police. As soon as we drove into Assiut, however, our escorts disappeared and we were left alone. We drove past the University of Assiut, one of the most respected learning institutions in Egypt. Then we passed through the downtown area, where students were staging a small protest rally against Israel's policy toward the Palestinians. I wanted to stop and photograph the protest but the driver would have no part of it. Instead he sped up and soon we found ourselves at the Assiut press office.

We were here to pick up our press guide, but such a thing is not so easy in a country where most of the jobs involve working for the government and the ritual of drinking tea is the accepted form of handshake.

Kees and I were escorted to the office of the director of the press center, a gracious and charming woman named Samia Fadil Iskander. Soon we were joined by a number of press officers for tea, where we talked about a variety of things, including my project and the news in the Middle East.

It was late afternoon by the time we got out of the press office and back on the road to Dronka. Two press officers joined us with their own driver. As we left Assiut we were met again by two truckloads of security police.

"We do this for security but you have nothing to worry about," said one of the press officers in our car as he pointed at the armed soldiers in the truck in front of us. "This used to be the hotbed of fundamentalism ten years ago. Now you can still find bullet marks in the walls, but no fundamentalists."

They were, he said with assurance, dead, in jail, or "gone to Afghanistan."

We were heading southwest out of Assiut and out of its green agricultural zone. Ahead of us were the bleak western mountains, barren
crags that get no water from the Nile and little from the sky. Midway
up the mountain ahead of us was what looked from a distance like a
gaping wound in the rock, a slash from a giant sword. Stuffed into that
slash and growing all around it were rows upon rows of buildings. Most
of the buildings looked like hotels and apartment houses, but as we drew
closer, church steeples became more visible, as did other buildings.

We drove up a long and wide drive to reach the gate. When we got
out of the car I just stood and stared. I was as taken by the size of the
complex as I was by its emptiness. There were rows upon rows of hotel
rooms and apartments that ran up the side of the mountain. A broad
pedestrian boulevard led into an enormous cavern that had once been a
stone quarry for the pharaohs, who were insatiable builders in their time.
But this too was the product of an insatiable builder. What Ramses II
was to the ancient Egyptians, Bishop Mikhail had become to the modern
Copts. He was the great builder of monuments to the Holy Family.

But there was one problem. There was hardly anyone here.

The loneliness gave this site an eerie feel. Where I had expected to
be alone at smaller sites, being among few people at this one was like
being at Disneyland after closing time.

Zahar, our man from the press office, did not share my discomfort.
Instead, he found the lack of people a relief.

"In August it is so packed you can hardly stand it," he said. "There
are thousands and thousands of people here, all praising God."

He was not exaggerating the numbers, Kees said. When the believers make their pilgrimage for the Great Procession for the Virgin Mary,
there are estimated to be as many as a half million people here. The pilgrimage continues for two weeks and then Dronka empties out, host-
ing a small but steady stream of visitors the remainder of the year.

Being from Arizona, I could imagine coming here in the stifling heat
of the summer with tens of thousands of other people, standing shoulder
to shoulder, listening to a pilgrimage sermon. Dronka suddenly seemed
very small.

We went inside the mountain. It reminded me of an underground
football field. Across the room were various religious stations. There
was a baptistery with several tanks of water lined up in a row. This was
used for mass baptisms, when hundreds of parents would wait in line
with their children to receive the holy immersion.

There were rows of chairs set up in the middle of the room, maybe five hundred or more. This was a church without walls, where pilgrims could catch a quick sermon. Cut into the stone at the back of the quarry were rooms that were blocked from the public by iron gates. We could look through the gates at the massive paintings of Mary holding the baby Jesus, but that was as far as we could get. They were, we were told by Sister Lydia, among the holiest spots in Dronka.

"Several years ago, a bright light came from this part of the cave," said Sister Lydia, who was introduced to us by a monk because she spoke English thanks to years of study at American University in Cairo. "No one could actually see a face in the light, but it was assumed that the light was a message from the Virgin Mary. The light made us believe that this was the place where the Holy Family stayed when they were here in this cave."

Since the appearance of that light, this cave is treated as a special place that can be entered only during the procession of deacons in August, when they carry an icon throughout the entire site as a display of reverence.

There have been many miraculous appearances of light here at Dronka, said Sister Lydia, who has been here since 1970. Happily she began to recount them for us.

"In 1968 the Virgin appeared here after she appeared in Zeitoun," said the sister, her smile beaming as she spoke. "Last year during the pilgrimage there were lights that many people thought were the Holy Family. In October we saw lights in the bell tower of the church. And then, of course, there are frequently lights above the Church of St. Mark in Assiut."

"How do you interpret these lights?" I asked.

"They are from the Holy Family," said Sister Lydia. "They are telling us that these areas are blessed."

Many agree with this assessment of the light apparitions. Light visions have been reported in many forms and at many times. Some take the form of the Virgin Mary. Sometimes the Virgin is said to be surrounded by flashing lights and white pigeons. Other times the light seems to spray down from the heavens, bathing the steeple of St. Mark's. Thousands of pilgrims rush to these areas when visions of light are reported.

When they happen in Assiut, many people assume that it is the heavens demanding peace in Fundy Land. When they happen in Dronka, they are frequently associated with the appearance of Bishop Mikhail during his pilgrimage sermons.

In August 2001, Claudia Wiens, a German photographer, visited Dronka during its annual celebration. When she arrived, a monk told Wiens that she had come at the right time. "For five nights the Holy Virgin has kept appearing to us every night when the bishop is talking to the people."

She noted that lights began flashing when he held his cross high. Suddenly, she said, "the light was bright, coming irregularly from all sides, sudden and fast. Nobody could see a shape but people assumed it had to be the Holy Virgin."

Wiens was more skeptical than the believers around her. She began to search for any technical source of light but was unable to find one. Still, she noted, every time the bishop held up his cross more light "seemed to appear." She referred to the sermon as a perfectly produced fireworks display, one that became more and more exciting as the bishop moved his cross up and down in the form of a cross.

Although she never found the source of light, Wiens never believed in the holiness of what she saw.

"Was that heaven talking to us? Or might there be a smart character behind it who wanted to strengthen his position? Somebody who wanted to prove his holiness? That would be a huge manipulation of thousands of people," wrote Wiens. "Who knows? I can't tell. I only saw light but no source. But I can tell you that it happened the next day again at exactly the same time. I must say, heaven is on time."

I didn't ask Sister Lydia if she was ever skeptical about the heavenly light shows. I knew what her answer would be. I also knew that after leaving Dronka I would be given the chance to interview Bishop Mikhail himself. He would be able to fully explain for me the meaning—and possibly the source—of the apparitions of light that this region was so famous for.

That interview was not to be, however. As we toured Dronka with Sister Lydia, a monk approached Kees with bad news. Bishop Mikhail would not be able to keep his interview appointment. The bishop was extremely busy and was forced to cancel.

"The bishop does not usually speak to the press, so I was surprised that he agreed to an interview to begin with," said Kees, clearly distressed by the cancellation.

Since Dronka was officially the end of the Holy Family trail, Kees had hoped to finally snag an interview with the elusive bishop of Assiut. Now that was not to be. Our voyage would end with no explanation of the mystery of the lights.

"You should not be surprised," said Sister Lydia. "The bishop is known to be reclusive. You must accept that he may change his mind."

As Kees spoke to the monk, I continued to talk to Sister Lydia about Dronka and the surrounding area. Sister Lydia had an idea. Now that we had extra time on our hands we could examine Dronka more closely or perhaps visit the cave church that was nearby.

Frankly, I was not interested in seeing more of Dronka. After traveling the entire Holy Family trail and seeing ancient sites like Tell Basta, Ashmunayn, and Deir al-Muharraq, Dronka felt very plastic. It reminded me more of a modern religious amusement park than an ancient Holy Family site in Egypt. At the time I felt a pang of guilt for thinking this way. In retrospect, though, how else could I feel? After visiting truly ancient sites, what kind of appeal could a newly built site really have?

But another cave church—now that sounded interesting. "Where is it?" I asked Sister Lydia.

"It is in Rifa, just a few kilometers south," she said. "The priest there thinks that his church was visited by the Holy Family, too. He thinks it was there that they hid from the soldiers of Herod."

I told Kees what the nun had said and soon our caravan was back on the road, headed for the dusty outpost of Rifa. Although close to Dronka, this town had clearly seen few pilgrims. Tired and crumbling, Rifa was off the main road about half a mile and appeared to exist only to service the military base that bordered it on the north.

We drove into town like an occupation force and parked in front of the pink-domed church. Before we could open the car doors, a large priest positioned himself in front of the gate as though he was about to make his last stand. Sister Lydia could not remember his name, so we had not been able to contact him by telephone from Dronka. The site of such a large contingent of official vehicles showing up unannounced made him suspect the worst.

Kees left the car immediately and began to explain the purpose of our arrival. As he did, the priest's defensive posture softened and a smile came over his face. He began pointing toward the mountains behind the town, the ones that were laced with dozens of caves, several of which had entrances with pillars that made them look like Greek temples.

Father Joel of Rifa has declared the caves above his town a possible hideout for the Holy Family.

"He has said that the Holy Family could have come here, too," said Kees, translating the words of Father Joel, who was shaking my hand like I was a long-lost relative. "He said they could have come here just as easily as they came to Dronka. In fact, it would have been safer. These caves are much smaller and attract less attention than the big cave at Dronka. Everyone would look for them at Dronka. Here no one would have looked."

This made sense to us, at least as much sense as the Holy Family continuing to Dronka from Deir al-Muharraq. If they went as far south as Dronka, why not travel the extra few kilometers to a less visible set of caves? We wanted to examine the caves more closely.

After an hour of negotiating with the commander of the army base, which had jurisdiction over the caves, we were allowed to go up there as long as we took no photographs. Our caravan grew again, as soldiers were sent to watch us and make sure no pictures were taken. We now had a grand total of sixteen armed security people, eight to watch out for us, and eight to watch us. Once we reached the level of the caves, I knew why they were so concerned about photos. This high road gave us a strategic view of the army base, but it also put us on a special army road, one designed specifically to move army equipment quickly up and down the country. We were on top of a mountain with a top-secret view.

I left my camera inside the car and followed Father Joel into a cave that looked the same as the dozens of other caves that lined the road. We walked down a short tunnel and into a room that was illuminated by candlelight. There, next to an ancient altar, was an icon of the Virgin Mary holding the baby Jesus. Over their heads floated two angels. The icon was clearly very old, as was the iconostasis that was behind the altar. Father Joel said it was 273 years old. The stone altar, he said, was the same as the stone altar found at Deir al-Muharraq. Both, he said, were made from stone cut in pharaonic times.

We didn't have the heart to tell him that the altar stone in Deir al-Muharraq was now of questionable origin. That information, we decided, would come to him through official sources. Rather, we just took the moment to appreciate where we were: in a very old church in a land of myth and mystery.

"This is where we think the Holy Family stayed," said Father Joel.

He believed this, he said, because this is a very old church and because it has always been said that the Holy Family stayed here. He shrugged as if to say, *Why would I need more evidence?*

We left the cave church and walked a narrow path to the next cave. It turned out to be a large pharaonic temple with eight shafts for burying mummies. Then we took a treacherously narrow and steep path to a Ptolemaic temple that, like the other, had been cut out of the mountain. Inside this temple was a seventh-century Christian church that had been built out of mud brick.

"This is all a sign that the Holy Family stayed here," said Father Joel, standing by the altar of this church within a temple. "There are many good places for them to hide in these mountains. And there are signs that they stayed here. Why else would these churches be built here? They are built here because they were an honor to the Holy Family."

The deacons and the soldiers and the man from the press office all nodded in agreement. There were many questions about proof that could have been asked at this time, but it didn't seem appropriate to question such strong faith. Everyone here was happy. They were bathed in the knowledge of their heritage, surrounded by a history of their own making. I saw nothing wrong with letting belief go unquestioned, at least this time.

"Our church is a blessed place," said Father Joel.

I could see what he meant.

16. The Dimension
of the Impossibles

Father Joel shook our hands and willingly posed for pictures with the caves of Rifa in the distant background.

"Be sure to include us in your book," he said, placing his beefy hand on my shoulder. "It was here where the Holy Family hid in the mountains from Herod's soldiers. This is certainly true."

The bearlike priest walked Kees and me to the car. Once we were inside he pushed the door closed and waved goodbye.

It was then that I realized my voyage was over. I had covered the entire official Holy Family trail from start to finish and then some if you included this unofficial extension to the route.

"I've done it," I said to Kees.

"Yes, you have," he said, shaking my hand. "You have done what few people in the world have done—you have covered the entire Holy Family trail. An act like this makes you among the most faithful. You are truly Saint Paul from Arizona."

I thought the adventure was now over but I was wrong.

"Let's stop in Assiut so you can at least see the Church of St. Mark," said Kees. "Even though the bishop won't see you, you should at least see his church. It is very famous."

"Certainly," I replied. "Why not? I won't be in this part of the world again for a while."

It was well after dark when we arrived back in the thriving river town of Assiut.

"We should tell someone that an American is in town so they can demonstrate against you," said Kees. "Here you have been to Fundy Land and no one has been hostile to you."

Kees was joking, of course. Still, I did find it surprising that so little anger had been directed toward me this entire trip. Before leaving the United States, I had been warned to expect hostility. Now I was at the end of my voyage and nothing more unseemly than civil arguments had taken place between me and the citizenry of Egypt. At one point I asked the owner of a cab stand if he was angry at America for bombing Afghanistan. He politely pointed out that Afghanistan was two thousand miles from Egypt and "a world away" in thought. "Please tell America that we are not Afghans," he asked.

We drove down the esplanade next to the Nile and then turned down a couple of dark streets until we were directly in front of the Church of St. Mark.

There was nothing special about its architecture and nothing particularly ornate or attractive about its steeple. I had seen better on this trip and I had certainly seen worse.

"Let me take a picture and then we can get back to al-Qussia," I said to Kees.

I rested my Nikon digital camera on top of the car and turned the lens upward so it would capture the steeple from a low angle. Then I pushed the button and removed my hand so the camera would not shift while it took a time exposure.

I expected a photo of the white steeple against the dark sky. What I got, though, was something quite different. The white steeple stood in sharp contrast to the sky, all right, but the sky wasn't black. It was as though a crack in the heavens had developed and bright light was spilling down like rain.

A crowd had gathered, as always happened when I took photos. This time, though, when the picture came up on the screen, the crowd began to swoon with reverence.

"That is the light vision that people see," exclaimed a Muslim policeman. "It is very special to see it."

"I have seen this heavenly lighting many times," said a Muslim police lieutenant. "It appears to people of all faiths."

"It is the Virgin Mary," declared Zahar, our Assiut press office guide.

The author photographed a spray of light coming down from the heavens over the Church of St. Mark in Assiut. Such lights, called "visions of Mary" by the faithful, have been seen for many years by thousands of people.

When I pointed out that it was only light and enveloped no human form, he shrugged. "It is the Virgin Mary."

A dozen or so people viewed the photo that night. All swore that it was the mystical light that had visited the Church of St. Mark so many times in the past.

"Congratulations," said Kees. "You are the first Westerner to photograph the lights of St. Mark."

It is a good day when you can complete the trail of Jesus in Egypt and capture an apparition of light on film. I was ready to let things go at that, but I would soon find out that I could not get off that easily.

Zahar, the man from the press office, left our group and went directly to the office of Bishop Mikhail, where he told a deacon about the photograph.

As we drove out of Assiut and headed north on the agricultural

road, a call came over Kees' cellular telephone. He grinned as he talked
to the person on the other end.

"This is the deacon who works for Bishop Mikhail," said Kees. "It
seems the bishop wants to meet with you right now. He wants to see
the photo."

I thought about turning back for Assiut but decided against it. Our
security police were tired and were already complaining about the
length of their workday as it was. Plus the road to Assiut is deadly at
night, in part because so many think they can save gas by driving without their headlights. On top of that, the bishop's office had already
canceled one interview session with us; I did not feel confident that the
bishop himself would actually be present for an interview if we did
return.

"Tell them we will show them the picture another day," I said to Kees.

We returned to Al-Qussia and were having a cup of hot tea when
another call came over Kees' cell phone.

"That was a priest representing the bishop," said Kees, hanging up.
"He said he will meet us at the train station tomorrow to get a copy of
the picture."

"I can't give him a copy," I said. "There is no printer here to print it
with."

"I told him that," said Kees. "So the priest said he will follow us to
Cairo and get one there."

"They are persistent," I said.

"You have no idea," said Kees. "He is on a mission from the bishop
of Assiut. He won't stop until it is fulfilled."

As we were drinking tea in the dining room of the guest house, Bishop
Thomas arrived from his trip to Cairo. Although it was nearly mid-
night, he made the rounds of his staff, asking them what had transpired
since he left and giving them their orders for the next morning, when
he would leave again, this time for Wady el-Natrun, where he was
putting the finishing touches on a retreat center in the near western
desert. Bishop Thomas was an energetic man with a slight limp, a reminder of a near-fatal car accident that had taken place a few years earlier on the deadly desert road. He had a round face and a quick and
bright smile that made him look much younger than his forty-three
years.

Kees said that Bishop Thomas was considered one of the "five-star bishops" because of his first-class bishopric, with its excellent food and efficient staff. Clearly, Bishop Thomas was a brilliant man, with a mind as quick as his smile. He was fluent in English and had become one of the Copts' most effective overseas fund-raisers as a result. Just as valuable as his language skills was his ability to translate the customs and traditions of Egyptians to others. I had met very few people on my Holy Family voyage who could speak English, but even fewer who could explain clearly the intricate cultural motivations behind the beliefs and practices of the Copts.

We made small talk and then I asked the bishop if we could confer with him for a few minutes to clarify questions I still had about the Holy Family's visit to Egypt. He agreed immediately and had his deacon dim the lights in the red-walled sitting room. "A darker room like this has an atmosphere more conducive to talk," he said, sitting in a high-backed chair lined with faux gold filigree. He was right about that. The few minutes we requested turned into two hours of wide-ranging conversation that shone new light on my mysterious voyage.

"I have just tonight completed the entire Holy Family trail from El-Arish to Deir al-Muharraq," I told the bishop, getting right to the point. "I hope this question doesn't offend you, but how many of the Holy Family trail stories do you think are actually true?"

The bishop thought for a moment and as he did he picked up his cup of tea and balanced it in his palm.

"I understand your question, but before I address it, I want to talk for a moment about the mentality of the Copts. I can do that with this cup. If I were to say that this cup is in my hand and my hand is in this cup, people would think I was crazy because they can see that I am holding this cup in the palm of my hand. Either I have it in my hand or my hand is in it. It can't be both ways at the same time.

"But the Copts have the belief of another dimension. They think that it could happen both ways. They believe this because of Bible verses that they read in a real way, not in a symbolic way. For example, Christ said in the Bible, 'I am in you and you are in me.' Many people who read the Bible would take this in a symbolic way to mean that goodness is in all of us. But the Copts would say, 'No, it is real, a part of Jesus is in me and a part of me is in Jesus.'"

"So they don't take things metaphorically?" I asked.

"Sometimes they do," he said. "But they also believe that 'impossibles' can happen, even if at times it seems as though they couldn't."

I must have looked a little confused because Bishop Thomas put his cup down and leaned back.

"The beliefs of the Copts are like water," he explained. "If I come to you, a great writer, and I ask you to explain to me the taste of water, you would write and write and write but you would not be able to explain to me how it tastes. But you know the taste of water, I know the taste of water, little kids know the taste of water. There is a certain deep knowledge that cannot be pronounced. That deep knowledge may be different in each of us and cannot be explained easily to other cultures."

For the Copts, said Bishop Thomas, this deep knowledge involves the "dimension of impossibles," the belief in religious mysteries and miracles that are around us every day. This belief in the "impossibles" has a strong influence on how Copts interpret—and even embellish—the events that took place on the Holy Family trail. In that sense, said the bishop, almost every village that lays claim to a visit by the Holy Family has a regional twist to its story.

"For example, if you go to Meir you can hear a story that the Holy Family stayed three nights in a house," said Bishop Thomas. "That is a great story in itself and they should be very proud that it happened. But then the storytellers in the village give it another dimension. They want to add a little power to the site, so they say that no one has ever died in this house where the Holy Family stayed. The logic in this story doesn't meet with the mainstream Christian philosophy about death. But the storyteller adds this little bit of spice anyway, to make the village have a special connection to Jesus."

These embellishments don't bother him, said Bishop Thomas, as long as they don't detract from the basic purpose of the Holy Family's visit to Egypt as well as the message of Jesus.

"The Holy Family did not come to Egypt just for fun," said the bishop. "They came here because it was a fulfillment of the prophecy in the Old Testament book of Isaiah. It is important to remember it."

Bishop Thomas picked up a Bible and in the dim light read the verse from Isaiah that Egyptians believe is marked by the house where the Holy Family lived in the center of Egypt at Deir al-Muharraq: "In that day shall there be an altar to the Lord in the midst of the land of Egypt, and a pillar at the border thereof to the Lord."

Bishop Thomas closed the Bible and smiled brightly.

"The arrival of the Holy Family in Egypt was a fulfillment of Old Testament prophecy. Because of that I have no doubt that the Holy Family was actually here," he said. "And I think you can actually feel the presence of something holy when you visit these areas. They have strong forces and an energy. I can feel these forces myself when I am there; it is something real. And I respect that there is a need for these people to express their village culture by adding spice to these stories. There is a place for this expression as long as it is connected to the philosophy of salvation expressed by Jesus."

I told Bishop Thomas that many of the stories told by the Copts match those told in the Infancy Gospels, those apocryphal books that are not included in the Bible. But nowhere in Egypt had I found Copts who had read the Infancy Gospels. And many of the clergy turned up their noses at the mere mention of these books.

"That is because the Church is very strict in declaring that the Bible we have is the one and only word, and anything outside of that is not to be looked at," said the bishop. "There may have been a time when these books [the Infancy Gospels] were condemned, so people are not allowed to read them. I don't know what happened that people are not aware of these books. Some of these books were even found in Egypt and were written by Egyptians, but they are not read because they do not meet with our mainstream philosophy."

"But how is it that so many of these stories are the same?" I asked.

"This is not hard," said the bishop. "In the same ways that the gospels were passed on orally for years and years, before they were written down, so too were these stories of the Holy Family in Egypt passed on from the first century, when they actually happened. Then they were finally written down. For Copts they were solidified by the Vision of Theophilus."

The fourth-century Vision of Theophilus was not the beginning of the Holy Family tradition in Egypt, as some Copts believe. Rather, it was the seal of approval for all the stories already in circulation, said the bishop.

"The history of the Holy Family could not have started in the fourth century because no one would have accepted it," said the bishop. "The Vision of Theophilus was a collection and an approval and a seal for the already existing tradition of the Holy Family."

In the same way that gospels are a collection of oral traditions that have been written down, Bishop Thomas felt that the Vision of Theophilus was a collection of oral traditions expressed through a vision.

"He was traveling from Alexandria to Deir al-Muharraq and I feel like maybe he was moving from one village to another and hearing all of these stories," he said. "And then he ended up in this place, the house of the Holy Family, when he was full of all these stories and he prayed to know what was real."

"So did he have a vision or a dream?" I asked.

"He had a vision," said Bishop Thomas without hesitation. "I respect very much the Vision of Theophilus. But I don't think that the history of the Holy Family started with his vision. Instead these stories were approved by his vision."

Despite being a thoroughly modern cleric, Bishop Thomas was a great believer in visions. As a boy of seven, he had seen the vision of the Virgin Mary at Zeitoun. It was one of those things, he said, that will stay with him all his life.

"This apparition was very clear," he said. "Zeitoun is a story that we can depend upon because so many people saw it. I could not say I need tangible evidence that it happened, because the fact that it happened is enough for one who has seen such a vision. But the storytellers have added their spice even to that vision. Storytellers will say that the Virgin looked them right in the eyes and wrapped her arms around them. To them I say, 'Enjoy your story.' It doesn't take away the reality of that apparition; it just adds a little spice to it."

"What do you think of the visions of light that have been seen over the church of St. Mark in Assiut?" I asked the bishop.

"I did not see it myself because as a person I do not run after such things," he said. "A lot of people have seen it, though. But I just take this as a blessing and stop. I don't go more than that."

Almost reluctantly, I turned on my digital camera and scrolled through the day's photos until I came to the apparition of light that I had captured only hours earlier. As he looked at the photo in the camera's viewing screen, I told him the entire story—how we had stopped to get a quick photo of the church and when I checked the picture I had taken there was this spray of light coming down from the heavens. I told him how the people around us had reacted, especially the Muslims who said they had seen this light before and the other people in the crowd who said that this was indeed the apparition of light that has so famously appeared over the church steeple in recent years.

"Yes, this could be what people are seeing," said the bishop, examining the picture. "I myself can see that it is fact, that it happened. You took this picture and the light appeared. I would not go more than that. It is mysterious enough. I do not need to add other mystery."

"What does it mean, though?" I asked.

Bishop Thomas paused for a few moments and then smiled brightly.

"There is a light here and it's mysterious and it's a blessing," he said. "But maybe it is a very personal message for you. You must receive it in the way that you feel it."

⊹

We left the next day by train for Cairo. By the time we arrived we were being pursued by three people from the bishop's office, all asking for copies of the photo.

I asked my friend Shems Friedlander, the head of the Graphic Arts Department at American University of Cairo, to please make a print. When the bishop's people learned of Shem's involvement they descended on his office and wouldn't leave until the print was made. Then they rushed it back to Assiut by the afternoon train and put it into the hands of the awaiting bishop.

His verdict was a quick one.

"This is another spiritual phenomena from the heavens," said the bishop in a message relayed by e-mail through a priest named Yakoob. "Our Lord allowed you to have the bless[ing] to see this phenomena and enjoy with it."

The syntax of the message was a little off but its meaning was clear. I had been given the divine opportunity to photograph a phenomenon. I was blessed.

"What do you think?" I asked Kees.

"I think this is your opportunity to ask Bishop Mikhail a few questions," he said. "He is known to be a very spiritual bishop, so he will certainly be the best one to address questions about apparitions to."

⊹

With only a few days left in Egypt I wrote a note to Bishop Mikhail through Father Yakoob.

Dear Father Yakoob:

Thank you very much for showing the photo to His Grace, Bishop Mikhail. I am very excited to find that I photographed a "spiritual phenomena from the heavens." As far as I know I am the first American to photograph this phenomenon. I truly feel chosen.

I don't believe you know this, but my purpose for coming to

Egypt was to write a book about the Holy Family trail. On the day
that I photographed this light, I had just returned from Dronka,
which was the last stop in the Holy Family voyage, according to
His Grace.

   I have two questions that I would like you to ask His Grace:
   1. Why do these visions of light appear to some people and
       not to others?
   2. Also, I photographed this phenomenon on the last day of
       my research. Is there a spiritual message in such an event,
       especially when it takes place at the end of a voyage
       covering the entire Holy Family trail?

In short order I received a reply from Father Yakoob. It read:

Dear Mr. Paul Perry:
   I have showed your last email to his grace Ava Mikhail the
Bishop of Assiut and he answered as follows:
   Regarding question number one:
   Why do these lights appear to some people and to some not?
It is supposed that heaven loves all and the Lord rises his sun over
all people. But with the light apparition there are some people
who exist with their bodies, while at the same time they are away
with the heart, soul, and mind. [Personal note: I assume this
means that some people are more spiritual.]
   You captured that photo while you were just returning from
the visit of the Convent of Virgin Mary in the hills of Assiut. Just
the Lord wants to show you the link between that convent and the
place holding the Church of Saint Mark.
   Regarding question number two:
   Is there a spiritual message in photographing such a vision
after covering the entire Holy Family trail? You have seen and you
have checked exactly like the Eastern Magis whom God showed
the star upon the Holy Christmas of our Lord Jesus Christ. As the
Lord used the Magis, He also used you, too, and your witness will
be more evident than ours as there is an important principle that
says, "we see with the eyes of others first, then we let the
phenomena explain about itself."

I understood what the bishop meant. I had spent months examining the impact of Jesus and the Holy Family trail on the people of

Egypt. What I found truly surprised me. Jesus was not another abstract Egyptian deity, like those found on the walls of pharaonic temples. His presence in Egypt announced the arrival of a brave new religion, one that still survives two thousand years later. I had seen nothing to confirm the actual existence of Jesus in Egypt—at least nothing that would withstand the scrutiny of Western archaeology. But I had seen plenty of sites and heard dozens of stories, all of which have made the Holy Family a living, breathing presence for millions of believers. Although it was impossible to "see" Jesus the way one would see the image of a pharaoh on a temple wall, signs of His presence had been everywhere. To use one of my favorite allusions, it was like being in a lifeboat on a foggy sea and being passed by a large ship. You might not see the ship for the fog, but you will certainly hear its engines and feel its wake as it passes by.

It was the same here. The historical Jesus had eluded me. Yet the effects of His passing were everywhere. The wake of Jesus had spread far and wide in this ancient land of myth and magic.

I sat in my rented apartment in Cairo and reminisced about the Holy Family trail and the sites I had visited. It was a trail that began at the troubled border with Israel and ended near Assiut, the troubled center of Fundy Land. I had traveled from trouble to trouble through this volatile land, yet had encountered no troubles of my own. Being an American at a time of international tensions made me more visible, but at no time did I feel as though it made me a target of any hostilities. Rather, when people discovered the reason for my presence, I became a target of best wishes and grace. "Jesus brings us all together," said a church member in Sakha, where the stone with the supposed footprint of Jesus is enshrined. "Whether Christian or Muslim, He is common ground because His message is one of peace and love."

Sitting in the relative quiet of my apartment, I could relive the voyage and feel the *baraka* of the people along the trail.

I remembered the woman in Ishneen who invited me into her home so I could photograph her and her children with their prize possession, a calf that occupied her living room along with sheep, rabbits, and ducks.

And how about the two men who had led me down an alley in Cairo to show me a religious site that was beneath a building's stairwell? What was it in their eyes that gave me trust enough to follow them?

Then there was the imam in Dairout, who gladly let us examine the well in his mosque to see if it was a well created by Jesus, even though the Muslims in the area considered it the well of a Companion of the prophet Muhammad. What was it he had said? "We don't mind if you come here looking for Jesus because we believe in Jesus, too."

The presence of Jesus in this land has made it a holy land for the people who live here. The sites are living proof of the presence of the Holy Family, just as the visions and homilies have confirmed the stories handed down from mouth to mouth.

Were these stories true? I didn't know. Discovering their historical truth was not possible and no longer significant, at least for me. What was important was their effect on the people who believed them. The presence of Jesus in their country had made the Egyptians feel blessed. His presence and blessing had been ensured by the prophecy of Isaiah in the Old Testament: "Blessed be Egypt my people." The impact of the Old Testament and the New wrapped neatly around the oral tradition, visions, and homilies to provide *baraka* for the blessed people of Egypt.

I recognized the impact of the Holy Family's voyage on Egypt, but had I recognized its impact on me? That was the challenge I saw in the bishop's cryptic response to my second question. By visiting the sites and talking with the people, I could "see with the eyes of others," as the bishop's e-mail phrased it. But the bishop also challenged me to "let the phenomena explain about itself."

How do I do that? I wondered. I had approached my subject as a journalist, visiting the Holy Family sites and observing firsthand the importance of Jesus to the Egyptians. Somewhere along the line, though, I crossed the line. I became a participant. A believer. I realized how important Jesus is to me and to my own culture. Was He truly the Son of God, as the Holy Bible says? Or was He one of the great prophets, as the Muslims proclaim, someone who communicated with God as they believe Muhammad and Moses did? Perhaps the answer to either question is yes. It has been argued both ways persuasively for centuries by the wisest of men and women. Yet no one knows the true nature of Jesus. There is no science on the subject, no hard facts, only faith, defined as a devotion to something without logical facts. What was important, however, was the message of Jesus. He preached a philosophy of forgiveness and understanding. He turned the other cheek when faced with the anger of others, fed the poor, treated the sick. In every way His teachings were the gold standard of compassion.

I still had questions about whether I had truly photographed a heavenly apparition or whether it was just a reflection of light from a more terrestrial source. I honestly didn't know and I don't know to this day. After a while I chose not to ponder it further. As Bishop Thomas told me, "You must receive it in the way that you feel it."

In the spirit of inner guidance, I turned off my intellect and let my heart be my guide. When I did that, the message of the apparition became very clear to me.

I picked up the telephone and dialed Kees at home.

"There is something I have to do before I leave," I said to him.

The next evening found us in the medicine clinic of the Church of the Holy Virgin and St. Athanasius the Apostolic in Dar el-Salam, an area of Cairo that is so poor it is not even found in tourist guidebooks.

I call it a "medicine clinic" because that is what it was, a room inside the church that was filled with outdated medications that pharmacists had given to this church instead of throwing them out. There were stacks of pharmaceuticals lined up across the small room and people coming in and out to drop off donated meds, pick up new ones, or just visit with Father Daniel.

Father Daniel had the stocky looks of a baseball player and a good sense of humor that exceeded what it should have for the job he was doing. He was assigned to work for the "Brothers of the Lord," a euphemism for the underprivileged. Father Daniel's job in this parish was to make sure that the poor Christians of Dar el-Salam received as much help as they possibly could.

We listened as he arranged medication and food assistance for a widow who had just had breast cancer surgery. Then he greeted a pharmacist who came in to donate time. "It is better to have people treated by a pharmacist," he told the man. "Because they end up at the pharmacy anyway."

With a lull in activity, he then turned his attentions to us.

"It is nice what you want to do," he said. "Poverty is darkness and it is difficult for many people to see it."

He telephoned a deacon who lived in a nearby apartment and soon the man showed up. He was tall and big-chested and looked like the husky English actor Oliver Reed when he was in his prime. Father Daniel told him what we wanted to do and where to take us. He told us that we would have to transfer the boxes of food we had brought from Kees' car to his. The road to the house was very rough and narrow and the street very dark, he explained. It would be best if we took his older car.

We piled into his car and soon we were crawling through a street so rutted I dubbed it "the street without mercy." It fit that name in other ways, too. Walls were crumbling from the groundwater that seeped into them, and the smell of raw sewage hung in the air.

Finally we stopped and the deacon got out and knocked on a door. A haggard-looking woman answered and then another came and stood behind her. The three spoke for a moment and then we were invited inside.

"I told them why you have come and they are very grateful," said the deacon.

One of the women—her name was Sadia Latif—brought sodas to each of us. The other woman, Noha Amal, joined us. From another room came several young women and one young boy. They were surprised to see a foreigner.

There were no husbands. They had died several years ago, leaving these two women to pool their meager pensions to care for their families in this apartment. Uneducated, middle-aged women are unemployable in Egypt. Their only hope for a decent old age was that their children would complete college and land one of the few jobs available in this job-impoverished country. As a result, the two women were pushing their children through school.

We made nervous small talk for a while and then we brought the boxes of food from the car and gave it to the two widows and their families. Then, with the help of the deacon, the landlord was contacted and I paid the rent on their apartment for six months, a total of three hundred Egyptian pounds, roughly sixty American dollars.

I didn't tell them about the voyage I had been on to seek out Holy Family sites. Nor did I tell them about the apparition of light that I had photographed in Assiut, nor how it had motivated me to create a small wake of my own in a large sea of poverty. Instead I took the advice of Bishop Thomas to heart: to keep the message a personal one and "receive it the way that you feel it."

The women shook our hands as we left, holding them too long, as though we might have been apparitions ourselves and everything we had brought would disappear when we did. We stayed as long as they wanted and then drove the battering road back to the church.

A verse from Matthew came to mind that seemed fitting to this night as well as the day two thousand years ago that Jesus brought his blessing to Egypt.

Neither do people light a lamp and put it under a bowl. Instead they put in on its stand, and it gives light to everyone in the house. In the same way, let your light shine before men, that they may see your good deeds and praise your Father in heaven.

Acknowledgments

On the morning of September 11, 2001, I was planning my trip to Egypt when my wife told me that an airplane had just struck the World Trade Center. I ran to the television and was shocked by what I saw. Like most of my countrymen, I suddenly saw this as a conflict between "us" and "them," the people of the Middle East.

I nearly canceled my trip several times during the next month while I watched the Middle East being portrayed in the media as the type of place a sensible American wouldn't go. What prevented me from canceling the writing of this book altogether was the fact that this was my only chance to fulfill a longtime dream. If I didn't go now, I would probably never have the time to do it again. So I pressed on.

Once I arrived in Egypt, my fears melted away. Almost everywhere I went I was treated like a cousin rather than an enemy. People approached me on the street to express their outrage about the terrorist acts of September 11, or to talk about world politics in general. It didn't take me long to realize that the vast majority of Egyptians want what most of us want, namely peace and harmony.

I know that it's a broad gesture to thank the Egyptian people for helping me with this book, but I want to do that just the same. Their courtesy and hospitality was heartfelt. May we all have peace in our time, *insha'allah.*

On an individual level, special thanks go to Drs. Cornelis "Kees" Hulsman. His knowledge of his adopted country is encyclopedic, and his connections among its people are vast. He collected the contact information relentlessly for so many sources on our trip that one day I speculated that if he were being boiled in oil, his last act would be to ask the cook for his phone number. He responded, "Well of course, you never know when you'll need a good chef."

It is with Kees that I explored many of these Holy Family sites and it is with him that I hope to do it again. I also want to thank his gracious wife, Sawsan, and his wonderful children—Petra, Johan, Paul, and Filip—for making me feel at home.

Through Kees I met Bishop Marcos, Bishop Thomas, Bishop Dimetrius, Bishop Paphnutius, Father Yu'annis, Father Stephanous, Father Philoxenos, and a host of other faithful who helped guide us on our path. Ra'ed El-Sharqawi, the enthusiastic guide on my first research trip, was an endless source of information and good conversation.

Mounir Ghabbour, the owner of the Sonesta Hotel in Cairo, was a gracious host. As chairman of the National Egyptian Heritage Revival Association (NEHRA), he has been largely responsible for the restoration of many of Egypt's most important Coptic sites. Without the hard work of people like Ghabbour, these sites would soon fade away.

Shems Friedlander, director of the Apple Center for Graphic Communication at the American University in Cairo, has been a longtime friend and was a great source of moral support in Egypt.

On the home front, I thank my family for supporting this book adventure, as they have the many others I have been involved in. Tim McIntire's knowledge of the Bible has provided hours of thought-provoking conversation, and my oldest friend Chuck Kelly has given me excellent editorial advice and spared no red ink. Vicki Wolfe also provided many constructive comments.

Leona Nevler acquired this book for Ballantine, and Tracy Brown became its editor. Both saw early on what it could be, and I hope it has lived up to their expectations. Special thanks go to Tracy, whose patience and guidance have been welcomed.

Finally I want to thank my literary agent Nat Sobel. We have been friends and associates for more than twenty years, which is proof that business and pleasure do mix.

To have the help of all of these people in writing this book has been a source of *baraka* for me. I hope that I have given some back to them as well.

The Bible and all of the stories that surround it are a constant source of conversation. If you would like to continue the dialogue about the voyage of the Holy Family into Egypt, please contact me at:

P.O. Box 13255
Scottsdale, AZ 85261

or at my Web site:

www.jesusinegypt.com